Making Moral Decisions

THEMES IN RELIGIOUS STUDIES SERIES

Series Editors: Jean Holm, with John Bowker

Other titles

Making Moral Decisions

Edited by

Jean Holm

with John Bowker

PINTER
PUBLISHERS
LONDON, NEW YORK

Distributed exclusively in the United States and Canada by St. Martin's Press

Pinter Publishers Ltd.
25 Floral Street, London WC2E 9DS, United Kingdom

First published in 1994

Distributed exclusively in the USA and Canada by St. Martin's Press, Inc.,
Room 400, 175 Fifth Avenue, New York, NY 10010, USA

British Library Cataloguing in Publication Data

A CIP catalogue record for this book is available from the British Library

ISBN 1 85567 096 8 (hb)
ISBN 1 85567 097 6 (pb)

Library of Congress Cataloging in Publication Data

A CIP catalog record for this book is available from the Library of
Congress

Typeset by Mayhew Typesetting, Rhayader, Powys
Printed and bound in Great Britain by Biddles Ltd., Guildford and King's Lynn

Contents

Series Preface

The person who knows only one religion does not know any religion. This rather startling claim was made in 1873, by Friedrich Max Müller, in his book, *Introduction to the Science of Religion*. He was applying to religion a saying of the poet Goethe: 'He who knows one language, knows none.'

In many ways this series illustrates Max Müller's claim. The diversity among the religious traditions represented in each of the volumes shows how mistaken are those people who assume that the pattern of belief and practice in their own religion is reflected equally in other religions. It is, of course, possible to do a cross-cultural study of the ways in which religions tackle particular issues, such as those which form the titles of the ten books in this series, but it soon becomes obvious that something which is central in one religion may be much less important in another. To take just three examples: the contrast between Islam's and Sikhism's attitudes to pilgrimage, in *Sacred Place*; the whole spectrum of positions on the authority of scriptures illustrated in *Sacred Writings*; and the problem which the titles, *Picturing God* and *Worship*, created for the contributor on Buddhism.

The series offers an introduction to the ways in which the themes are approached within eight religious traditions. Some of the themes relate particularly to the faith and practice of individuals and religious communities (*Picturing God, Worship, Rites of Passage, Sacred Writings, Myth and History, Sacred Place*); others have much wider implications, for society in general as well as for the religious communities themselves (*Attitudes to Nature, Making Moral Decisions, Human Nature and Destiny, Women in Religion*). This distinction, however, is not clear-cut. For instance, the 'sacred places' of Ayodhya and Jerusalem have figured in situations of national and international conflict, and some countries have passed laws regulating, or even banning, religious worship.

Stereotypes of the beliefs and practices of religions are so widespread that a real effort, of both study and imagination, is needed in order to discover what a religion looks – and feels – like to its adherents. We have to bracket out, temporarily, our own beliefs and presuppositions, and 'listen in' to a religion's account of what *it* regards as significant. This is not a straightforward task, and readers of the books in this series will encounter a number of the issues that characterise the study of religions, and that have to be taken into account in any serious attempt to get behind a factual description of a religion to an understanding of the real meaning of the words and actions for its adherents.

First, the problem of language. Islam's insistence that the Arabic of the Qur'ān cannot be 'translated' reflects the impossibility of finding in another language an exact equivalent of many of the most important terms in a religion. The very word, Islam, means something much more positive to a Muslim than is suggested in English by 'submission'. Similarly, it can be misleading to use 'incarnation' for *avatāra* in Hinduism, or 'suffering' for *dukkha* in Buddhism, or 'law' for Torah in Judaism, or 'gods' for *kami* in Shinto, or 'heaven' for *T'ien* in Taoism, or 'name' for *Nām* in Sikhism.

Next, the problem of defining – drawing a line around – a religion. Religions do not exist in a vacuum; they are influenced by the social and cultural context in which they are set. This can affect what they strenuously reject as well as what they may absorb into their pattern of belief and practice. And such influence is continuous, from a religion's origins (even though we may have no records from that period), through significant historical developments (which sometimes lead to the rise of new movements or sects), to its contemporary situation – especially when a religion is transplanted into a different region. For example, anyone who has studied Hinduism in India will be quite unprepared for the form of Hinduism they will meet on the island of Bali.

Even speaking of a 'religion' may be problematic. The term, 'Hinduism', for example, was invented by western scholars, and would not be recognised or understood by most 'Hindus'. A different example is provided by the religious situation in Japan, and the consequent debate among scholars as to whether they should speak of Japanese 'religion' or Japanese 'religions'.

Finally, it can be misleading to encounter only one aspect of a religion's teaching. The themes in this series are part of an interrelated network of beliefs and practices within each religious tradition, and need to be seen in this wider context. The reading lists at the end of each chapter point readers to general studies of the religions, as well as to books which are helpful for further reading on the themes themselves.

Jean Holm
November 1993

List of Contributors

Jean Holm (EDITOR) was formerly Principal Lecturer in Religious Studies at Homerton College, Cambridge, teaching mainly Judaism and Hinduism. Her interests include relationships between religions; the relationship of culture to religion; and the way in which children are nurtured within a different cultural context. Her publications include *Teaching Religion in School* (OUP, 1975), *The Study of Religions* (Sheldon, 1977), *Growing up in Judaism* (Longman, 1990), *Growing up in Christianity*, with Romie Ridley (Longman, 1990), and *A Keyguide to Sources of Information on World Religions* (Mansell, 1991). She has edited three previous series: *Issues in Religious Studies*, with Peter Baelz (Sheldon), *Anselm Books*, with Peter Baelz (Lutterworth) and *Growing up in a Religion* (Longman).

John Bowker (EDITOR) was Professor of Religious Studies in Lancaster University, before returning to Cambridge to become Dean and Fellow of Trinity College. He is at present Professor of Divinity at Gresham College in London, and Adjunct Professor at the University of Pennsylvania and at the State University of North Carolina. He is particularly interested in anthropological and sociological approaches to the study of religions. He has done a number of programmes for the BBC, including the *Worlds of Faith* series, and a series on Islam and Hinduism for the World Service. He is the author of many books in the field of Religious Studies, including *The Meanings of Death* (Cambridge University Press, 1991), which was awarded the biennial Harper Collins religious book prize in 1993, in the academic section.

Stewart McFarlane is a Lecturer in Religious Studies at the University of Lancaster, specialising in Chinese Religion and Philosophy;

he is also Visiting Professor at the Chung-Hwa Institute of Buddhist Studies in Taiwan. Dr McFarlane has published numerous articles and chapters on Buddhist ethics and society. He is a member of the editorial board of the *Journal of Asian Philosophy* and is currently writing a book on 'Culture, Identity and Power in Chinese Martial Arts'.

Douglas Davies is Professor of Religious Studies in the Department of Theology at the University of Nottingham, where he specialises in teaching the social anthropology of religion. He trained both in theology and social anthropology and his research continues to relate to both disciplines. His interest in theoretical and historical aspects of religious studies is represented in a major study of the sociology of knowledge and religion, published as *Meaning and Salvation in Religious Studies* (Brill, 1984), and in a historical volume, *Frank Byron Jevons 1858–1936, An Evolutionary Realist* (Edwin Mellen Press, 1991). He is also very much concerned with practical aspects of religious behaviour and is a leading British scholar of Mormonism and, in addition to various articles, is author of *Mormon Spirituality* (Nottingham and Utah University Press, 1987). He was joint Director of the Rural Church Project, involving one of the largest sociological studies of religion in Britain, published as *Church and Religion in Rural Britain* (with C. Watkins and M. Winter, T. & T. Clark, 1991). As Director of the Cremation Research Project he is conducting basic work on Cremation in Britain and Europe and has already produced some results in *Cremation Today and Tomorrow* (Grove Books, 1990).

Gavin D. Flood is Lecturer in Religious Studies at the University of Wales, Lampeter, where he teaches courses on Indian Religions and New Religious Movements. His research interests include Śaivism and Hindu Tantra, ritual, and the understandings of the self in Indian religions. Dr Flood has published articles on Kashmir Śaivism and is author of *Body and Cosmology in Kashmir Śaivism* (Mellen, 1993).

Clinton Bennett is a Lecturer in Study of Religions at Westminster College, Oxford, and a Baptist Minister. His research interests include Islamic theology and philosophy, historical and contemporary encounter between Muslims and non-Muslims, Islam and anthropology, and religious beliefs as agents of social transformation. Dr Bennett, who edits *Discernment: An Ecumenical Journal of Inter-Religious Encounter*, is the author of *Victorian Images of Islam* (Gray Seal, London, 1992), has travelled and worked in the Muslim world, and was a member of the World Council of Churches' (WCC) working party that produced *Issues in Christian-Muslim Relations: Ecumenical Considerations* (1991). He currently serves on the WCC's 'Consultation on the Church and the Jewish People'.

Norman Solomon is founder and Director of the Centre for the Study of Judaism and Jewish/Christian Relations at the Selly Oak Colleges, Birmingham. He is Visiting Lecturer to the Oxford Centre for Postgraduate Hebrew Studies, adviser to the International Council of Christians and Jews, and Vice Chairman of the World Congress of Faiths. Among his many publications is *Judaism and World Religion* (Macmillan, 1991). Rabbi Dr Solomon has a particular interest in Christian–Jewish dialogue and has been a frequent participant in international dialogue events with the World Council of Churches, the Vatican and the Ecumenical Patriarchate. He is also involved in trilateral dialogues of Jews, Christians and Muslims.

Indarjit Singh is the Founder Editor of the *Sikh Messenger* – a quarterly English language magazine founded in 1984 about Sikh history and religion, and generally regarded as the main voice of Sikhism in the western world. He has contributed to and advised on numerous publications on Sikhism. He is the author of *Strangers in our Midst* and co-translated *Rehat Maryada* – a guide to the Sikh way of life. He won the 'United Kingdom Templeton Award – 1989', a national award for the furtherance of spiritual understanding – this was the first time it had been won by a member of the non-Christian community. He was also awarded the 'Interfaith Medallion – 1991', which was presented jointly by the Council of Christians and Jews and the BBC for services to religious broadcasting.

Introduction: Raising the Issues

John Bowker

What ought I to do? Or not to do, as the case may be? What 'the case' is turns out to be all-important: the answer that we give to those questions depends very much on what the circumstances are which have led to their being asked. If I want to make a Christmas cake, what ought I to do? Look up a recipe? Ask for advice if I have never made one before? Check that the right ingredients are in the house before I start? 'Ought' questions of that kind are answered by relation to facts (what factually counts as a Christmas cake?) and competence (can I do it?).

But 'ought' questions rapidly move into areas where facts are relevant to the answer but not decisive in giving the answer. I see reports on TV news about starvation in Africa: what ought I to do? Give some money? Write to my MP about overseas aid? Nothing? Decide to spend a year working overseas? Once again, a practical, as opposed to a theoretical, answer is limited by competence: not everything that I might like to do in theory is possible for me, although it might be for someone else. But what is different about *this* kind of 'ought' question is that facts are relevant to the answer (although they are characteristically very complicated: what, for example, are the facts about the relation between overseas aid and local initiative?), but they do not tell you what you ought to do. Thus the sight of a starving child in Africa will make most people react with pity and a desire to do something to help. But *what* they ought to do is not held within the fact itself. And then again, not everyone looking at the same facts will see them as making an 'ought' demand upon them: not everyone will see even a starving

1

child as demanding some response from them; they may simply walk by on the other side of the road.

Facts and values

'Ought' questions lie along a line or spectrum. At one end are questions where the facts of the case tell you what you ought to do if you are going to hit a particular target or goal: what ought I to do if I am to draw a straight line between two points? Take out a ruler and a pencil and connect them. At the other end are questions where the facts of the case are relevant to the answer, but do not in themselves tell you what the appropriate, or best, action is: what ought I to do to reduce the greenhouse effect and global warming? And here, to complicate matters still further, even the facts are in dispute.

Already we have begun to introduce words like 'target', 'appropriate', and 'best'. These are all words which imply, or involve, *evaluation*. All human beings are aware of the future, but none of us has any certain knowledge of what is going to happen tomorrow. This means that we live toward unknown futures and, consequently, any action which we project into the future requires us to evaluate how it is going to work, what its consequences will be, whether it is worth undertaking, and so on.

Moral life begins with this kind of inevitable evaluation. But, of course, that evaluation may be nothing more than a calculation of what might be most advantageous to *me*. In other words, it might be entirely selfish. The evaluation becomes specifically moral when we build into it the value that others have, and consider the effects of a decision for them, not just for me and for my advantage. These 'others' do not have to be other humans alone, they may be animals, for example, or the planet itself. I feel an obligation to them which has to be built into my evaluation of what is the right or the appropriate or the just action, if it is to count as being good.

So one of the deepest marks of being human, as opposed to being a stone or a star (excellent things in themselves, but not the same as being human), is when we feel the pull of obligation within us and do something about it. It is when we simply feel that we ought to do something, even before we can find reasons for doing it, or even when reason tells us that we would be foolish to do it. That basic tug of a tide within us, the pull of obligation which is as strong as the swing of a needle in a compass to the magnetic pole, is common to all human beings. It is the beginning of what is known as 'conscience'. Of course we are capable of suppressing conscience, or of overriding it: '"I wish I had known all this before," said Pippin [in J.R.R. Tolkein's *The Lord of the Rings*]. "I had no notion of what I was doing." "Oh yes, you had," said Gandalf. "You knew you were behaving wrongly and foolishly; and you told yourself so, though you did not listen."' But that 'override' does not alter the fact that in the exercise of conscience, deciding what is right and acting on that decision, we are being most characteristically, and most splendidly, human.

But still the fact remains that, no matter how strongly we feel a sense of moral obligation, we cannot always be certain what exactly we ought to do. The philosopher, David Hume (1711–76), believed that that must be the case, because we do not, and cannot, observe directly the moral obligation in any event or situation. The sense of obligation or value has to be added on to the basic observation. So he argued:

> Take any action allowed to be vicious; wilful murder, for instance. Examine it in all lights and see if you can find that matter of fact . . . which you call *vice*. In whichever way you take it, you only find certain passions, motives, volitions and thoughts. . . . The vice entirely escapes you, as long as you consider the object. You never can find it till you turn your reflection into your own breast, and find a sentiment of disapprobation, which arises in you, towards this action.
>
> (*A Treatise of Human Nature* (1777), Book III, 'Of Morals',
> ed. L. A. Selby-Bigge, Oxford, Oxford University Press, p. 468)

Hume argued that people do not *see* a moral demand, still less agree that they have seen it, in the way that they see and agree that a circle is a circle and a square is a square.

This argument has dominated reflection on the nature of moral judgement for two centuries, and has led to the strong distinction between facts and values. This is usually expressed by saying that facts do not lead you to values as clearly as they lead you to the judgement that this is a circle, or that book is red. To put the point more briefly (as it is often put) – you cannot get an 'ought' from an 'is', you cannot get values from facts.

3

Morals as matters of opinion

But if facts do not lead us to agreed moral judgements, perhaps it has to follow that moral judgements are a matter of feeling and opinion. Thus I may have a strong feeling of anger or disapproval if I see a child starving, and I may feel that I and others ought to do something about it; but if I try to convince other people by argument, they may simply disagree and remain unconvinced. They may think, for example, that the overpopulation of the planet has to find its own correction, or even be helped to find that level of sustainable population by us.

This belief, that moral judgement is a matter of feeling and opinion, has had enormous consequences in virtually all aspects of life, particularly in the western democracies. If we look at some of these consequences, we can see how important they are in understanding the relation between religions and moral decision making at the present time. First, this belief reinforces and endorses the way in which western styles of democracy give a 'preferential option to options' – that is to say, they allow the maximum freedom of opinion, within the limits which are necessary for a society to function at all and which are set by law. For example, we are free to drive, but we must first prove competence (by passing a test), and we are not free to 'stop' at a green light and 'go' on red. The drawing of those limits is contested: ought it to be legal to take cannabis, or altogether illegal to drink and drive? The view that moral judgements are a matter of opinion which not everyone can be expected to share, makes a society diverse and pluralistic, within a boundary of commonly accepted law. It is the kind of society envisaged and created in the American Constitution of the eighteenth century.

But this raises a second issue. The American Constitution also rested on a conviction that certain truths are *not* matters of opinion: 'We hold these truths to be self-evident, that all men are created equal, that they are endowed by their Creator with certain inalienable Rights, that among these are Life, Liberty and the pursuit of Happiness.' But why should these be regarded as anything other than matters of opinion? Perhaps rights too are a consequence of *cultural construction*; that is to say, the view that moral judgements are a matter of feeling and opinion will have no difficulty in saying the same of such things as 'rights': they may be deeply embedded in our languages and our political systems, but they are still constructed and endorsed by us as opinions which many of us agree to and rely on. But then *all* such constructions would seem to be relative to the cultures or societies in which they occur, and to have only the validity of the particular culture which accepts them. This is known as cultural relativity. The anthropologist, Führer-Haimendorf exemplified the point in this way:

> To a western audience, the situation of a son passionately in love with his step-mother appears fraught with tragedy, and it seems inevitable that the drama should end with the hero's doom. A Tibetan audience would not understand what all the excitement is about, for Tibetans see no harm in the sharing of one wife by father and son. An arrangement which one society considers the height of immorality, is thought natural by another.
>
> (C. von Führer-Haimendorf (1967) *Morals and Merit*, Weidenfeld and Nicolson, p. 1)

Cultural relativity means that all moral judgements *may* be contested. If there are no absolute standards by which rightness and wrongness can be measured, then who is to say what will count as right or wrong?

Consideration of this question moves us on to a third point at issue. The answer, perhaps, may be that those who can find facts which are *relevant* to judgement, even if they cannot compel the agreement of all people, may be able to state what is right or wrong. One of the major consequences of the belief that moral judgements are matters of opinion and feeling is the search for more general principles which will act as a guide. The best known of these is Utilitarianism. In its crudest possible form, this means searching, in any decision or action, for the greatest good of the greatest possible number. But this is at its weakest precisely where we need guidance – in difficult cases. How do we calculate the proportion of benefits when, for example, we are faced with competing claims for finite resources? If I have three patients, one of whom needs a heart transplant, another a lung transplant, and a third a kidney transplant, ought I to take a young man who has turned up in Accident and Emergency with a broken arm, and, on the principle of the greatest good for the greatest number, cut him up and reallocate the necessary parts? The fact that the example is absurd nevertheless points to the difficulty of the necessary calculations, and it has led to great sophistications of utilitarianism in the present century to make it more usable as a guide. But however usable it may be, it is still extremely different from moral systems which believe that moral judgements are rooted, not in matters of calculation or of opinion, but in conformity to commands and laws – either the commands of a natural law (a recognition of what is good and right that lies in human nature and in the natural order to which we belong), or in the commands of God (as, for example, in the revelation of his law, or of *dharma*, life-way).

But, fourthly, the belief that facts do not lead all people to see the same value in them, and that consequently an 'is' does not lead coercively to an 'ought', has brought those views about natural law and the law of God seriously into question. How do we *know* what God has commanded when religions differ so much on what they believe him to have said? How does it come about that God appears to have commanded things which seem to others (and not just to other religions) to be deeply immoral? Does it mean that things become good simply because God commands them? Or does God command them because they are, in any case, good? If we do things and regard them as good because God has commanded them, are they any longer *moral* actions – since it is no longer our own decision, but simply an act of obedience? Where the natural law is concerned, the familiar questions return: if there *is* a natural law, how does it come about that different cultures and different periods of history have failed to recognise or identify it? Of course, they may claim to have identified laws which transcend particular moments and particular societies but, so far, these claimed universal laws have turned out to be exactly those matters of opinion which later ages have contested. Consider, for example, the claims made about the 'natural' nature of slavery or of the subordination of women to men.

So the fifth and largest consequence of the last two centuries, in which the belief has been gaining ground that moral judgements are matters of feeling and opinion, is that we live on a balance between the opportunity of extreme moral maturity and the possibility of complete moral anarchy. On the one side, morality is no longer a matter of conformity to rules and laws unless we see that those rules and laws do as a matter of fact (fact for us) constitute the right and the good way to live; but in any case, the emphasis will be on our own decision to live a moral or an immoral life. On the other side, there will be no particular reason (since reasons, on this view, are not compelling) why we should not live in ways which have traditionally seemed horrendous: Hitler, Stalin, Verwoerd and Pol Pot were not isolated in the evil they did – plenty of people acted with them.

Religious and moral facts

All this must seem to call in question the religious style, or the religious foundation, of moral decision-making. But we need to bear in mind two things: first, that there is much in this account that religions agree with, and which they say in their own words. Thus religions, in general, do not believe that morality can be translated into conforming with the laws of God without question. They agree that being moral is a strenuous business. They also take evil a great deal more seriously than most secular accounts of morality do, and recognise – when they talk in the East about ignorance (*avidya*) and *karma*, and in the West about sin – that we are not entirely in rational control of our own lives.

But secondly, we need to bear in mind that religions, in general, contest one of the most basic points in the post-Hume account of moral decision making, and that this disagreement is increasingly shared by non-religious accounts of the matter, given by artists and philosophers in particular. Religions hold that humans are capable of seeing directly what is right and wrong, good and evil, and that these values are not always added on to a more neutral observation. Frequently we do see some situation or event as inextricably value-laden. We do see vice (i.e., that which is vicious) when we see someone beating a dog. Our judgement may turn out to be mistaken (perhaps the dog had just attacked someone), and our observation does not tell us what we ought to do – though it may be signalling to us that we ought to do something within the range and limits of competence. But those necessary qualifications do not alter the basic human ability to see the morally good and the morally bad directly and immediately, and not just as an optional value added on.

So the foundation of moral decision making lies in the religious insistence that the recognition of value is a human universal. All human beings distinguish between right and wrong, good and evil, true and false. What *counts* as good or right differs from culture to culture, from one moment in history to another, from one person to another and even within a person during the course of a life, but the human ability to make such distinctions does not differ. If people seem to be incapable of making or operating the distinctions, we know that they have put themselves outside the human community, and in our own culture we label them 'psychopaths'.

Recognising values

To be human, therefore, is to recognise value, including moral value. And just as humans are those who discern value, so also are they the bearers of meaning and value in their own lives. The values of goodness, beauty and truth are not limited to one time or one place; they can occur to humans at any time and in any place, no matter how much the content of what is discerned as beautiful or good may be specific to a particular moment. That is why such values are known as 'absolutes': they transcend particular moments and lives, while always occurring within particular moments and lives. But if these values are transcendent and absolute, it is not surprising that we ask where they come from. Is it just a lucky chance? Or is it not more likely that values come from a source of value who is the good, the beautiful and the true? And that, at least for a start, is what we mean by God.

If that is so, it will no longer be surprising to find that there is, between societies and from one historical moment to another, a great deal more convergence in what counts as good than we would be entitled to expect if morality were indeed a matter of opinion and cultural construction. We begin to see that there are limits set on what can count as a good or wise or appropriate life, which are as non-negotiable as the laws of nature. We cannot live successfully if we suppose that we can ignore the law of gravity and step off the roof of a building with impunity; and we cannot expect to live successfully if we suppose that we can ignore the claims of others upon us and regard the murder of children as 'all right for me'.

Natural law and biology

The kind of argument expounded above underlies attempts to re-found moral decision-making in nature and in natural law. The most common form of this argument currently lies in what is known as 'sociobiology'. This is the view that we, and, all other organisms, are 'gene-survival machines'. The genes hold the instructions (often, but misleadingly, called 'information') to build the proteins, which build the bodies which, in turn, reproduce that same genetic information in another generation. In evolution, the small changes or mutations in the genetic information either help an organism to survive and transmit the new gene-set into another generation, or that particular variation goes to extinction. Thus genes, according to this argument, sit inside a defensive system (in the case of humans, inside the skin), until their DNA and RNA are replicated in another 'gene-survival machine'. But in the case of humans, the survival machine is extremely complicated, not least because the human genes have built a very sophisticated brain – a brain which is able to plan strategically, to evaluate, to cooperate or to compete, especially through language, with other humans. In other words, humans have built a *second* defensive skin around themselves, and that second skin is called 'culture'.

In this context, religions can be recognised as the oldest cultural systems we know of. Religions, as we first encounter them, organise the whole of life for a village or a society, and they supply to individuals the codes of language (through myths, rituals and symbols) through which the common enterprise of life becomes possible – or, as the sociobiologist would say, through which the replication of genetic material and the nurture of children are defended and made more likely. Morals emerge as the customs (the word 'moral' comes from the Latin word for 'custom') which a family or a village or a society adopts as the code for itself emerges; and either that sum of choices is rewarded by the replication of the genetic material, or that group goes to extinction. So, on this view, religions are related to moral decision-making as the earliest and still most widely prevalent systems for the protection of genetic information and the nurture of children, which is why religious morality seems to be so preoccupied with sex and food.

Self-sacrifice

The basically biological view of morality discussed above seems a very restricted one. After all, many religions put a high value on martyrdom, or on laying down one's life for others. They may also

9

put a higher value on celibacy than on replicating one's own genetic material. Sociobiologists reply to this objection with the concept of 'kinship altruism'. This means that, from the point of view of the genes, it is the set of genes held in a kinship *group* that matters, not the genes of any one particular individual.

But how then are we to explain the willingness of religious people to be celibate or to lay down their lives for those who cannot possibly belong to their own kinship group? Religions do of course supply metaphors of a human family. But sociobiologists are more inclined to say that religions have supplied motivation for the sacrifices required by gene-serving moralities, by offering to their adherents rewards which make the morality 'worthwhile', even though it is no longer directly connected to gene protection. Originally these rewards and punishments were restricted to this life, but eventually a belief developed that there might be eternal rewards and punishments, and it was then, according to the sociobiologist, that the power of religions in relation to morality became dominating.

There is undoubted truth in this account, which religions are unwise to deny. But it is only a partial account of the role of religions in moral decision-making. In particular, it fails to see how religions frequently militate against reward-based moralities, indeed, regarding them as immoral. As the Christian hymn puts it:

My God, I love thee, not because
I hope for heaven thereby,
Nor yet because who love thee not
Are lost eternally.

E'en so I love thee, and will love,
And in thy praise will sing,
Solely because thou art my God,
And my eternal king.

Religious moralities often contain the note of reward and punishment, but they also contain the truth of value – the truth that in the recognition of goodness and beauty we are drawn into behaviours which often turn back on gene-based programmes and contradict them; they set as goals, not reward, but holiness. It is this which constitutes what is known as 'ethical vitality'.

Ethical vitality

The concept of ethical vitality comes from the field of social anthropology and is of considerable use in understanding moral decision-making in relation to social life and the religious idea of salvation. In an important essay entitled, *The Ideology of Merit*, S.J. Tambiah described the way in which, in some Buddhist traditions, boys become monks for limited periods of time. They observe the necessary Buddhist rules of life by sacrificing their own wishes and desires. It is believed that they earn or make merit through this sacrificial form of religious duty and use it to offset demerit in the lives of their families. Tambiah expresses the issue in these terms:

> Youths become temporary monks to make merit for the elders and community members. In effect . . . the older generation persuades its youth temporarily to renounce its vitality and sexual potency and undergo an ascetic regimen. In a sense it is the sacrifice of this human energy that produces ethical vitality which can counter *karma* and suffering.
>
> ('The Ideology of Merit', in E. Leach, *Dialectic in Practical Religion*, Cambridge, Cambridge University Press, 1968, p. 105)

One way of understanding how this process of merit-making works is to remember that humans are both social and self-conscious. As social beings we live in organised groups with rules to control our communal existence. The ideas of goodness and badness behind these rules are related, as we have seen, to the group's survival and welfare. As social beings we also invest our rules with emotionally-charged value. This emotional power binds people to central cultural values which seem so real and true that they are placed beyond contradiction.

As self-conscious beings we reflect upon these rules of life and realise their importance for our worth or even our survival. Here the word 'moral' comes very close to meaning the same as 'social', so that when we say something is morally good we regard it as good for society too, just as something that is morally bad is thought to work against the welfare of society. Thus, as Durkheim realised, long before sociobiology had emerged as a discipline, religions create the realities of society, not least by supplying the rituals and the

11

symbols through which our bonding to each other can be given objective form. Indeed, Durkheim regarded religion *as* society in externalised and symbolised form. Thus the social reality of a school can be summed up in a symbolic figure (a mascot, for example) which summarises one's participation in, and loyalty to, the school. The symbol, or totem, becomes revered and sacred, and it evokes from individuals a willingness to give up their own selfish priorities in favour of society.

This, for Durkheim, is the foundation of moral decision-making, and it makes such decision-making inescapably religious.

Once again, this is clearly too simple an account of morality and religion as a whole. But it does remind us of the deep entanglement of religion *and* society in the creation of moral judgement. Not surprisingly, anthropologists of religion have explored the many different ways in which religions validate fundamental social interactions and behaviours. Thus, to give only one example, all societies have to enable and control the interactions of obligation and (to give it its technical name) reciprocity.

Reciprocity – give and take

Reciprocity is the technical term for the process of give and take operating between members of society. From their earliest days, children are taught how to respond when things are given to them, later they are taught how to share, and finally they are taught how to give to others. Among adults this process of reciprocity can become quite complicated. It is also complex in terms of what one nation gives to another, as in the case of rich nations in their dealings with poor nations.

In 1909 the French anthropologist, Marcel Mauss, published a book about gifts and gift-giving which opened up a very useful approach to the world of human relationships. He argued that many different sorts of relationship between people are created and fostered through the giving and receiving of gifts. Gifts, he suggested, are not always the innocent objects they so often appear to be. What is more, when people say 'it is the thought that counts', when they get a gift that is less than expected, they are not, strictly speaking, telling the truth. It is not the thought that counts but the actual gift given and received. It is as though people keep a mental account book of what others have given them and what they need to give in return to keep a rough balance between all parties. A gift may be said to enshrine within itself attitudes towards a relationship. Central to Mauss' gift theory was the idea of obligation, and this concept is of fundamental importance for the study of religion.

For Mauss, the person who receives a gift is obliged to give a return gift. The donor puts the recipient under obligation. In one sense, the donor has a power over the receiver. The very fact that the recipient takes the gift involves a recognition of this power and implies acknowledgement of it. Some people may not want to be under obligation to someone else and may avoid receiving gifts; others may be only too pleased to be linked to a powerful person capable of giving weighty gifts.

Gifts themselves are of many kinds. The idea of a gift probably makes us think of objects, but the word 'gift' is really a label that describes a broad category of things from material presents of chocolates, to the loan of a book, or to a bribe of money. Further still, it may embrace the time which someone 'gives' when helping us do some job. It can also cover the more abstract idea of devotion or love. There is some sort of obligation involved in all these cases.

Reciprocity, identity and meaning

It is through these processes of 'give' and 'take' that social life comes to take on meaning for us as human beings. We learn 'who is who' as we come to know what we may expect from them and what they may expect from us. The child knows that a present from a family relation must be appreciated no matter how inappropriate it is, just as the child also knows it must not accept gifts from strangers. So it is that our duties and obligations are spelt out to us through gifts in the broad sense, while the various schemes of reciprocity that make up our lives help us to define the world and give us a sense of our place within it. Our sense of identity is itself partly made up through acts of reciprocity.

This point links in with another aspect of life which needs some explanation – the idea of causation. Life becomes sensible and intelligible to us in complicated ways, involving learning the language and ideas of our culture and learning how to behave in particular circumstances. One feature that is especially important in all societies is learning about cause and effect, about the laws or principles by which things operate.

13

There are, of course, different sorts of cause and effect. Science, for example, explores the laws governing cause and effect in the natural world of atomic and chemical reactions, and in the ways living material operates in plant and animal life. In economics, sociology, and psychology, other links between patterns of action and reaction in social and personal life are explored. Very similar ideas of cause and effect also work in the realms of both religion and morality. To understand this it is useful to start with the ordinary life of human beings before moving to their religious life.

Meaning, cause and morality

There are two distinctive features lying at the heart of human morality and of religion: the first is that human beings seek meaning and the second is that they seek moral meaning.

Seeking meaning is basic to human life. We want to know about the world around us and about ourselves. The emergence of language and of all sorts of knowledge is a witness to what amounts to a human need. Science is perhaps one of the best examples of this drive for meaning as it strives to give clearer and increasingly more definite answers to the question of 'how' it is that things are as they are. But what of moral meaning?

Seeking moral meaning is a development, based on the necessity for evaluation, of the ordinary drive to make sense of the world. Its distinctive feature comes from the fact that humans are social animals and not simply rational creatures. In social life we find people caught up in many sorts of relationships with each other under the influence of rules of behaviour. Each society comes to a sort of agreement about what it believes to be good and what it believes to be bad. These rules of morality are powerful because they carry with them what we might call emotional loads or emotional charges. People often feel strongly about moral rules, because they are attached to them by tradition and precedent, and also because these rules help form an individual's own sense of identity.

These emotional charges make moral rules very powerful in social life, more so than purely rational or scientific laws. Our attitude towards the law of gravity, for example, is not the same as our attitude towards the law against murder. Each society, and each group within that society, tends to have special laws which help keep their way of life safe.

14

Just as scientific laws help explain the physical world to us, so moral laws help explain the social world and our own identity. Identity itself comes to be one form of explanation as it describes who we are and what we are as members of our own particular society. This sense of identity involves a strong emotional dimension because we are not neutral about ourselves; we are deeply concerned about our status and place in the world and about how others treat us. Our security and survival often seem closely associated with our sense of identity.

The sociologist, Hans Mol, has argued that whatever confers a sense of identity upon an individual is, itself, placed above contradiction. The source of identity may become so precious that it is invested with sacred qualities. Such a source or focus of identity certainly helps explain the world to the individual or group concerned; it may also be part of a complicated scheme of reciprocity, in the sense that the worship people 'pay' to their deities is a form of return gift, responding to the identity that has been received. Adulation of footballers or pop stars is a secular example.

The idea of salvation or of ultimate release can be seen as one of the greatest examples of identity conferred upon someone by religion. Such ideas usually explain why the world is as it is and how individuals can overcome the flaws present in worldly life. So even the religious idea of salvation can be seen as an extension of the human drive for meaning, but in this case, a meaning which has a strong moral dimension to it.

Good and evil

What this means in practice is that religions take all the dimensions of time seriously in relation to moral decision-making. They take the past seriously, because they know that things have been done in the past for which forgiveness, penitence, atonement, restitution, retribution are necessary. They take the present seriously, because they believe that a moral life is one in which the self has to lose or abandon its self-interest, at every present moment, if it is to find itself for what it truly is. And they take the future seriously, because all religions live toward the horizon of hope. They believe that the good life is eventually rewarded, although they differ very much on how far that reward can be earned by good works, or can be received only as a gift of grace.

15

Religions, therefore, differ greatly in what they identify as a good action or a good person. They differ greatly in the status they give to laws and rules in the forming of moral life. But they agree, very profoundly, in their belief that human beings are capable of distinguishing between good and evil, or right and wrong, and of acting on the basis of those judgements. It follows that all religions ought (if they are not to contradict themselves) to be at the forefront of every campaign to ensure that people have the opportunity to make those judgements and to act upon them. Those judgements may be strongly constrained by many things – by previous experiences, by family upbringing, by genetic inheritance, and we may be much limited in what we can actually do for ourselves. We may, in other words, need help, whether from God by way of grace, or from *bodhisattva* by way of compassion, or from community support, or from spiritual guides and *gurūs*, or from revealed guidance by way of text and law; all these are exhibited in the religions reviewed in this book. But all religions believe that we have at least some competence to take charge of our own programmes and to allow moral considerations to act upon our decisions. This is what it means to be human. If there is a basic human right, from which other rights in turn may follow, it is the right to be human in this way, with the opportunity to see what is good and to act upon that judgement.

In this book, therefore, you will find many variations on the human theme of evaluation and judgement. The question to be asked is how these variations can, if at all, be brought to bear on the problems which now confront us, not simply as local or individual moral problems, but also as global problems, transcending national boundaries. The major religions have centuries of experience in transcending national boundaries. In what ways might that experience help us as we address the problems which concern us all?

1. Buddhism

Stewart McFarlane

An initial impression of Buddhist teaching and practice would suggest that for the Buddhist, moral decision-making is not problematic. The detailed training rules of conduct and deportment (*pāṭimokkha*) for the monks and the five precepts (*pañca-sīla*) for laypeople, are apparently straightforward behavioural, moral and ritual guidelines. All that appears to be required of the Buddhist is to follow these guidelines as best they can, with little need for moral reflection and analysis. In reality the situation is more complicated for practising Buddhists and for observers seeking to understand the moral dimensions of the tradition.

The fundamental distinction between monk and layperson is only one of a whole range of levels of spiritual and moral attainment that are acknowledged in Buddhism. Not only are the behavioural requirements varied according to the level of attainment reached, but the understanding of the moral and psychological theory will differ according to the spiritual level of the individual. Ordinary lay people and untrained monks do not generally understand the detailed psychological theory underlying the notion of *karma*, the notion of the correlation between intentions, actions and their consequences in the life or future lives of the individual. Still less are they expected to have achieved an experiential understanding of the workings of *karma* in action. Such experience is only available to advanced level meditators who are systematically pursuing the Buddhist path (*magga*) to liberation (*nirvāṇa*), the cessation of suffering or supreme awakening (*saṃbodhi*). However for the advanced levels of practice and for adepts (*asekha*) who are expected to teach and direct others, such levels of meditational experience and understanding are necessary.

Another factor which makes Buddhist moral reflection more problematic, is the fact that the time-scale and cosmology on which Buddhist moral processes take place are very different from western assumptions about the nature of human life and the functioning of the universe. The historical Buddha, Śakyamuni, and the legendary material about him illustrate these differences very clearly. Buddhists understand the Buddha's final lifetime as one dedicated to his primary role as a teacher and exemplar of *dhamma* (Sanskrit-*dharma*). *Dhamma* is the truth or teaching which provides the way to the cessation of suffering which is *nirvāṇa* or Supreme Awakening. *Dhamma* is such an important concept that it comes to take on the meaning of truth or reality itself, because it is the means by which the liberated state is achieved. In the Buddhist understanding, Śakyamuni's career began thousands of years before his final lifetime, when, as an ordinary human being he expressed the wish to be awakened, and the previous Buddha, Dīpankara, observing his virtue, spiritual worth and aspiration, predicted that he would be the next *buddha* (Conze 1959: 19–24). The progress of the *bodhisattva* or *buddha*-to-be is partly recorded in the legendary but very important material of the Jātaka stories, which describe numerous incidents over a whole series of lives in which the *buddha*-to-be demonstrates his virtue and refines his understanding as preparation for his final life as the fully awakened Buddha; his full knowledge and understanding of the nature of that process, largely a matter of an experiential understanding of *karma*, is not attained until immediately prior to his awakening (Robinson and Johnson 1977: 38–39). The Jātaka stories themselves are important sources for examples of Buddhist ethics in action, albeit in an exaggerated 'mythic' framework. The notion of successive lives of the Buddha, and the progressive spiritual development and moral refinement he undergoes, provides an ideal model for the process of refinement and progression which Buddhism tries to institute for all beings.

Realistically, of course, it is just as possible for beings to decline morally and spiritually through successive lives. This kind of time-scale and the underlying moral theory associated with it explains why the Buddhist view of human nature and the cosmos is both developmental and hierarchical. Beings living at the same time are clearly at different stages of moral and spiritual development. Therefore, different types of teaching and guidance are going to be appropriate to different beings. Traditionally Buddhist teaching is not a generalised activity, but is carried out with regard to specific individuals and groups at certain levels of attainment. Texts were only available after the traditional method of teaching was established, and for many centuries 'texts' were memorised and transmitted within the monastic order (*saṅgha*), and were not generally available. The developmental and hierarchical nature of Buddhist assumptions about the universe means that considerable flexibility is applied in the practical teaching offered by Buddhist authorities. Even straightforward teachings on moral matters can be modified, sometimes intensified, sometimes relaxed in the course of teaching and transmission. Examples of this will appear throughout this chapter. This process has also happened historically, as Buddhism has been transmitted to diverse cultural and religious environments. The examples of meat-eating and Buddhist attitudes to violence will be considered later.

We return now to the developmental and hierarchical nature of the Buddhist understanding of the universe and of the human place in it. A sophisticated vocabulary of technical terms is adopted in Buddhist texts, which reflect this type of understanding. Some examples and their meanings are:

1. *lokuttara* (supermundane)   *lokiya* (worldly)
2. *asekha* (adept)   *sekha* (learner)   *puthujjana* (ordinary man)
3. *paramattha-sacca* (ultimate truth)   *sammuti-sacca*
                                        (conventional truth)
   paramārtha-satya   "   "   *samvṛti-satya*   "   "

The way moral decisions are reached will depend on what level of understanding is being expressed and addressed. Another distinction now frequently employed by western scholars was that developed by M. Spiro. It is not an indigenous classification, although it does closely relate to the types of distinction and classifications used above. Spiro classifies Theravāda Buddhism into three different types.

1. Nibbanic Buddhism relates to the teachings, practices and concerns of the 'spiritual élite' within the *saṅgha* (monastic community), who are directing their practice to the attaining of liberation (*nibbāna/nirvāna*).
2. Kammatic Buddhism (relating to *kamma/karma*) is concerned

19

with the performance of wholesome actions, and through them the attaining of a desirable rebirth, either as a god, or as a wealthy and powerful man, or as a monk who will then be in a position to follow the path to liberation more fully. Spiro sees the orientation and concerns of the majority of Theravāda Buddhists as participating in this type of Buddhism.

3. Apotropaic Buddhism (i.e., Buddhism which supplies the means whereby evils and threats are 'turned away' and resisted) is concerned with using the 'magical' or meritorious power of *buddha-dhamma* and its representatives to protect people from natural and supernatural calamities. It includes using Buddhist ritual chanting to protect against such things as demons or droughts, and in exorcism and healing procedures.

Spiro acknowledges the extent to which the activities and concerns within these categories can interact and overlap. He clearly does not present them as self-contained systems or as completely rigid categories (Spiro 1971: 12). Despite some criticisms of Spiro's terminology and classifications, which often turn out to be criticisms of an over-rigid use of them, his analysis has considerable value in understanding the complexity of Buddhist ethical, social and soteriological thinking.

The structure of Buddhist ethical teaching

Given that Buddhism traditionally operates with hierarchical and developmental notions of spiritual understanding and moral attainment, it follows that beings at different levels of understanding will be given teachings and methods which are appropriate to their level of understanding. This means that general statements about the nature of Buddhist teachings must be treated with caution, as the level of teaching and the kind of group or individual to which it is directed needs to be considered. This applies to questions about moral decision-making in Buddhism, as it does to other issues of *buddha-dhamma*. One clear example of the hierarchical and developmental nature of Buddhist teachings, which is of special importance for Buddhist ethical teachings, is the *dharma* formula, or summary of the structure of Buddhist teaching which occurs over twenty times in the Pāli Canon (the basic authoritative texts of Southern or Theravāda Buddhism). A significant part of the content outlined in this formula is concerned with applying an understanding of *karma (kamma)* to the practical implications of ethics, cosmology and spiritual attainment. The structure of the formula is as follows:

1. Step-by-step discourse: a) first part: giving (dāna), precepts (sīla) and the heavens [i.e., the different levels of refined existence, which correspond to levels of refinement in consciousness and moral practice]: b) second part: the defects of sensuality and positive gain in freedom from it.
2. The particular teaching: the Four Noble Truths, suffering, its arising, its cessation and the path to its cessation.

(Cousins, in Hinnells (ed.) 1985: 300)

The detailed content which provides the specific message within this formula was adapted according to the circumstances in which it was delivered. In some texts it occurs in little more than the summary provided above. In others it is expanded with detailed explanation and examples. As Lance Cousins points out, the texts often describe the Buddha delivering this teaching, followed by the hearer of the teaching gaining a direct perception and heightened understanding of *dharma*. The Pāli term for this perception and sudden understanding is *dhamma-cakkhu* (*dharma* eye or spiritual vision); it marks the person's entry on to the supermundane (*lokuttara*) path, and so their serious commencement of higher practice and attainment. One dramatic example of this attainment taking place suddenly, and to an unlikely candidate, is the case of Aṅgulimāla. He was a murderer and bandit, who pursued the Buddha one day with the intention of killing him. The Buddha used his psychic mastery to outpace the running Aṅgulimāla, without appearing to move quickly at all. The Buddha gave the perplexed Aṅgulimāla a very brief *dhamma* talk on harmlessness, and the would-be assassin attained the *dhamma-cakkhu*, threw away his weapons and became a monk. Shortly after this he attained liberation as an *arahant* ('Worthy One' who has attained the highest goal short of being a *buddha*).[1]

It is important to notice that the 'step-by-step discourse' is predominantly directed towards ethical concerns and teachings. It could therefore be said to relate to 'kammatic' (pp. 19–20) concerns. Within this teaching there is a subtle shift from the external features of moral conduct in the first part, to more psychological aspects of

21

ethical teaching in the second part. These two parts of the step-by-step discourse provide a platform of moral behaviour and mental stability, so the follower is ready to achieve a fuller understanding of the particular teaching of the Four Noble Truths. These are obviously soteriological in orientation, and constitute what Spiro has classified as 'Nibbanic Buddhism'. The difference in content between the two types of teaching should not blind us to their conceptual and functional inter-relatedness.

The first part of the step-by-step discourse begins with giving (*dāna*). This is understood as a formal religious act rather than a generalised act of charity. It is directed specifically to a monk or spiritually-developed person. Its ethical and religious significance is often ignored in doctrinally orientated western accounts of Buddhism. Originally, *dāna* was taught as a non-violent replacement for the brahmanical sacrifice. It has the effect of purifying and transforming the mind of the giver:

> The inner intention of the giver is reflected in the care, attention and joy with which the giving is performed. The higher the state of mind the more powerful the action (*kamma*). Important too is the state of mind of the recipient, made infectious as it were by the special nature of the act of giving. Either of these is sufficient to make the act effective. The two together are even more powerful.

> (Cousins, in Hinnells 1985: 301)

The emphasis on the intention and attitude underlying the act is characteristic of Buddhist ethical teaching and practice. The popular understanding of the merit (*puñña*) which results from the practice of *dāna* is an important feature of lay Buddhist practice in all Buddhist countries (see Gombrich 1988: 124–7). For those aspiring to systematic practice and attainment on the Path, *dāna* helps the preliminary settling of the mind, and reduces selfishness, and provides a natural preparation for undertaking the Precepts (*sīla*). For the laity there are normally five precepts. Again the formal undertaking of the precepts, which usually follows the 'going for refuge' to Buddha, *Dharma* and *Saṅgha*, constitutes a religious act which brings about benefits and merits. The refuges and precepts are therefore chanted at the outset of most formal Buddhist activities. The wording of the precepts is significant; it translates as follows:

I undertake the training rule of refraining from:

- destroying life;
- taking what is not given;
- wrong behaviour in regard to sense pleasure;
- untrue speech;
- causes of intoxication.

The precepts are formulated not as imperatives or commandments, but as training rules voluntarily undertaken to facilitate practice.[2] For the laity there are no externally imposed sanctions for transgression of the precepts. According to Buddhist action theory (i.e., *karma*), unwholesome acts will result in unpleasant tendencies and results. Spiro observed in Myanmar (Burma) that the main motivation for complying with the precepts was fear for the 'karmic' consequences of non-compliance, rather than the positive meritorious benefits of compliance (Spiro 1971: 99). Behaviourally, one could argue that this amounts to the same result, but Spiro is rightly concerned with the psychological or motivational factors behind moral behaviour.

In his study he lists the set of conventional Burmese beliefs about the specific consequences of failure to comply with specific precepts. They are as follows: for adultery, the man will be reborn with a small penis, the woman will be reborn as a prostitute. For adultery with a married woman, the consequence is hell. For killing, the consequence is usually an interminable period in one of the hells, the length of duration depending partly upon the moral, spiritual and 'biological' status of the victim, and sometimes on their relationship to the killer. Killing a monk or one's parents is clearly among the gravest of offences. Killing other people or animals is certainly serious but the time in hell will be shorter. For less grave cases of killing, a short human life rather than hell may be the result. Killing mammals is graver in its consequences than killing reptiles; killing invertebrates is the least grave. Stealing will result in an impoverished future life; the consequences of white lies can be removed by meritorious acts. As Spiro points out, there are many variations in the detailed 'karmic' correlations which ordinary Burmese people maintain (Spiro 1971: 98–102).

Spiro observed that among the Buddhists of Myanmar positive acts such as giving (*dāna*), the support of monks or building pagodas, or the purchase and release of animals intended for slaughter, are considered more effective methods of acquiring merit rather than simple compliance with the precepts (Spiro 1971: 103–113). Similar findings have been observed among Thai Buddhists.[3] Unfortunately Spiro tends to interpret such beliefs only in rather mechanistic terms, and formally separates considerations of merit accumulation from considerations of morality. This procedure seems to be informed by western assumptions about the nature of moral worth, and ignores the extent to which positive accumulation and avoidance of unwholesome acts form a complementary process; and one makes little sense without reference to the other. As Lance Cousins points out, the cultivation of giving (dāna) and moral conduct (sīla) will themselves refine consciousness to such a level that rebirth in one of the lower heavens is likely if further practice and entry on the Path are not developed (Cousins, in Hinnells 1985: 304).

It should be emphasised that there is nothing improper or un-Buddhist about limiting one's aims to this level of attainment. Many of the ways in which Buddhist practices and institutions actually function represent a very subtle fusing of 'popular' concerns for the accumulation of merit and a beneficial rebirth, with 'élite' monastic concerns over the dissemination of buddha-dhamma, and the continuation of lay support.

One perfect illustration of this fusion of concerns and interests is the traditional phenomenon of temporary monkhood, which is still widely practised in Myanmar and Thailand (cf. the discussion of ethical vitality in the introduction, p. 11). In it young boys are temporarily admitted to monasteries as 'monks'. The age of the boys is generally eleven, and the period of this temporary monk status is traditionally three months, but there are wide variations (Spiro 1971: 247). The temporary ordination procedure serves a number of functions. From the 'kammatic' and popular point of view, it achieves considerable merit for the boy and his sponsor (usually his family). In ritual or 'apotropaic' terms the actual ordination ceremony generates considerable magical and protective power for the boy and his sponsors.

From an institutional point of view, the monastery is gaining revenue for the service and, even more important, it is establishing a clear link between that individual and the saṅgha which will influence his attitude to Buddha, dhamma and saṅgha for the rest of his life. He will in adult life expect to be a donor or supporter of monks if his resources allow. In a small number of cases the boy decides that he finds the life of a monk rewarding or worthwhile, or possibly less harsh than the life of work and hardship in the world, and decides to remain as a monk. In other words, the ordination can be an important means of recruitment to the *sangha*. Finally, from a dharmic point of view, he is being exposed, albeit in a diluted form, to the discipline of monastic life and the value of restraint. Spiro (1971: 105) tends to minimise this dimension of the procedure, but it should not be ignored.

In Buddhist societies both past and present, 'Nibbanic Buddhism', or the systematic following of the Path (*magga*), with the overt intention of rapidly gaining liberation and the spiritual status of *arahant* (Sanskrit: *arhat*; 'worthy one' – the highest ideal for Theravāda Buddhists) is the concern of a minority of monks within the *sangha*. The majority of devout Buddhists, including most monks, are concerned with what Spiro describes as the 'proximate salvation' offered by 'kammatic Buddhism'. The concepts relating to and derived from the 'radical salvation' sought in 'Nibbanic Buddhism' are of course highly important. They have an indirect influence on all forms of Buddhist practice and belief. But the temporary salvation offered by improving one's status and destination in the next life through the accumulation of merit (*puñña*) is the more common concern of the majority of devout Buddhists.

The second part of the step-by-step discourse moves on to address the dangers of attachment to sensory experience. These dangers include the distortion of mental clarity, partiality, selfishness, craving, grasping, violence, dishonesty, theft. The most direct and positive antidote to these states is the cultivation in meditation of the four *brahmavihāra*, or sublime states, of loving kindness (*mettā*), compassion (*karuṇā*), sympathetic joy (*muditā*), and equanimity (*upekkhā*). It has been convincingly demonstrated that these states are meditational achievements and are concerned with attitudes, rather than with practice or providing the direct motivation to social or ethical action.[4] Aronson distinguishes these states from the more general socially motivating qualities of 'simple compassion' (*karuṇa*) and 'sympathy' (*anukampā*) which are available to all Buddhists whether they are proceeding to an advanced level of practice on the Path, or ordinary householders. He points out that it was this primary motive of sympathy which caused the Buddha to arise and teach in the first place. The sublime states cultivated in meditation will produce a refining of consciousness to such a level that rebirth in a less corporeal realm of existence will be possible. Alternatively meditators may choose to follow the path to a higher level of attainment, cultivate their meditational practice and so move on to the level referred to in the 'particular teaching', which is concerned with an understanding of the Four Noble Truths and the advanced levels of meditation practice (see Cousins, in Hinnells 1985: 305–309).

The importance of karma

It is clear that underpinning and pervading the whole of the Buddhist teaching on the Path, at both ordinary (lokiya) and supermundane (lokuttara) levels, is the notion of karma. Because a general knowledge of Buddhist teaching about karma is now quite common in the East and West, it is easy to underestimate the impact of the Buddha's innovative reworking of a traditional brahmanic concept. This impact is dramatically described in early texts dealing with the Buddha's final stages of attainment and his enlightenment. In these accounts, the fourth higher knowledge (abhiññā) gained by the Buddha is of his own previous lives, and how his wholesome actions give rise to beneficial consequences. This is followed by the fifth higher knowledge, which is the ability to observe the previous lives of all living beings, giving a vivid and direct understanding of the nature of their actions and the attendant consequences (karmavipāka). The sixth superknowledge consists in the knowledge of the destruction of the influxes (āsava), unwholesome tendencies and mental states, followed by the Buddha's direct experience of the nature of the human condition as suffering or imperfection, its cause, its cessation and the Path to its cessation, i.e. the Four Noble Truths.

The Buddha's important contribution to the theory and concept of karma has been to give an ethical and psychological orientation to the brahmanic notion of karma, which referred to effective ritual action. The emphasis in Buddhism is on the determining or volitional intention behind the action, and it is this which produces the seeds and tendencies which affect or determine future states and conditions. In the Buddhist context, the meaning of karma has shifted from ritual act to volitional act or intention. 'It is choice or intention that I call *karma* – mental work – for having chosen, a man acts by body, speech and mind.'[5] This is reflected in the traditional Buddhist emphasis on the need for controlling and understanding the mind if moral practice and spiritual training are to be cultivated to their higher levels.

The emphasis on the psychology of intentions in traditional Buddhist ethical teaching and spiritual practice should not lead to the undermining of physical behaviour and actual consequences. It would be incorrect to say that the intention or will to perform an unwholesome act, which was not actually carried out, would produce the same effect as the actual performance of such an act. The subtlety of levels of intention and the relationship between intention and behaviour are acknowledged. For example, the casual thought, 'I wish X were dead', is certainly unwholesome, and will produce some unfortunate result. But the results would be much more serious in the case of someone who wishes X dead and makes detailed plans for murder. The results would be even more grave in the case of someone who raises the initial thought, plans and then actually carries out the murder. The degree of intention or volitional energies (*saṃskāra/saṅkāra*) involved in the final scenario are clearly greater than those involved in the first two.

It is clear that the notion of *karma* permeates all levels of Buddhist teaching and practice. A generalised 'knowledge of the ownership of deeds' greatly facilitates cultivation of giving and moral conduct. It is also clear that a full understanding of the detailed operation of *karma* and its implications is available only at the highest levels of attainment and practice. It is interesting to note that it is only at this level of practice and attainment, when intentional acts producing harmful consequences are no longer performed, that a full understanding of the nature of that action and results is achieved (Robinson and Johnson 1977: 38–39). This does not mean that beings at this advanced level no longer act. The teaching career and activities of the Buddha and the *arhat*s (worthy/enlightened ones) disproves this. It simply means that their acts are of such a quality that they no longer generate fresh tendencies and consequences in performing them.

Given the causal processes involved in the operation of *karma* at the lower or provisional levels, and given the more subtle processes operating at the higher level, we can describe the Buddhist ethical and spiritual path as a form of spiritually rarified utilitarianism (p. 5). What counts as 'good' in Buddhism is understood in terms of liberation or overcoming suffering. The subtle pleasurable nature of meditative states (e.g., the *brahmavihāra* and *jhāna* states and resultant heavenly realms) is often overlooked. *Nirvāṇa* itself is frequently characterised as supremely blissful, peace, etc. The incentive value of the pleasurable aspects of the path is employed at both popular and higher levels. Here again, the thinking underlying such uses is distinctly consequentialist.

The moral rules of the *Saṅgha*

The issue of the training rules or precepts (*prātimokṣa/pātimokkha*) of the monastic order (*saṅgha*) is one of supreme importance in understanding the functioning of Buddhist ethical thought. The training precepts and rules constitute the core of the Vinaya Piṭaka (Discipline Collection) section of the Buddhist Canon. They are a list of offences recited regularly at the confession ceremony known as *uposatha*, which occurs on the days of the new moon and the full moon. The early form of this ceremony involved the confession of any transgression before the whole community (*saṅgha*). Gombrich notes that the developed procedure involves the confession of offences in pairs, followed by the communal recitation by all the monks present (Gombrich 1988: 109).

It nevertheless remains true that the formal and public dimensions of this ritual are central to the maintenance of the *saṅgha*. It is important to note that a monk's transgressions can be officially acknowledged only if they are confessed voluntarily by the monk himself. Many offences are concerned with details of deportment and decorum, and the simple confession of them incurs no further consequences. Gombrich notes that 75 of the 227 offences in the *pātimokkha* code of the Theravāda tradition are of this nature (p. 108). Only four types of offence result in permanent exclusion from the *saṅgha*. These are: killing a person, engaging in sexual intercourse, theft, and the false claiming of higher knowledge and powers. Lesser offences may result in temporary exclusion. Gombrich has rightly indicated the importance of the fortnightly confessions of offences and communal recitation of the *pātimokkha* in Buddhist history (Gombrich 1988: 106–114).

It is clear that it is the sharing of a common *pātimokkha* which is crucial in determining an ordination tradition, and it is the common *pātimokkha* and ordination tradition which is what defines and determines a sect (*nikāya*). Although to an outsider the differences between the *pātimokkha* of the different sects seem to be inconsequential, it is the preserving of the integrity of these lists of offences in detail which gives the sect its continuity and ensures that lineage's identity. As Gombrich observes, the formation and definition of a sect (*nikāya*) in traditional Buddhism is much more a question of observance and corporate ritual identity than primarily a matter of doctrinal agreement (Gombrich 1988: 110–114).

The *sangha*, ethics and society

For the issue of Buddhist morals and society, what is of equal importance is how the personal practice of the individual monk interweaves with the communal and institutional dimensions of the *sangha*. Gombrich (p. 72) has described early Buddhism and the Theravāda tradition as representing a form of religious individualism (i.e., relying only upon one's own resources and efforts to realise a goal). Early Buddhist texts describe the Buddha identifying the Path by his own example and providing the means for beings to find liberation. It is up to self-reliant individuals to employ these means and follow the Path through their own efforts. Buddhist traditions have been virtually unanimous throughout Buddhist history that the most effective and reliable way of following the Path is within the community of the *sangha*. This necessarily involves engaging with the social dimensions of the *sangha*, which is best seen as a communal institution with a soteriological orientation, in Gombrich's words, 'an association of self reliant individuals' (p. 89). This dual nature of the *sangha* and its effective embracing of individual spiritual concerns and communal institutional concerns has given rise to considerable discussion by western scholars and commentators. It has often been at the heart of some of the more obvious conflicting characterisations of Buddhism in scholarly accounts. One dimension of the *sangha* has often been emphasised at the expense of the other.

One example of a difference in emphasis in modern scholarship, which relates to the above issues, is to be found in the differences between T.O. Ling and R.F. Gombrich. Ling sees early Buddhism as a psycho-social philosophy which incorporates 'a theory of existence consisting of a diagnosis (of the human malaise) and the prescription for a cure'.[6] He rightly takes the teaching of no-self as central to Buddhism, but interprets it specifically as a teaching designed to overcome the 'disease of individualism'. He sees the communal life of the *saṅgha* as providing the context and environment where individualism can be most effectively broken down. On the issue of the relationship between *saṅgha* and lay society, Ling maintains that the Buddha consciously modelled the *saṅgha*'s constitution and organisation on the methods of government of the tribal republics of north India, and that these principles were ideally seen as a model for government for society in general. His case for the latter largely rests on his interpretation of the 'conditions of welfare' passage in the *Mahāparinibbāna sutta*. In this text, King Ajāttasattu of Magadha plans to invade the neighbouring states of the Vajjian Confederacy. The king asks the Buddha about the likely outcome. The Buddha replies that, providing the Vajjians continue to hold their regular public meetings, take decisions in concord, and honour their established traditions and institutions, then they will survive and prosper. Shortly after, he says that providing the Buddhist *saṅgha* operates along the same lines, and upholds its own rules and institutions, then it too will survive and prosper. Ling is suggesting that in this text, the Vajjians are regarded as democratic, and that their system of government is presented as a worthy model, for the *saṅgha* and for society as a whole (Ling 1981: 144–152, McFarlane in Pauling 1986: 98–9).

Ling's emphasis here is upon the observance of collective decision-making, as well as a moral orientation, and it is these which are seen as the signs of a strong tradition, state or institution. Ling concedes that, in practice, the early *saṅgha* had to come to terms with the reality of increasingly powerful centralised and expansionist monarchies in north India in the fifth and fourth centuries BCE. It would appear that the characterisation of early Buddhism offered by Gombrich reflects a radically different perspective. He sees Buddhism as an early form of religious individualism with a theory of effective individual action which appealed to an increasingly important mercantile class (Gombrich 1988: 72–81).

Despite the apparent differences between Ling and Gombrich in their characterisations of early Indian Buddhism, it is possible to reconcile significant aspects of their positions. One could argue that a soteriological religion of self-help and individual responsibility, with its ethic of merit at a popular level, and spiritual endeavour at the élite level (Gombrich), would be forced to confront the psychologically and spiritually damaging implications of its own individualism. Taking this process further, efforts of an individual and inherently 'self-authenticating' kind must be made in order to overcome or uproot the notion of individualism and its attendant excesses. One can, of course, interpret this as an impossible and paradoxical vicious circle; or one can assume the Mahāyāna Buddhist perspective of skilful means and see it as using a thorn to take out a thorn.

Mahāyāna Buddhism

The ethical and social teaching of Mahāyāna Buddhism will now be considered in more detail. Although not exclusive to the Mahāyāna traditions, it was among these that the concept of the *bodhisattva* was refined and developed into an ethical and spiritual practice and ideal in its own right (*bodhisattva* means literally 'Being of Awakening'). It is impossible to treat Mahāyāna Buddhism as a single unified entity, but the *bodhisattva* as the embodiment and exemplar of supreme wisdom (*mahāprajñā*) and supreme compassion (*mahākaruṇā*) does provide the nearest thing to a core concept for all the diverse traditions and practices of the Mahāyāna. Many of the familiar virtues and meditational states exemplified in traditional Buddhism reappear in the qualities and practices of the *bodhisattva*, known as the perfections (*pāramitā*). These are: giving (*dāna*), moral conduct (*sīla*), patience (*kṣānti*), energy (*vīrya*), absorptive meditation (*dhyāna*), and wisdom (*prajñā*). Some later texts add skilful means (*upāyakauśalya*), resolution (*praṇidhāna*), strength (*bala*), and knowledge (*jñāna*).

A feature evident in this combination of perfections (and in many Mahāyāna texts) is the tendency to universalise or generalise central concepts and values. In this way, ideas and norms which for earlier traditional forms of Buddhism would have been restricted to the spiritual élite within the *saṅgha*, are extended or made available to the laity as well. Frank Reynolds and Robert Company have noted this tendency and have identified the concept of the *bodhisattva* as 'an ideal that combined the social virtues of a righteous householder with the ascetic ideals of a meditating monk, bridging what was

31

perceived by its proponents as a gap between monastic and popular Buddhism' (Reynolds and Company, in Eliade ed. 1985 Vol. 2: 501).

One feature of this universalising process is the replacing of the supposedly narrow and 'self regarding' goal of *nirvāṇa* as achieved by the *arahant* or *śrāvaka*, with the universal goal of supreme enlightenment (*saṃbodhi*) for all beings, as exemplified by the *buddha*s and *bodhisattva*s. In theory, the *bodhisattva* Path is open to all whether monk or layperson, man or woman. In practice, its higher stages are more likely to be achieved within the context of the *saṅgha*. Further evidence for the process of universalising or generalising at the level of values and norms can be found in texts which take ethical requirements previously confined to the *saṅgha* and teach them as norms for the laity. For example, the Chinese Mahāyāna version of the *Brahmajāla sūtra* requires both monks and lay people to abstain from violence and involvement with military affairs. In the Pāli version such requirements are clearly limited to members of the *saṅgha*.[7] Similarly, not killing animals and showing compassion to them, which are encouraged in early Buddhism (Horner 1967: passim), become requirements in the Mahāyāna; hence instructions for *bodhisattva*s to avoid meat are to be found in the Mahāyāna *Brahmajāla sūtra*.

This process is also evident in doctrinal matters. One of the great heroes of the Mahāyāna is the Bodhisattva Vimalakīrti, a wealthy householder with a family and many concubines, who teaches the senior monks and whose wisdom and skill equal that of Mañjuśrī.[8] A number of other Mahāyāna texts give prominence to advanced lay teachers of *dharma* (see Williams 1989; 21, 125, 129, 154). I agree with Williams that it would be incorrect to conclude from such texts that the Mahāyāna represents a product of innovations developed by lay Buddhists (1989: 22–26). With the exception of the modern Japanese lay Buddhist movements such as the Soka Gakkai, the *saṅgha* has always remained at the centre of Mahāyāna religious life and doctrinal development. It is almost certain that these spiritually egalitarian *sūtra*s were inspired and transmitted by monks.

There are philosophical or doctrinal reasons behind the Mahāyāna tendency to universalise across the *saṅgha*/householder distinction. One of the fundamental insights of the Mahāyāna is the non-differentiation of the round of craving, grasping, suffering, rebirth (*saṃsāra*), and the cessation of suffering in the liberated state (*nirvāṇa*), because all states and appearances are manifestations of

32

the same underlying *buddha*-nature (Jap., *bussho*), which is empty of self (*śunyatā*). The non-differentiation of *saṃsāra* and *nirvāṇa* was articulated by Nāgārjuna, and developed in relation to Mahāyāna thought and practice in the 'Perfection of Wisdom' literature and all later Mahāyāna systems. Such an undifferentiated insight tends to facilitate a kind of spiritual egalitarianism which sees no ultimate distinction between monk and householder, ordinary being and *buddha*. However, Mahāyāna texts and teachers accept that it is at the level of delusion and differentiation that beings need to be taught and guided. So the methods and teachings must be carefully moderated and adapted to the level of understanding appropriate to such beings. The crucial importance of teaching at the conventional level of truth should not be underestimated. In articulating the distinction between ultimate truth (*paramārtha-satya*) and conventional/provisional truth (*saṃvṛti-satya*), Nāgārjuna makes it clear that it is only by recourse to the conventional that the ultimate can be attained (trans. in Williams 1989: 69).

One aspect of the skilful means (*upāyakauśalya*) of *buddha*s and *bodhisattva*s is their ability to know which expressions of conventional truth to employ in order to bring beings to the Path to liberation most effectively. The Mahāyāna identification of levels of truth means there is no real tension between the spiritual egalitarianism expressed in some Mahāyāna texts and the more traditional Buddhist acknowledgement of a spiritual and moral hierarchy.

The problem for commentators is that different levels of truth and different means (*upāya*) interweave in the same passages and texts. This is perfectly illustrated in the context of Mahāyāna ethics, psychology and soteriology, in the account of Mañjuśrī's 'attempt' to kill the Buddha, in a text extant in the Chinese *Mahāratnakūta* collection. The whole incident is a skilful means devised by the Buddha in order to rid five hundred *bodhisattva*s of the spiritually debilitating knowledge of the heinous offences in past lives. The Buddha causes Mañjuśrī to attack him with a sword, then instructs Mañjuśrī that the real way to kill him is to see the Buddha (or any being) as possessing self or person. In reality, the Buddha, all beings and all *dharma*s are empty of self. To see them otherwise is actually to 'kill' them. In as much as they are ultimately without self, form or person, then killing them is an impossibility. On realising the emptiness of all *dharma*s, the five hundred *bodhisattva*s abandon their remorse over past crimes and continue their practice. One of the interesting features of this account is that in creating this skilful means the Buddha ensures that all the novice *bodhisattva*s of lesser understanding simply do not see the incident or hear the resulting discussion on emptiness and *karma*. This clearly demonstrates the principle of accommodation to different levels of ability and understanding which is central to the concept of skilful means.

It is clear from a wide range of Mahāyāna texts and teachings that the compassion and skilfulness of *buddha*s and *bodhisattva*s may permit or even require them to set aside traditional moral or doctrinal norms. The *Lotus sūtra (Saddharmapuṇḍarika sūtra/ Myoho-renge-kyo)*, which exerted such an influence in far eastern Buddhist teaching and practice, contains many such cases. For example, in chapter eight the Buddha declares that *bodhisattva*s may appear to adopt deluded and heretical views in order to gain the confidence of beings and lead them to liberation.[9] The most famous case of skilful means occurs in the third chapter of the *Lotus sūtra*, where the deception of a father (the Buddha), in promising toys which he does not have to his sons, is justified because the promise tempts them out of a burning house (*saṃsāra*).

The underlying principles of skilful means are apparent in early Buddhist texts, even though the technical vocabulary and detailed theory are lacking. One striking example is where the Buddha shows the lovesick monk, Nanda, the beauty of the nymphs in a heavenly realm to break his attachment to his new wife, and so causes Nanda to renew his efforts in meditation, in order to be reborn there. In fact, Nanda progresses to become an *arhat*, and forgets all about his desires for either human or heavenly maidens (Pye 1978: 122).

Texts dealing with skilful means, non-duality, emptiness, and other central Mahāyāna concepts frequently resort to extreme rhetorical exaggerations to make their point. There is a clear intention to shock conventional Buddhist hearers or readers out of their prosaic assumptions. These considerations are evident when *bodhisattva*s are described changing their sex at will,[10] or when the Buddha, in a previous life, breaks a vow of celibacy and lives with a woman for twelve years to prevent her death (Chang 1983: 433). In another life he kills a bandit with a spear to save five hundred traders, who are really *bodhisattva*s, and in doing so saves the man from the consequences of his intended actions.

It is clear from the circumstances of these and similar accounts, and from the high spiritual status of the performers of these deeds, that they are not intended to be employed as blanket justifications of moral transgressions in ordinary situations, outside the context of spiritual training and practice (McFarlane, in Pauling 1986 Vol. 1: 101–102). In scholarly treatises associated with the great Buddhist philosopher, Asanga (fourth or fifth century CE), there is evidence of attempts to formulate a dharmically and karmically coherent rationale for such transgressions. In these discussions and in the challenging examples used, there seems to be a willingness to test to the limit the demands of compassion and skilful means. Asanga's most challenging statement on these matters occurs in his *Bodhisattvabhūmi* treatise.

> There are certain offences of nature which the *bodhisattva* may practise through his skilful means, whereby he commits no fault and indeed produces much merit. For instance, when the *bodhisattva* sees a thief or bandit ready to kill many hundred beings, even great beings such as *śrāvaka*s, *pratyekabuddha*s, or *bodhisattva*s. Seeing this, he refines his thought and reflects: 'If I kill this being I will be reborn in a hell, but I am willing to suffer it. This being may later act in such a way as to avoid hell'. Resolving in this way, the *bodhisattva*, with kind thoughts towards the being, one with him in his heart, with compassionate regard to his future and abhorring his act, kills him. He is free from fault and produces much merit.
>
> So, too, is the *bodhisattva* when there are kings or great ministers who are excessively cruel and have no compassion for beings, intent on causing pain to others. Since he has the power, he makes them fall from command of the kingdom, where they cause so much demerit; his heart is compassionate, he intends their welfare and happiness. If there are thieves and bandits who take the property of others, or property of the *sangha* or a *stūpa*, making it their own to enjoy, the *bodhisattva* takes it from them, reflecting, 'Let not this property be a disadvantage and misfortune to them for a long time'. So he takes it and returns it to the *sangha* or to the *stūpa*. By this means, the *bodhisattva*, though taking what is not given, does not have a bad rebirth, indeed much merit is produced.[11]
>
> (Asanga, *Bodhisattvabhūmi*, Wogira (ed.) 1930: 165–7)

Such examples and arguments are certainly open to casuistic exploitation, though the explicit use of the concept of skilful means to justify or rationalise known cases of moral transgressions is actually quite rare. However, it would be misleading to suggest that they never occurred. One notable example is the celebrated assassination of the Tibetan king, gLand dar ma, by the monk dPal gyi rdo rje, in 842 CE. The king was violently persecuting the *saṅgha* and the monk acted to save the *dharma*, and save the king from perpetuating his own wicked acts and their consequences (Williams 1989: 190). It is significant that even though the Mahāyāna ethic of skilful means theoretically justified the act, the offending monk admitted his offence and excluded himself from ordination ceremonies. In another supposedly historical incident, which is typical of the kind of rhetorical extremes already mentioned, the great Mādhyamika teacher, Aryadeva, invokes the notions of emptiness and non-duality, and the illusoriness of the victim and perpetrator of murder. He does this not to justify an act of killing on his part, but rather when he has just been fatally stabbed by an assassin, to whom he proceeds to teach the above *dharma*, and who he provides with the means of his escape (Khantipalo 1964: 174–5).

Vajrayāna Buddhism

Like other major developments in Buddhist teachings and methods, the Vajrayāna (Adamantine Vehicle) represents both a continuity with the Buddhism from which it emerged as well as a creative departure from it. The antecedents of the Vajrayāna are basically twofold:

1. The radical emptiness teaching of the 'perfection of wisdom' (*Prajñāpāramitā*) and Mādhyamika texts, which asserts the non-differentiation of *saṃsāra* and *nirvāna* (pp. 32–3), and the ultimate 'sameness' of all *dharma*s, and so encourages dispassion and detachment with regard to *dharma*s.
2. A strongly devotional or affective type of Buddhist practice, which was familiar with the magical potency of Buddhist ritual. This could be classified using Spiro's category of 'apotropaic'. It should be acknowledged that even the perfection of wisdom texts and their related practices are not devoid of this magical dimension of Buddhist practice (Conze 1959: 96–100, 118–125).

The aim of practice in Vajrayāna is to focus the mental, volitional and physical energies of the initiate, and refine them through meditational, mantric and ritual means, eventually transforming them to a point where their qualities are the same as those of the body of a *buddha*. In other words, it is to use the ordinary qualities of the body, speech and mind, and transform them into the extraordinary qualities of the *dharmakāya* (true body of all *buddha*s).

Some more radical Vajrayāna treatises or *tantra*s (*tantra*s are ritual texts attributed to the Buddha, which offer access to spiritual mastery and power), seem to start where Asanga and the extreme cases in the *sūtra*s cited above left off. Some appear to insist uncompromisingly on the initiate's demonstration of the non-differentiation between *saṃsāra* and *nirvāna*, or between pure and impure. Actions such as the following are all recommended, in the appropriate circumstances: killing (usually restricted to killing beings about to commit actions which would take them straight to hell), lying (usually recommended in the interest of *upāyakauśalya*), stealing (usually to prevent those who crave possessions from stealing themselves), adultery (usually to provide human rebirths for the recently deceased who are in danger of descending into a hell), wine drinking (usually to sever attachments and overcome discrimination between fellow initiates and worldlings), consorting with low caste women (usually explained as a means of overcoming attachment to the 'pure' and aversion to the 'impure', i.e. a practical demonstration of sameness and non-discrimination).

Although Vajrayāna Buddhism developed in India from as early as the fifth and sixth centuries CE the bulk of the commentarial literature on the *tantra*s (a form of esoteric Buddhism initiating a devotee into higher levels of attainment) is preserved in Tibetan texts, although some *tantra*s are preserved in Sanskrit. These texts and their commentaries continue to perplex many western scholars, who are generally approaching the texts in isolation from the meditational and ritual practices associated with them, as well as from the rich oral tradition which supports their practice.

Two excellent recent studies of the ways of interpreting complex Vajrayāna texts are those of Michael M. Broido and Robert A.F. Thurman (both in Lopez ed. 1988: 71–118, 119–148).[12] Broido points out that there are clearly intended multiple levels of explanation apparent in these texts. He demonstrates how the fundamental distinction between a *neyārtha* (provisional or exoteric) level of explanation and a *nithartha* (final or esoteric) level, is explicitly applied to one such text (Broido, in Lopez ed. 1988: 72–82). The *neyārtha* explanation follows very much that outlined above. But the *nithartha* explanation treats the language of killing, lying, stealing, adultery, etc. as a detailed code for a variety of specific meditational, physiological and mantric procedures, largely concerned with the generation of internal heat through sound (*mantra*), and the retention and redirection of semen. A very general relationship between mental/behavioural control and mental/physiological control could perhaps be argued for in attempting to relate the two levels of explanation here, but it would be difficult to sustain with any real conviction. What is clear is that tantric texts and their commentarial material cannot simply be taken at face value.

Conclusion

The diversity, complexity and flexibility of moral practice and moral reponse to be found in Buddhist traditions make generalisation about the nature of Buddhist moral decision-making extremely difficult. The apparent simplicity of the precepts for lay people and the training rules for monks, serves as a guide for the ordinary follower, and alleviates the need for detailed reflection on the nature of moral or karmic processes. The implicit message for the ordinary Buddhist is to follow the moral guidelines provided by *dharma*, and, even in the absence of a full understanding of the detailed operations of *karma*, a happy future life will be achieved. Even underlying this implicit message is a pragmatism which is typical of all Buddhist thinking. The soteriological and pragmatic orientation of higher levels of Buddhist practice (Nibbanic Buddhism), means that considerable flexibility is apparent at the level of practice. Hence for the advanced *bodhisattva* in the higher levels of Mahāyāna practice and teaching, breaking the formal precepts may be expedientially necessary. In such cases, of course, the overriding consideration remains a moral one, in that the *bodhisattva* only acts in such a way in the interests of great compassion (*mahā-karuṇā*). He uses desperate measures and skilful means only in particular and exceptional circumstances; and does so only in the interest of benefitting or teaching deluded beings. The underlying motivation remains both moral and soteriological.

The Vajrayāna tradition, despite its strange, coded language and apparently bizarre practices, operates on the same underlying assumptions as the Mahāyāna tradition from which it emerged. The aim of literal transformation into the form and attributes of an enlightened *buddha*, also entails an engagement with the fundamental qualities of supreme wisdom (*mahā-prajñā*) and supreme compassion (*mahā-karuṇā*). It should also be emphasised that the extreme measures sanctioned by Asanga and other Mahāyāna authorities, and the sometimes bizarre sounding rites of the Vajrayāna tradition were generally envisaged as being practised by monks, who were normally following the discipline and restraint of the training rules of the *saṅgha*, and who were always under the direct supervision of an experienced teacher. In such a context, transgressions, even in the context of skilful means for the sake of others, were seen as the exception and not the rule.

NOTES

1. Horner, I.B. trans. (1975) *Middle Length Sayings*, London, Pali Text Society, vol. 2, pp. 284–92.
2. See Bowker, J. (1983) *Worlds of Faith*, BBC Ariel Books, p. 132.
3. Tambiah, S.J. (1968) 'The Ideology of Merit and the Social Correlates of Buddhism in a Thai Village', in E.R. Leach (ed.) *Dialectic in Practical Religion*, Cambridge University Press, pp. 69–70.
4. See Aronson, H.B. *Love and Sympathy in Theravāda Buddhism*, Delhi, Motilal Banarsidass, Ch. 5, and 'Motivations to social action in Theravāda Buddhism', in A.K. Narain (ed.) *Studies in History of Buddhism*, Delhi, B.R. Publishing Corporation, pp. 1–12, both 1980.
5. *Anguttara Nikāya*, quoted in M. Carrithers (1983) *The Buddha*, Oxford University Press, p. 67.
6. Ling, T.O. (1973) *The Buddha*, London, Temple Smith, p. 120.
7. Rhys Davids, T.W. and C.A.F. Rhys Davids (1969) *Dialogues of the Buddha* (Digha Nikaya) part 1, London, Pali Text Society, Part 1: 4, 5, 13.
8. Lamotte, E. (1976) trans. S. Boin *The Teaching of Vimalakirti*, London, Pali Text Society, Ch. 8.
9. Hurvitz, L. (1976) *Scripture of the Lotus Blossom of the Fine Dharma*, New York, Columbia University Press, p. 160.
10. Paul, D.Y. (1985) *Women in Buddhism*, London, University of California Press, Ch. 5.

11. With thanks to my colleague David Smith for the help with the translation of the Sanskrit text.
12. In Lopez, D.S. (ed.) (1988) *Buddhist Hermeneutics*, Honolulu, University of Hawaii.

FURTHER READING

Asanga (1930) *Bodhisattvabhūmi* Wogira, U. (ed.) Tokyo.

Chang, Garma C.C. (ed.) (1983) *A Treasury of Mahāyāna Sutras*, Pennsylvania State University Press.

Collins, S. (1982) *Selfless Persons*, Cambridge, CUP.

Conze, E. (1959) *Buddhist Scriptures*, London, Penguin.

Cousins, L.S. (1985) 'Buddhism', in J.R. Hinnells (ed.) *A Handbook of Living Religions*, London, Penguin.

Gombrich, R.F. (1988) *Theravāda Buddhism*, London, Routledge and Kegan Paul.

Horner, I.B. (1967) *Early Buddhism and the Taking of Life*, The Wheel Publication No. 104; Kandy, Sri Lanka, Buddhist Publication Society.

Khantipalo, P. (1964) *Tolerance: A Study from Buddhist Sources*, London, Rider.

Ling, T.O. (ed.) (1981) *The Buddha's Philosophy of Man*, London, Dent.

McFarlane, S. (1986) 'Buddhism', in L. Pauling (ed.) *World Encyclopedia of Peace*, Vol. 1, Oxford, Pergamon.

Pye, M. (1978) *Skilful Means*, London, Duckworth.

Reynolds, F.E. and R. Company (1985) 'Buddhist Ethics', in M. Eliade (ed.) *The Encyclopedia of Religion* Vol. 2: 498–504, New York, Macmillan.

Robinson, R.H. and Johnson, W.L. (1977) *The Buddhist Religion*, California, Dickenson.

Spiro, M.E. (1971) *Buddhism and Society* London, Allen & Unwin.

Williams, P. (1989) *Mahāyāna Buddhism*, London: Routledge.

2. Christianity

Douglas Davies

Making moral decisions involves living in accord with the principles of a religion, and this lies at the heart of religious faith where issues of good and evil come into sharp focus. To understand the moral laws of a religion we need to grasp the principles motivating them and to see not only how they give shape and pattern to people's lives, but also how they motivate believers in living the good life. How, then, should Christians make moral decisions, what are the motives that control their way of life?

Like Jesus, many early Christians were Jews. One consequence of this was that Christianity inherited the Jewish belief that morality starts with God and reflects the very nature of God. God was believed to be specially concerned with both holiness and justice in individual and social life. Israel, and especially its prophets, realised early on that God was as much concerned with honesty in ordinary affairs as with the dutiful performance of religious ceremonies (Isaiah 1: 12–17; Micah 6: 6–8). The early Christian communities in some of their writings also stressed the importance of an inward love for the laws governing human life.

The word 'communities' (in the plural) is important, because it is a reminder that there was no one, single, 'Christianity' from the earliest moments, but rather a quest for the meaning and significance of Jesus, which took many different forms. It included disputes and conflicts. It is true that in general Jesus was recognised as Lord, as the one who had lived and died and risen from the dead in order to reconcile us to God and to each other. But when Jesus was also recognised as Christ (as the Messiah for whom the Jews had been waiting), what would the consequences of that recognition be for moral life and behaviour? Did the detail of the Law remain in place, as a control over life? Or had the detail of the Law been sub-ordinated to a new command of love? Is a good life to be achieved by works (feeding the hungry, visiting the sick, clothing the naked), or is it to be accepted as a work of God's grace and of the working of the Holy Spirit within individuals? The New Testament does not display one answer to these questions, but rather a struggle to see and understand more clearly what answers are in accord with 'the mind of Christ'.

The last phrase is not entirely vague. From the outset, followers of Jesus clearly felt that they were to make moral decisions in accordance with the teaching which Jesus gave and the life which he led. This dual emphasis on teaching and example was to remain important in later Christian history. In the Sermon on the Mount (Matthew 5–8) we have several examples of Jesus challenging people on the way they should live. For example, Jesus tells his listeners that they have all heard the traditional Jewish law that they must love their neighbour as themselves, but now he tells them that, in addition to loving their neighbours, they must also love their enemies (Matthew 5: 43–46). The reason for loving enemies comes from God's own moral nature, which all can see in the fact that God gives the benefit of sun and rain to all alike, irrespective of their attitude towards God. In other words, God is generous and not discriminatory.

Jesus finishes this part of his argument with the very simple point that even non-religious people are kind to those from whom they expect some benefit in return. Everybody knows that such 'give and take' is basic to life: I shall treat you well so that you will treat me well. This is part of being worldly-wise, but, in the teaching of Jesus, it is not true wisdom according to the values of the Kingdom of God. God's values are characterised by generosity, where people get more than they give, and certainly more than they deserve. All this is very pointedly taught towards the end of Matthew's Gospel in the story of a man hiring workers for his vineyard (20: 1–16). Men are hired at different times of the day, but, when pay-time comes, they all receive the same amount of money. Those who have worked all day long are disappointed at being paid the same as those who had done only one hour's work, even though they are given what they had originally agreed upon. We are not told the reaction of those who received a whole day's pay for just one hour's work, but we are told that the employer is a very generous person. In other words, the basis on which this employer operates is not the normal scheme of things.

Those hearing Jesus' teaching would have to get used to operating in a similar way if they too wanted to be disciples. Their moral decisions also would have to be based on the values of generosity and love. Just as important is the fact that without this knowledge they will misunderstand the way God treats them and the way they treat God. These simple points lay the foundation for understanding how Christians should set about making moral decisions and living morally themselves in their personal, social and private lives. Matters of morality on a nation- or state-wide level raise different (or at least additional) issues, as in the case of war, which need separate consideration (see further, pp. 62f.).

'Give and take' in daily life

Rules governing ordinary social life are often linked to the rules of religion. Sometimes they parallel each other but they may also be contradictory.

We have already seen (in the Introduction, pp. 12–13) how anthropologists understand reciprocity and obligation, and how it affects moral life and being. In the case of Christianity, the moral meaning of relationships is focused on an entirely new answer to the question, 'And who is my neighbour?' The question was asked by the lawyer who had already asked Jesus what he should do to inherit eternal life. Jesus told him in reply that he already had the answer in his own religious tradition: the absolute love of God, and the love of his neighbour as himself. 'But he, seeking to justify himself, said, "And who is my neighbour?"'

The parable of the good Samaritan extends the boundary of obligation to everyone and reduces the expectation of reciprocity to zero. This constitutes the identity of a Christian believer in a correspondingly new relation to God, with the content of obligation (in terms of ritual observance) reduced to zero (or at least 'near-zero') as a priority in human life, and with the expectation of reciprocity increased to the maximum, because it is recognised that everything is received as gift, including life itself. ('You see how he clothes the flowers of the field . . .? Shall he not much more clothe you, O you of little faith?') Thus the moral life and being of a Christian become a radical attack on idolatry, far more profound

43

than breaking carved images of God. The point here is that if human beings do tend to invest the other sources of their identity with great significance, even to the extent of seeing those sources as sacred, then idolatry may be only a step away.

Identity, worship and idolatry

In Christian thinking, idolatry occurs when God as the ultimate reality is replaced by some lesser concern. It is perfectly possible for individuals to gain their sense of identity from their family, spouse or children, from their career, profession, or hobby. A total focus on money, sex, or some other aspect of life may also serve the same end, giving an individual a sense of meaning and purpose in life. But in Christian thinking such things are secondary to God. So if individuals draw their identity solely from such partial things they are caught up in idolatry. The temptation to become selfishly focused on these items may lead to ethical choices which are the opposite of God's open generosity. In this sense, it is easy to see the miser as one who idolises money and is certainly not generous.

This situation is also the opposite of true worship in one important sense. Idolatry reinforces the individual's own sense of self. Worship, by contrast, stresses the centrality of God, and directs the worshipper away from self towards the divine. Such a movement from self towards God is one form of transcendence. It is basic to worship and closely related to ethics or the way people ought to live the good life.

This raises the question of reciprocity once more. In idolatry individuals give because they expect to receive benefit in return. They may offer to the gods to receive back as much. The form of prayer that goes with such idolatry takes the line: 'If you, O God, save me from this trouble, I will give money to the Church'. In contrast, in worship the believer offers thanks or praise to God simply because of the nature of God. In ethical decisions the believer acts in accordance with the nature of other people, who are made in the image of God. There is no expectation of benefit or return. This brings us to the important issue of self-sacrifice and self-offering.

The goal of Christian living is self-sacrifice. The believer lives for others and for God because Christ lived in that way, and because Christ lived and died for the sake of all people. The sacrifice of Christ draws out a response of self-sacrifice in the believer (Romans

12: 1). The Letter to the Galatians (2: 20) expresses it in this way, 'I have been crucified with Christ; it is no longer I who live, but Christ who lives in me: and the life I now live in the flesh I live by faith in the Son of God, who loved me and gave himself for me'.

Moral decision-making

What has been said so far is important as the foundation for morality. Christian morality, focused in the love of God, revealed in Jesus Christ, is grasped in such a way that a response is expressed in social justice. In other words, moral decisions are Christ-focused and socially enacted; they are also closely related to the idea of salvation.

Salvation is the identity of the Christian granted by God. This is a very important idea since it sets the boundaries for the way people think about themselves, and that perspective itself influences the way people think about others and act towards others. Salvation involves the believer in a new set of 'obligations' to God and to others. This is a very delicate area of debate and needs careful spelling out. One interesting way to do this is by relating the social ideas of gift and reciprocity to the theological ideas of grace and merit.

The Hebrew Bible set the social basis for salvation within the framework of God's covenant with Israel. God had promised a chosen people that he would cause them to flourish and to have a land for their own possession. In return, they were to live justly according to divine laws. The one problem with this view was that individuals might ignore their personal responsibility by putting the emphasis upon the group to which they belonged. As a counter-measure against this evasion of personal responsibility there is a trend of thought in the Hebrew scriptures which underlines the fact that all individuals are responsible for their own personal sins. Both Jeremiah and Ezekiel quote the same proverb ('The fathers have eaten sour grapes, and the children's teeth have been set on edge') in order to stress the point that a child should not suffer for the sins its parent committed, but rather that individuals should take responsibility for their own sin (Ezekiel 18: 1; see also 2 Kings 14: 6). The law of God was applicable both to the nation and to individuals within it.

Among the followers of Jesus and in the early Christian community there was much debate about whether this Jewish law of God also applied to Christian Jews. And what of Christians who were not Jews at all? In other words, did God's covenant with Israel embrace Christianity?

One reason why these were real and pressing problems was because early Christianity quickly came to establish itself as separate from Jewish identity and community life. Some of the early Christians were probably not Jews themselves, some of them were freed slaves or people who did not belong to fixed communities. The Christian churches of the first and second centuries came to provide an alternative community for many who lacked a community of their own. What would be the rules controlling these new congregation-communities, both within their own life and as far as the wider world was concerned? This became an even more pressing question because of the early Christian belief in the value of individuals in their own right, irrespective of their national, religious, or even their gender differences. In the teaching of Jesus, each individual has to decide on how to live after hearing the message of the Kingdom of God. Part of the process of making moral decisions lies in knowing that you have to decide for yourself, and that each believer is a responsible agent. Tradition was insufficient. One answer to these questions on how the new Christian community of otherwise unrelated yet 'saved' individuals should be governed emerges in the letters and theology of Paul. Central to his argument is the issue of grace and merit, which was to prove increasingly important throughout the future history of the emergent Christian Church.

Grace, merit and salvation

God is the central starting point in Paul's thought. God is the first to act both in creation and in salvation. It was God's decision to save humanity from its evil state. God did this through Jesus of Nazareth, who was himself God's appointed Messiah and was also in some distinctive way God's 'son'. Not only did Jesus live a perfect life, but his death was a sacrifice which paralleled the sacrifices of the Jewish Temple and also went far beyond them. This intense, spontaneous activity of God was grounded in divine mercy and love towards the human race. Humanity, by contrast, is depicted as being quite unable to rouse itself to any activity at all. All are, in Paul's terms, quite dead. Salvation originates in God and comes to men and women to enliven them, enabling them to respond to God's love.

Grace is the divine attitude of generous love revealed to needy human beings through Jesus. In the Letter to the Romans, Paul describes men and women as not only helpless and ungodly, but as enemies of God (5: 6, 10). In a vivid expression, Paul speaks of God's love being poured into human hearts; as dying from thirst, they are revived, saved by a love which forgives their sins and creates them anew to love God and to serve others. Paul goes to great pains at this point to argue that human effort plays no part in God's process of salvation. Nobody can boast that their own religious life or endeavours have won them God's favour; it was God who came and lavished riches upon them. Once individuals appreciate just what it is that God has done, they become touched by this expression of divine generosity and thus find it possible to become generous themselves.

We might even interpret 'faith' as this new sense of being generous. Faith is not the outcome of human endeavour: it is newly created in individuals as grace makes an impact upon their lives. There is a sense, then, in which grace and faith are true partners: grace expresses God's generous love, and faith expresses humanity's open acceptance of it. But this is where the problems start.

Because human beings are so used to living by reciprocity, they think that religion works on the same basis. In everyday life there is cause and effect in matched payments of give and take. Work produces wages and nobody ever gets anything for nothing. On that approach to life you would expect God to favour humanity because of some human endeavour or action. Paul's firm conviction is that nobody anywhere has any reason to think like that as far as the Christian message is concerned.

Grace and morality

Through Christ a new morality has been created. It resembles the Old Testament scheme of God's prime action towards a chosen people, but this new scheme is grounded in God's self-sacrifice in Christ and has resulted in a people of faith. The ethic or rule by which this people must live is the new commandment of love, which is not based on a balanced reciprocity. This rather technical term, 'balanced reciprocity', means that people expect to be repaid for what they do. 'A fair day's work for a fair day's pay' is one example of balanced reciprocity, and it underlies most social life. Christ's

47

ethic argued against such a careful give and take. He argued that if someone takes your coat you should give him your cloak as well (Matthew 5: 40). This outlook is grounded in generosity, and modelled on God's generosity to humanity.

In a very basic sense the teaching of Jesus seems to start on the normal assumption of reciprocity, that you should do to others what you expect them to do to you. This has a basic logic to it which all can understand (Matthew 7: 12), and it is sometimes even called the Golden Rule. But then Jesus passes on to an ethic of love which involves loving your enemy, an idea contrary to normal reciprocal rules. In human life enemies exist to do evil and harm; they are to be resisted and opposed, not only by individuals but by society at large. Christ's teaching throws a question mark over such normal views. Grace and faith together describe this new style of living. Ethical decisions should be taken on the basis of this ethic of love, according to the Sermon on the Mount; by so doing believers will truly reflect the generosity or 'perfectness' of God (Matthew 5: 48). The problem comes when people confuse ordinary reciprocity with the model of divine generosity. This is one of the best ways of understanding what is often called the 'faith-works' issue in Christian thought.

As this occurs in the letters of Paul (particularly in Galatians, 1 Corinthians, 2 Corinthians, Romans, to give them in the probable order in which they were written), it is the tension between, on the one side, the radical incapacity of humans to earn their own salvation, above all through an attempted obedience to the commands of law, and on the other side, the language of command which Paul uses, when instructing Christians how to live. Christian life is summarised in the love of God and the love of one's neighbour, but what does that general principle mean in detail and in practice? J.W. Drane summarised the issue in the title of his study of it, *Paul, Libertine or Legalist?*: 'The least we can do', he argued, 'is to observe that whereas in Galatians Paul was able to reject legalism in all its forms, in I Corinthians he reintroduces the *form* of legal language, which in turn leads him into a position in I Corinthians not so very much different from the legalism he had so much deprecated in Galatians' (p. 65).

But in the context of gift-giving and reciprocity, the apparent conflict dissolves. If we have received all things as a gift, including the Holy Spirit – the capacity to 'walk in newness of life' – then the language of a human life will become one of love, joy, peace, etc.

Some behaviours so contradict the utterance of the Spirit that they can be condemned; others so exemplify it that they can be commanded. But they are not commanded as bribes (gifts from ourselves to God of a coercive kind) to ensure our own salvation. Justification is not a statement that God has decided to overlook our sins because now we are doing a little better, but rather it is a statement that he has cancelled altogether the condemnation that we all undoubtedly deserve.

But although we can see now how the apparent tension between grace and works in relation to salvation might be resolved, the fact remains that the whole of Christian history has been an exploration of emphasis between these two, as they affect the practice and worth of morality.

The ideas of human endeavour, merit and reciprocity, can all be seen within Christian doctrine in the debate about salvation conducted by Augustine and Pelagius in the early fifth century. Augustine was a philosopher who converted to Christianity, and became Bishop of Hippo in North Africa. Pelagius was a lay monk who went from the British Isles to Rome and then on to Africa.

Augustine and Pelagius

Augustine thought that individuals were saved from the consequences of sin because God willed that they should hear the message of divine mercy and respond to it. He developed the idea of predestination, which is already found in the Bible, and said that God chose some people to believe in divine grace while others were not so chosen. Here the great stress is on God's wise decision and on the fact that salvation is a gift given to men and women. It is by God's mercy that they are able to understand their plight and sinfulness, and by God's mercy that they come to decide to live as Christians. The idea of 'prevenient grace' has been used to describe God's grace 'preventing' or, in a modern meaning of that term, 'going before' an individual on the road to faith. This made great sense to Augustine, as it did later to Martin Luther, against the background of human moral weakness and God's plan of predestination. What is important, as far as the earlier discussion of reciprocity is concerned, is that grace stands out as a gift in this scheme of salvation. Because all of God's actions are free and not

49

conditioned by human activity, so too with grace; grace is free and unmerited, and shows God's goodness and love.

This pattern of faith which stresses God's initiative above anything that a person does, is typical of those who have been described as 'twice-born' individuals. This descriptive term was elaborated by the psychologist and philosopher, William James, in his important study, *The Varieties of Religious Experience* (1902). There he spoke of people who see the world as evil, and who feel themselves inwardly disturbed by guilt and other negative forces. This outlook he called the religion of the 'sick-soul'. But these individuals often experience a conversion and a sense of freedom from guilt through a kind of new birth. Paul, Augustine and Luther all seem to have had such an experience.

Another and different sort of life is led by the 'once-born' type of religious believer. William James spoke of these people as having a religion of 'healthy-mindedness'. They do not experience a critical moment or period of conversion but tend to grow into their religious faith over a life-time. They tend to stress the goodness of both God and human beings and do not emphasise evil and guilt. The once- and the twice-born styles of Christian religion can, in a very broad way, be related to the form of theology in more Catholic and more Protestant traditions. Catholic doctrine does speak of being born again, but means by that the ritual process of baptism through which a child is said to be born again, as the Holy Spirit works through the ritual of the Church. As far as the psychological and experiential life of individuals is concerned, there is no expectation that a moment of conversion will occur. Within the more Protestant tradition, the idea of a personal act of commitment to God is more directly related to a conversion involving an experience of change.

The Catholic, once-born, style of life lived through the sacraments of the Church corresponds with a disciplined form of existence. In fact this idea of discipline can be stressed to a marked degree. This was one of the features emphasised by Pelagius, Augustine's opponent. In some respects Pelagius resembles a 'once-born' Christian. Being a monk he knew the significance of a disciplined life as a means of improving himself. Humanity, he believed, possessed the capability to do good because God had made that possible, but it depended upon individuals whether they willed to do good or not. If the belief was too widely accepted that individuals could do nothing to help themselves as far as salvation was concerned, then they would cease to strive to be better and would then simply become worse.

Augustine could not agree with this. God alone, he believed, was the source of salvation. People could not choose and carry out morally good things, simply because they were not morally good themselves. The doctrine of the Fall was influential in Augustine's thinking. He argued that, although humanity was created morally good, all people have disobeyed God and have been tainted with evil ever since. The generations after Adam and Eve have inherited, and been influenced by, evil.

We are now in a position to see why this debate between Augustine and Pelagius on salvation is important for the total theme of making moral decisions. The question hangs on the nature of human beings and the capabilities they possess. Are they capable of making moral decisions on their own, unaided by divine help? Is human nature so corrupted by sin that nothing good can come of it? Or are human beings intrinsically good, and able, at least partially and perhaps fully, to do good deeds?

Moral theology

Generally speaking, most Christian traditions accepted that men and women are at least inclined to evil. The majority of modern theologians, who would not accept literally the idea of a historical Adam and Eve and their original disobedience, still recognise the radical human inability to do good and avoid evil at all times. But it makes relatively little difference whether we speak of the Fall as a historical event or as a metaphor of the fallenness of humanity as a present experience: the significance lies in the fact that men and women know themselves to be other than they ought to be. They have a sense of what it means to be good, they know that there are religious laws and general principles of goodness, and they know that they fail to keep them.

For Augustine, God is always good in electing people to be among those who believe. These, in turn, when they come to believe and to experience the merciful love of God, acknowledge that God is the source of their own goodwill. They speak of themselves as having received grace from God, and express a passive sense of having been helpless until the divine mercy worked within them. Other terms were used to describe different aspects of grace, and all show how vital the idea was to Catholic and Protestant traditions alike. Protestant theology, for example, stressed 'irresistible grace', which meant that even God's chosen ones might fall by the wayside if God did not ensure that grace worked for them irresistibly until they attained heaven itself. 'Actual grace' was a Catholic term for God's special help in assisting an individual achieve some great endeavour but which would not stay with that person permanently.

So when it comes to making moral decisions, many Christians are aware that deciding what is good is one thing, but actually doing it is another. To love God with all one's heart, mind and strength, and to love one's neighbour as one's self, are two great commandments which many people support but few are able to practise. The reason for this inability is the incapacitating power of sin. It is for this reason that assistance is needed from God. Just as Augustine argued that God gives grace to enable people to believe, so grace is needed to enable them to live as believers.

In the centuries following after Augustine, and especially with Thomas Aquinas in the thirteenth century, moral theology emerged as a special form of theology to help believers live in a Christian way. Rules were constructed using the Bible and the teaching of the Fathers of the Church, and employing human reason to interpret these sources. They were especially important for helping large numbers of converts to Christianity, and for guiding priests when they gave direction to people after confessions of sin.

Penance, grace and indulgences

The growth of the Church, with priests as leaders and an increasing lay membership, involved increased concern over discipline. By about the third century, Church members who behaved immorally were placed under penance and not allowed to attend the eucharist for a specified period. But if particularly worthy people, such as those awaiting martyrdom, prayed for them, then they could be let off some of their penance time and be readmitted to full fellowship. When the idea of purgatory developed, this idea of release from penance was transferred from this world into the next. Purgatory was where the souls of the dead were purged of remaining sin and guilt prior to finally gaining the ultimate vision of God.

Just as martyrs might pray for fellow Christians and their readmittance to fellowship, so the prayers of worthy believers would avail for the dead and speed their journey to heaven. It was here that the idea of merit became important. Within the total membership of the Church were some particularly meritorious people, not only Christ and the Blessed Virgin Mary, his mother, but martyrs and other saints. Together their good works constituted a kind of treasure chest of merit which could benefit less saintly Church members. By the twelfth century it was possible to be granted a portion of this merit in what was called an indulgence.

Church leaders granted these indulgences to believers for some endeavour such as engaging in the Crusades against the enemies of Christianity, performing some penance, making a pilgrimage, and so on. This was a system of reciprocity in which the freedom from a period in purgatory was given for some work done on earth. It depended on the idea of a 'treasury of merit' within the Communion of Saints of the Church, and on church leaders, especially the Pope and some others, administering the system.

Martin Luther

Indulgence was a system far removed from the New Testament, and was open to abuse. This was something that made a strong impact upon Martin Luther (1483–1546), a German scholar and monk, whose own search for a personal sense of satisfying religion had involved him in a conversion experience and a deep conviction that the grace of God was fundamental to salvation. He emphasised the doctrine of justification by faith, which was derived from Paul's Letter to the Romans and gained great support from Augustine. This argued that faith alone was the human side of that relationship with God which is one of grace. For Luther, it was Jesus Christ who fully expressed God's grace to men and women. In his own study of Paul's Letter to the Romans, Luther expanded this point at the beginning of chapter 12: Jesus is the foundation of Christian ethics, and that foundation is God's free gift to humanity.

For Luther, moral decisions emerged from the experience of God's grace, which made the Christian into a free individual. The salvation that came by grace and was received in faith gave to each individual a sense of freedom, a freedom from having to satisfy religious legal requirements, a freedom which could be used as a basis to serve other people. Having a knowledge of their own salvation, Christians need no longer strive to please God – since that was an impossibility for weak and fallen humanity – having been forgiven by God. They were now at liberty to serve God and their neighbour.

Merit and gift were two important ideas for Luther, but as this quotation from his Commentary on Romans shows, they were entirely focused on Christ:

> For if through the offense of one many died, much more the grace of God, and the gift, by the grace of one man, Jesus Christ, has abounded to many (Rom. 5: 15).
> The apostle connects grace and the gift of grace as if they differed from one another, but he does this in order to show clearly the nature of him who was to come, as he said, namely, that as we are justified by God and receive his grace, we do not receive this grace by any merit of our own, but it is a gift the Father gave to Christ in order that he should give it to men.

Luther adds a further note, that this grace of God is not like a gift one friend gives to another but is much broader, since it is the enemy of God – fallen humanity – that receives the gift of grace through Jesus Christ.

What is now obvious is that human endeavour is out of the question as far as salvation is concerned, and moral decisions cannot be taken in order to impress God or to achieve some merit which will contribute towards salvation. Moral decisions to serve and love one's neighbour must now, inevitably, spring up from the living faith which God's grace has created within the person of faith. Morality is a consequence of faith and an outcome of salvation, it is not a means of meriting salvation.

For Luther, as for many subsequent Christian thinkers, there is a powerful sense of freedom underlying this commitment to morality, even though he argues that the Christian is a divided person, being both justified and yet also a sinner. For Luther, Christian individuals are responsible before God for their lives. This focus on faith, the individual, and in particular the sense of freedom that comes with salvation, was to be even more important in Kierkegaard, a Protestant thinker of a later generation for whom the making of moral decisions constitutes the central process of becoming truly Christian.

Søren Kierkegaard: deciding to be yourself

Søren Kierkegaard (1813–1855) was a Dane. His own life experiences led him to be extremely critical both of the official Church and of contemporary philosophical trends. For him, truth concerned the inward and personal dimensions of existence rather than proofs about the objective world. Subjectivity, knowledge of self, rather than objectivity and knowledge of the world, lay at the heart of his outlook. This is the reason why many see Kierkegaard as the father of existentialism, a philosophical outlook focusing on the existence and experience of individuals. It has taken definite non- and anti-religious directions in the work of people such as Heidegger, Camus and Sartre, and more Christian directions with Karl Jaspers and especially Gabriel Marcel. Kierkegaard wanted individuals to be true to themselves, to discover their own identity through their own bitter experience of life. The greatest moral decision that can be made is the decision to face oneself and not to turn away into trivial pursuits.

This is an extremely important point as far as moral decisions in Christianity are concerned. We normally talk about morality in terms of making judgements affecting our behaviour towards others. We accept rules for life and act upon them. Kierkegaard asked something more of his hearers. He asked people to realise that the greatest of all moral decisions they would ever have to take was to decide to become themselves. Rather in the way that Jesus told his disciples that they had to take the great log out of their own eye before they could possibly see clearly to take a speck of dust out of somebody else's eye, so Kierkegaard calls individuals to see that they must actively decide to become themselves before they can act truly and with integrity towards God and towards others.

But this is no easy task. For as individuals begin to see themselves as they are, they encounter sin. It is not easy for one person to describe sin to another person, each individual must know his or her own sin. Sin involves a kind of dread or anxiety which comes over individuals as they learn about their own freedom and the many possibilities open to them. Freedom is part of the dread anxiety of being human, freedom is related to sin. Sometimes Kierkegaard speaks of a kind of 'dizziness' surrounding our sense of freedom, and it is this dizziness which gives us a sense of dread. But such an awareness is absolutely vital before individuals can begin to become themselves.

The dread must be accepted as an act of faith, but it can only be accepted through the paradoxical belief that God became an individual in Jesus Christ. To think that God became a particular individual on this earth is something that reason rejects, argued Kierkegaard, because it is so hard to understand. Objectively it cannot be proved, but Kierkegaard had abandoned such objective proof. It is subjectively and inwardly that individuals come to faith and believe that God became man in Jesus. It is as people begin to experience these things, and to act decisively on them, that they come to be themselves and come to be Christian. Prayer was important as an opportunity to be what each one is before God. The acting and posturing of social life must give way to becoming a real self before God.

Existence and ethical vitality

The idea of ethical vitality is raised and discussed in the Introduction to this volume (p. 11), and the reader should refer to that section.

Kierkegaard is regarded as a founder of European existentialism, a movement which placed much emphasis on the individual deciding what is morally right or wrong. But here, the Christian insight is very different, because it recognises how prone to error and sin individuals are. So instead of each individual being involved in gaining merit, it is the one person, Jesus Christ, who is the source of all merit. Thus, instead of thinking of a part of a youth's life being given up to live according to religious precepts, Christian theology sees the whole life of Jesus as being lived fully in accordance with the will of God. Then, when he is still a man in the prime of life, Jesus gives himself to death in actual self-sacrifice. This pattern of life and death produces the fullest possible degree of ethical vitality, so much so that Jesus is said to die for the sin of the whole world. The merit generated by his perfect life which is finally yielded up in death is enough to count against all the lack of merit of the rest of humanity.

In the teaching of Paul there is another application of ethical vitality directed to those who have already become Christians through the merits of Jesus Christ and not through their own efforts. Paul addresses believers in this way:

I appeal to you therefore, brethren, by the mercies of God, to present your bodies as a living sacrifice, holy and acceptable to God, which is your spiritual worship.

(Romans 12:1)

Because Christ's merit has already won salvation for believers they can now devote their own ethical vitality to living out their Christian lives, especially in service to their neighbour. But such freedom is very hard to live with, its acceptance is not easy. In moral terms, as we have seen, it may well be easier to have strict rules to keep than to be a free agent who has to decide how to live for the sake of others. Something of the same problem, arising from the pull between freedom and the need for certainty, emerges in the idea of the 'Protestant ethic'.

The Protestant ethic, the morality of work

The Protestant ethic is another idea derived from the social sciences, in this case from the German sociologist Max Weber. Originally published in 1904–05, this argument involves a fundamental attitude to the morality of work in the sense of labour. It deals with the relationship between wealth creation and salvation.

Weber believed that the Puritan religious outlook, which followed on from the Protestant Reformation in Europe in the sixteenth century, linked the realms of salvation and work in a very distinctive way. The Protestant Christian believed that salvation came from God to the extent that God selected or predestined people to be saved. This was all God's doing. There was, as we have already seen, no merit in human action by means of which men and women might save themselves. But people want a degree of certainty in their lives, and are not content with the idea that *perhaps* they are in the group that God has chosen to save rather than in the group God has chosen to damn. So a practical answer emerged as a way of coping with this dilemma: the Protestant ethic.

Christians set themselves the task of doing their work in careful and efficient ways, resulting in success and profit. They interpreted success as a divine blessing, and assumed that God would bless only those specially chosen for salvation. So wealth was an indirect proof of salvation. The moral decision to live carefully before God, and

57

not to waste the riches that were earned but to spend them in capitalist investment or charitable work, produced a whole cultural outlook.

Although the Protestant ethic is not normally associated with the idea of ethical vitality (pp. 11, 56), the two are very closely related. They are especially closely linked through the idea of asceticism. Max Weber saw Protestants who were dedicated to work as practising a sort of asceticism, which he called a worldly asceticism. Though they have not gone into a monastery and away from the world to control their life, they are still engaged in ascetic activities. Their life is highly organised, ordered and controlled. They do not waste their wealth indulging their appetites, and, just as much as monks, this commitment is for life. The similarity with monks, whether they are Christian or Buddhist monks, is obvious, in that life's energy is devoted to living according to strict moral principles related to salvation even if not causing salvation.

Here then, in Protestant ethical vitality, we have one important sort of moral decision. It is the decision to live a controlled and organised life to prove one's membership in God's company of elect people. The desire is still for a sense of certainty and approval rather than an open attitude of trust in God. But some, like the Protestant theologian Dietrich Bonhoeffer whom we consider below, find such an outlook on life and faith inadequate for genuine Christian morality. Given the long history in Christianity of debates about freedom and obedience, grace and works, the questions arise whether Christian moral decision-making is a matter of obedience to the law or authority of God, or whether it is a response to the grace of God which looks at every situation and tries to decide what the Holy Spirit urges as the best expression of love in that circumstance.

Absolute and relative morals

Those questions have to be asked in the context of more general questions: What is the basis for making a moral decision? Are there absolute moral values true for all times and places? Why can I not do as I like?

So far in this chapter, we have looked at the creative tension in Christianity as it has tried to answer these questions – the tension between grace and merit, faith and works, generosity and obedience.

There has been general agreement that moral values have an absolute character and can legitimately make a demand on all people, at all times and in all places. The idea that moral laws have been revealed by God is common to Judaism, Christianity and Islam. God is believed to be a moral being who has communicated the moral law to humanity, whose duty it is to accept and practise the good way of life. The question is, how to do so?

The Hebrew Bible contains instruction, law, or Torah, which Jews believe to have been given by God as the basis for the divine covenant relationship with ancient Israel. In the New Testament this Law is interpreted in a Christian way, especially by Paul. He thought that the Law showed people their own inability to keep it and therefore served as a means to bring them to trust in Jesus, the only perfect Jew, whose fulfilling of the Law became the basis for salvation. The demands of the Law were absolute and needed absolute observance, which all failed except Jesus.

A firm and fixed law of this sort can become a two-edged sword. On the one hand, everyone can be sure of how to live and need be in no doubt about what to do, but on the other hand, when failure occurs, because the law is not kept, then some penalty is encountered. The penalty can vary from a personal sense of guilt to the belief in damnation. This raises the important distinction between moral codes as a rule for life as opposed to moral codes as a guide in life.

The New Testament has no doubt that God revealed his will, in the form of specific commandments, to the people of Israel. The Ten Commandments (Deuteronomy 5: 7–21) might be summarised in the two great commandments, but they still represent an expression of absolute moral values. The covenant community is defined as those who live by those standards, by keeping the Law. Yet in general the New Testament writers no longer believe that the definition of a good or a right decision can be found simply by checking its conformity with the Law of the *old* covenant. The *new* covenant, or testament, is characterised by an application of rules and laws in the overriding direction of love. Put in a very extreme way, it was this perception which produced what is known as 'situation ethics'.

Situation ethics argue that love is the principle underlying Christian religion. If individuals genuinely have love at heart, and are open to learn from the traditional wisdom of the Church, then they can trust themselves to act morally in any particular situation. Certain fixed laws may be inappropriate in one specific context. It may, for example, be wrong to lie but it would be right to lie to a murderer, who was seeking his victim's whereabouts. Here the emphasis upon the individual takes over from rules laid down by an entire society. Situation ethics is one reflection of the modern trend to emphasise the significance of the individual, who must act on the basis of commitment to a moral principle applied in the light of the needs of others and the circumstances of the day.

In the Christian tradition, authority (coming from the will of God mediated through the Church) and individual responsibility to make moral decisions in relation to particular situations, are held together in the understanding of conscience.

Conscience

Traditionally speaking, conscience refers to the human ability to judge the difference between good and evil behaviour. It is often taken to be a given part of human nature. In the New Testament Paul speaks of the human conscience several times in his Letter to the Romans. The conscience of gentiles accuses or excuses them, depending on how they behave (Romans 2: 15). But this is not the whole story as far as Paul is concerned. Speaking for himself (later in the same Letter), he says that he knows the difference between good and evil, but his problem is that he cannot bring himself to do what is good. In other words he has an active conscience but his will to do the good thing is powerless (Romans 7: 15–24). For Paul, as for many thinkers in later centuries, the human conscience has to cope with imperfect human nature. Some think that the conscience itself has been spoiled through sin while others see the conscience as having to deal with an imperfect human nature surrounding it.

Nevertheless, the word 'conscience' stands for each individual as absolutely and solely responsible before God for the formation of her or his decision, thought or action. This is what is known as 'foundational conscience'. No authority, neither pope nor parent, can invade that conscience to control or coerce it. Each person stands before God. But each person is immersed in the issues and decisions of daily life. The individual exercise of judgement in detail is known as 'situational conscience'. Since no one can know all the relevant facts or consequences of a situational decision, it is here that the authority of scripture and of tradition becomes important, *informing* conscience. Even so, it cannot take over the foundational conscience, which is the individual decision before God and in the light of eternity.

The primacy of conscience over authority indicates why Dietrich Bonhoeffer (1906–45), a German pastor caught up in the political and moral problems of Germany in the Second World War, saw the human conscience as a means through which individuals come to a unity within themselves. It is a form of self-protection and self-control as individuals live in society, helping them to find integrity in their lives. Bonhoeffer argued that conscience 'is directed not towards a particular kind of doing but towards a particular mode of being. It protests against a doing which imperils the unity of this being with itself' (1955: 211).

But, says Bonhoeffer, the Christian conscience is more than this. If we talk only in terms of self-identity and protection we are in a realm of selfishness and self-rule. When an individual has Christian faith, such self-rule is no longer the goal. Jesus Christ replaces self-rule. The individual conscience can be full of ungodly self-justification, but for the Christian, Jesus Christ sets the conscience free from having to justify itself. In a most dramatic proclamation Bonhoeffer writes in a simple single sentence: 'Jesus Christ has become my conscience' (1955: 213).

Moral decisions can now be made in a different way and without fear of self. In a way that is not initially easy to understand, Bonhoeffer argues that the conscience which is set free by Jesus Christ will not be timidly afraid of what it does. It will even be free to 'enter into the guilt of another man for the other man's sake, and indeed precisely in doing this it will show itself in its purity'. The making of moral decisions is not something individuals do just for themselves. Following the example of Jesus Christ, they must live for others, and this will involve them in taking decisions that are risky and problematic. Such risk involves freedom and dangerous possibilities. It is the fact that Jesus Christ stands as the final judge of those who seek the good of others, and who risk acting in freedom to achieve this, which gives the courage to live. They hope for mercy from God rather than the praise of their own self-satisfied conscience.

Societies and social morality

Much of what we have looked at so far has focused on the individual. But individuals cannot live as Robinson Crusoes, each one an island, separate from everyone else. We live necessarily in societies and social groups (like families or schools), and morality concerns them as much as it concerns individuals. In groups or organisations, rules governing conduct are more likely to obtain, because there is no single person weighing up each situation; evaluation is diffused through an organisation, even though the decisions may be taken and expressed by authority figures. Individuals may agree or disagree (and that is a classic instance of conscience), but the rules and norms of the group or a society will continue.

But given that rules are likely to be prominent in groups or organisations or societies, and that these ultimately rest on a sufficient consensus among those who make up the membership, what happens when the rules of one group or society conflict with those of another? We have already seen in the Introduction (pp. 4–5) that cultural and moral relativity is a fact, at least in the sense that different societies endorse different items as good or evil (though they are, nevertheless, exemplifying the human universal of making judgements and distinctions of that kind). The Christian belief that the capacity to recognise goodness (however much we may fail to act upon it) is a human universal does not mean that the diversity of different life-styles has to be obliterated. There will be considerable agreement on some items, but equally important diversity in moral codes, which may nevertheless be regarded as good.

But what happens when there is a conflict between two systems, or societies? It is easy to talk theoretically about differences in moral codes. When morals clash in real situations, however, calm discussion may give way to action, as in the case of war. If one nation sees another being treated badly by a third party, what should it do? Did Hitler, for example, have the right to kill Jews because he wanted to eliminate them from his 'perfect' society? Should one country not respect the rights of rulers in another society to do what they want?

In the history of Christendom the idea of the Just War has explored some of these issues. Augustine (354–430) developed the idea of a Just War on the basis that war was commanded by God to restore the world to peace, and was not to be waged for personal benefit. This idea is reflected in Article 37 of the 39 Articles of Belief in the Church of England, where it says, 'it is lawful for Christian men, at the commandment of the Magistrate, to wear weapons, and serve in the wars'.

But in order to argue like this two distinctions have to be made: on the one hand, the distinction between the morality applicable to individuals and the morality applicable to nations; and on the other hand, the distinction between love and justice.

From what was said at the outset (p. 42), it is obvious that the teaching of Jesus applies directly to individual morality. Here one should love not only one's friend but also one's enemy. Waging war is obviously not a way to love, so war would have to be excluded from a morally acceptable way of life. But, as some subsequent Christian theologians have argued at length, the issue of justice takes the personal ethic of love on to another level of discussion. The theologian, Reinhold Niebuhr, who was born in 1894, was very much concerned with the way in which an ethical system for society could be related to an ethical system for the individual Christian. This he saw as relating the themes of love and justice within a world where sin was a fundamental problem affecting human behaviour. In his *Interpretation of Christian Ethics* (1935) he explored the idea of personal and social evil, and at one point came very close to a deep insight of a German contemporary, Dietrich Bonhoeffer.

Niebuhr argued that, 'There is no deeper pathos in the spiritual life of man than the cruelty of righteous people' (1956: 203). Here he tried to get at the fact that very religious people can be merciless and, through a false sense of their own goodness, adopt critical and unloving judgements. Love and justice do not coincide in a satisfactory way. More poignantly still, Bonhoeffer pressed the case of evil even more firmly. Involved in a plot to assassinate Hitler, he was caught and executed. His book, *Ethics*, was published in an incomplete form after his death. It is thus a work about ethics and Christian morality written amidst the most difficult themes of morality, those of war, justice, love, selfishness and self-sacrifice.

Today there are once more villains and saints, and they are not hidden from public view . . . They emerge from primeval depths and by their appearance they tear open the infernal or the divine abyss from which they come and enable us to see for a moment into mysteries of which we

63

had never dreamed. What is worse than doing evil is being evil. It is worse for a liar to tell the truth than for a lover of truth to lie . . . One sin is not like another. They do not all have the same weight.

(1955: 3)

This quotation powerfully illustrates the critical nature of his situation. From this modern theologian, we come to the heart of the matter – the title of a novel by Graham Greene which reminds us that fiction may make manifest more truth about the problems of making moral decisions than philosophy or biblical exegesis. Fiction acutely makes the point that it is in the struggle which is involved in the making of moral decisions (or in *not* making them) that human character is formed – not just 'human beings' but humanity in being. It is character which is the consequence of morality, either as a work of beauty, or as one of hideous deformity.

My moral choices

It is, then, our character which is reflected in the moral decisions we make, and which is, to a degree, created by those decisions. As we saw so clearly in Kierkegaard (p. 55), we have to decide to become ourselves. If we decide to steal or break the law we might well find ourselves convicted of a crime and becoming a criminal. If we decide to ride roughshod over people as part of our career development we may well find ourselves becoming callous and alienated from those who otherwise might be friends.

This is vitally important in the process of becoming a mature individual. As children we find many decisions taken on our behalf – we are taught how to behave. Becoming adult involves deciding how to behave. We have to take responsibility for our own actions and for the consequences of our actions.

There may, of course, be serious obstacles to our apparent freedom of choice. Indeed, this issue of freedom is a constant element in the Christian tradition of morality. In most Christian traditions the idea of sin is seen to weaken such freedom. We saw a classic expression of this in Paul, who knew what was good but felt unable to carry it out. The human state of sinful deprivation is often believed to require the grace of God to overcome it, both in the saving work of Jesus, and also in the power provided by the Holy

Spirit within individual lives. A similar idea of disability is also encountered in secular social opinion, as in the view that an impoverished childhood environment leads people into crime and delinquency. However, it is important to distinguish between ideas of determination and ideas of human possibility. Religious ideas of predestination and secular ideas of conditioning can both work against individuals taking responsibility for themselves despite the problems they have experienced.

Respect is an integral part of moral development. Respect for self and respect for others. In terms of Christian morality, both sorts of respect are grounded in our attitude of respect for God. The command to love our neighbour as ourselves is grounded in the command to love God with all our heart; it is important to notice that God, neighbour and self are all included in this outlook. Respect expresses the worth of a person. A sense of our own worth derives in Christianity from the belief that God both made us and loves us. We are worthy because God says so, through the acts of creation and redemption. This divine statement must take precedence even over any sense of personal unworthiness.

Sources of morality

'In the beginning is the decision'. This, for a Christian, might be said to be the first word on morality. All have to decide on the source and authority of morality for themselves. As they become alert to moral issues they must consider the laws of their society which, as citizens, they are obliged to obey. Why obey them? Should people make moral decisions at the personal level which match those of their society? This is not a simple decision as far as Christian morality is concerned. The law of the land may regard as legal things which some Christians take to be sinful. The longstanding issue of abortion is one such question. Some aspects of financial dealing and tax-paying might be others, as are forms of homosexual behaviour.

Traditional sources of morality for Christians have been the Bible, Church tradition, and the inward guidance of the Holy Spirit. Any or all of these can be emphasised in relation to our natural reasoning about life and the world. If making moral decisions is so important that we are formed through those decisions, then we could identify morality as part of the total creative process. In terms of Christian theology our morality should be grounded in love and not in fear. So fear as a source or justification for morality might have to be ruled out of court. The idea of hell as a punishment for the wicked is no basis for Christian morality. Not to sin because of the fear of consequences will not help a person become mature. Love as a respect for the worth of others is a far better motive for making moral decisions.

Other motives for morality include a sense of responsibility for the world of which we are all a part. The closing decades of the twentieth century have witnessed a tremendous growth in awareness of the danger to the earth's ecosystem from modern industry. This responsibility can be interpreted in Christian terms as part of our stewardship of nature, or it can have a secular origin in a human concern for our planet as the place of our survival and life.

Ecological morality highlights the major moral issue of whether my personal behaviour should be influenced by the good of others. My own freedom to use chemicals that are useful for my life but which endanger the lives of future generations is called into question. I am not the only person who matters. Here the profoundly religious theme of the disasters of the self-centred life are made real and observable in the necessity of shared living. We have to make moral decisions precisely because we live with others. To say that only the individual counts, and that my decisions must be based on what, for example, gives me pleasure, is to deny the Christian morality of mutual concern. The genius of Christian theology lies in the belief that morality helps us become more than we would be alone. Making moral decisions is part of the creative work of making persons.

FURTHER READING

Augustine (1945) *The City of God*, London, Everyman.
Bonhoeffer, D. (1955) *Ethics*, London, S.C.M. Press.
—— (1959) *Letters and Papers from Prison*, London, Fontana.
Drane, J.W. (1975) *Paul, Libertine or Legalist*, London, S.P.C.K.
Fletcher, J. (1966) *Situation Ethics*, London, S.C.M. Press.
Gill, R. (1985) *A Textbook of Christian Ethics*, Edinburgh, T. and T. Clark.
Hume, D. (1969) *A Treatise of Human Nature*, (ed.) E.C. Mossner, London, Harmondsworth, Penguin.

James, William (1902) *The Varieties of Religious Experience*. 1985 edn, Cambridge (MA), Harvard University Press.

Luther, M. (1961) *Luther: Lectures on Romans*, (ed.) Wilhelm Pauck, Philadelphia, The Westminster Press.

Niebuhr, Reinhold (1956. First Ed. 1935) *An Interpretation of Christian Ethics*, New York, Meridian Books.

Poggi, G. (1983) *Calvinism and the Capitalist Spirit*, London, Macmillan.

Weber, Max (1976) *The Protestant Ethic and the Spirit of Capitalism*, London, Allen and Unwin.

Westermark, E. (1923) *The Origin and Development of Moral Ideas*, London, Macmillan.

3. Hinduism

Gavin D. Flood

Hinduism is a term covering a wide and diverse range of Indian religious traditions. Indeed some, such as Wilfred Cantwell Smith, have argued that because of such diversity there is no such thing as 'Hinduism',[1] while others, such as Simon Weightman, make the point that it is legitimate to speak of 'Hinduism' as an 'umbrella concept' and to use the term because it exists in 'Hindu' self-perception.[2] This self-perception has arguably only developed with the rise of the Neo-Hindu movements in the nineteenth century and with the rise of Indian nationalism. Indeed the idea of a 'Hindu' as a self-conscious agent with a certain set of clearly delineated beliefs and moral code may be related to the development of an educated, urban class in India (Bharati 1982: 16–21). Bharati has contrasted this modern Hinduism with the rural Hinduism of the villages and the Sanskrit tradition of brahmanical learning and renunciation, which roughly corresponds to the distinction in anthropology between the 'little tradition' and 'great tradition' (Bharati 1982: 6–7). Throughout its history 'Hinduism' has displayed an astonishing diversity of ideas and practices, though it could nevertheless be argued that the Sanskrit, brahmanical renouncer tradition has to a great extent determined what is normative within 'Hinduism'. Indeed, a Hindu might argue that what maintains the unity of Hinduism is *dharma*, the normative duties and ethical code which governs all aspects of life, a code which is regarded as sacred and eternal (*sanātana*).

The brahmanical view of Hindu morality is thought to be based on the revelation (*śruti*) of the Veda, articulated in various law books, the *Dharmaśāstra*s, and in various philosophical systems, most notably the Mīmāṃsā, and becomes the practical ideology of the high caste Hindu householder. But this practical ideology is challenged by the heterodox traditions of Tantrism, which has ethical implications for the Hindu, as we shall see.

Bharati observes that strictly speaking to be a 'Hindu' is to be born within an endogamous group or caste of 'Hindu' society, regardless of belief system (Bharati 1982: 4). He notes that at the level of belief, the only 'minimal common denominator' in Hinduism, though by no means universally agreed, is acceptance of the sacred texts called the Veda as revelation (śruti). This would be largely true for all three kinds of Hinduism which he identifies, namely modern or urban Hinduism, village Hinduism and the Sanskrit, brahmanical tradition, though one must be aware that the Veda as primary revelation would not be accepted in some devotional (bhakti) traditions, nor on the whole in Tantrism.

If one takes the brahmanical Sanskrit tradition as in some sense normative, then apart from acceptance of the Veda as revelation, a key defining characteristic of a Hindu might be acceptance of the varṇāśramadharma, one's duty (dharma) in respect of class/caste (varṇa) and stage of life (āśrama), though again we must be aware that many Hindu traditions have rejected this model. Perhaps belief in the cycle of reincarnation (saṃsāra) and salvation or liberation (mokṣa) from this state might be added as common elements of Hindu ideology, though by no means universal. For example, for rural or village Hinduism, fate or the supernatural agency of malevolent spirits, might be regarded as a greater cause of suffering and death than action and its effects (karma).

Although the ideology of caste and admittance of the Veda as revelation are not universally accepted, they can nevertheless arguably be taken as starting points in arriving at an understanding of Hinduism. Rather than belief, what is more important in delineating the boundaries of Hinduism is action: 'orthopraxy' takes precedence over 'orthodoxy'. In other words, what a Hindu does in relation to his or her social standing and context is far more important than what a Hindu thinks. Indeed, there has been a proliferation of various Hindu ideologies – monistic, theistic and atheistic – but the overarching concern of most Hindus has been the primacy of correct action in accordance with one's prescribed duties and responsibilities determined by birth.

These duties and responsibilities, incorporated within the Sanskrit term dharma, are concerned with the fulfilling of social obligations to one's family and wider society, and the fulfilment of one's ritual obligations to the household deities and ancestors. Indeed, traditionally the high caste or 'twice-born' (*dvija*) Hindu is born with three debts (*ṛṇa*) to be paid: the debt of vedic study to the sages (*ṛṣi*) as a celibate student (*brahmacārin*), and, as a householder (*gṛhastha*), the debt of sacrifice to the gods (*deva*), and finally the debt of begetting a son to make funeral offerings to the ancestors (*pitṛ*). Correct action or ethical behaviour takes primacy over belief. This ethical behaviour (*dharma*), however, varies in different social contexts for different groups: *dharma* is, as Doniger observes, 'context sensitive' (Doniger 1991: xlvi)[3] (see below, p. 74).

Ethics and liberation

The famous Hindu law book, the *Manusmṛti*, says that once a man has fulfilled his moral (dharmic) obligations – that is, paid his three debts – he can retire to meditate and work for his liberation (*mokṣa*), though to seek liberation before he has fulfilled his moral obligations would be counterproductive and lead to hell (*Manu* 6. 35–38). This points to two areas of ultimate concern, *dharma* and liberation (*mokṣa*). These two areas of concern or realms of discourse have tended to be distinct in Hinduism: *dharma* has been the concern of the law books and the majority of Hindu house-holders at a practical level, *mokṣa* the concern of renouncers and Hindu philosophical discourse. K. Potter has remarked that while the idea of the Good, or moral perfection, has been the dominant or even ultimate value in western thought, in Indian thought, by contrast, liberation or freedom and control of self and environment have been the ultimate value most discussed in sophisticated philosophical discourse. He writes, '. . . the ultimate value recognized by classical Hinduism in its most sophisticated sources is not morality but freedom, not rational self control in the interests of the community's welfare but complete control over one's environment . . .' (Potter 1991: 3). Such statements, however, need to be qualified by the idea that liberation has sometimes been identified with the ultimate good (*niḥśreyasa*).[4] Indeed, liberation is minimally freedom from suffering, which is implicitly 'bad'.

While it may be true that liberation has taken priority in philosophical discourse, and is the ultimate goal of renunciation, and the many spiritual disciplines of Hinduism, it is also the case that ethics or *dharma* is the basis or foundation upon which liberation is achieved. *Mokṣa*, while transcending the relative opposites of 'good' and 'bad', nevertheless in orthodox Hinduism presupposes *dharma* which, at least according to the *Dharmaśāstras*, is a necessary condition for it. Although *mokṣa* is in some sense the opposite of *dharma*, it is nevertheless not *adharma*, 'unethical' or 'bad'. Indeed in the everyday Brahman householder's life, while perhaps liberation is a distant goal, *dharma* has taken precedence over world renunciation, as Madan (1987) has demonstrated. The Hindu householder (*gṛhastha*), while agreeing with the ideology of renunciation, has behaved at a practical level according to social and moral codes which see value not so much in their own transcendence through renunciation, but in their affirmation in daily life. Domesticity (*grāhasthya*) and its implied moral codes become more important than renunciation (*saṃnyāsa*) (Madan 1987: 17–47). Indeed *Manu* explicitly states that of the four stages of life (*āśrama*) the householder stage is the best (*jyeṣṭha*) because the householder supports the other three stages and this vedic activity is the supreme good (*śreyaskaratara*) (*Manu* 3. 77–78; 12. 86).

In contrast to the renouncer, the householder Brahman's supreme duties have traditionally been to perform vedic ritual, maintain his ritual purity and fulfil his other caste obligations. Action has therefore been his central concern, especially ritual action (*karma*), which originally referred to vedic sacrifice, but which in classical Hinduism came also to refer to the ritual obligations of deity worship (*pūjā*). Correct ritual action and correct patterns of behaviour determined by the tradition, have become central to the high caste Hindu's life. *Dharma* is inextricably linked with *karma* – the realm of its expression – and so is the primary concern of the Brahman householder, in contrast to the renouncer who must abandon dharmically prescribed ritual, *karma*, in order to attain *mokṣa*. For the renouncer, *mokṣa* entails the abandonment of *karma* – both in the sense of ritual action and in the sense of accumulated merit and demerit – and so is beyond the realm of the *dharma* which governs the householder's life, beyond the ethical codes which inform all aspects of the householder's existence.

This is illustrated in the Advaita Vedāntic theologian Śaṁkara's identification of the renouncer, who has abandoned ritual action (BSB 3. 4. 25. For abbreviations see p. 93), with the liberated man (*jīvanmukta*) who, by definition of being liberated, no longer acts;

71

his body merely unfolds or manifests what remains of his human destiny, his *prārabdhakarma* (see below, pp. 82–3). While the renouncer and the *jīvanmukta* have transcended the world of human transaction governed by *dharma*, the householder is obliged to maintain his household fires and pursue his worldly goals.

Traditionally, the high caste Hindu householder has had three goals of life (*puruṣārtha*) or 'three paths' (*trivarga*): the fulfilling of social and moral obligations (*dharma*), becoming prosperous or the acquisition of profit (*artha*), and the experience of pleasure (*kāma*) (*Manu* 2.13, 224, 7.27, 12.34). These three are collectively regarded as 'the good' (*śreyas*) in *Manu* (2.224). While *mokṣa* might be the highest goal of life according to the great tradition of renunciation, and indeed is added as a fourth to the three goals at a date later than *Manu*, *dharma* is its equal in the Hindu law books and in the householder's everyday existence; the householder's practical ideology of moral obligation and action takes precedence over the renouncer's ideology of actionless freedom. There are then competing goods for the Hindu householder, the good which is *dharma* and the good which is *mokṣa*.

The primacy of ethics as *Dharma*

The term *dharma*, as has been frequently pointed out, has no direct English counterpart, and we are faced with the difficulty of finding semantic equivalents which convey the various cultural resonances of the term. It has been variously rendered as 'religion', 'duty', 'justice', 'law' and 'ethics' (Coward et al. 1991: 2; Zaehner 1966 102–124). Although etymologies do not tell us much about the meaning of a term in the context of its use, Zaehner relates its root *dhṛ*, which means 'to hold, have or maintain', to the cognate terms in Latin *firmus*, 'firm' and *forma*, 'form'. He then defines *dharma* as 'the "form" of things as they are and the power that keeps them as they are and not otherwise' (Zaehner 1966: 2). In other words, *dharma* can be broadly interpreted as the force or power which controls or constrains phenomena in the universe. This is a very wide definition, yet, on the other hand, the term can also refer, much more narrowly, to a person's nature or an aspect of ritual action.

Our main concern here is the sphere of ethics, of which the term *dharma* is arguably the nearest Sanskrit equivalent; though whereas in the West 'ethics' can be discussed independently of 'religion', in

Hinduism *dharma* implies 'correct action', in the sense both of fulfilling moral obligations to one's kith and kin, and of fulfilling one's ritual obligations. It is therefore intimately connected with the idea of purity (*śuddha*) (see below).

Perhaps what is most striking about *dharma* is that it is both universal and particular; it refers both to a cosmic, eternal principle (*sanātana dharma*) and to specific laws and the contexts to which they are applied. *Dharma* is a cosmic principle which is responsive to different situations and contexts. This idea is illustrated in the Hindu law books, the earliest of which is the *Manusmṛti*, which reached its present form probably about the second century CE, and in the school of Hindu philosophy called the Mīmāṃsā, whose root text, Jaimini's *Mīmāṃsā-sūtra*, was composed around the second century BCE. The Mīmāṃsā, which along with the Vedānta or Uttara Mīmāṃsā, provided in the medieval period one of the main philosophies of the Brahman householder (Sanderson 1985: 193–7), offered an understanding of *dharma* as an eternal principle expressed at a human level as ritual obligation.

Jaimini defined *dharma* as that of which the characteristic is an obligation or injunction (*vidhi*) (MS 1. 1. 2). That is, *dharma* is an obligation enjoined by the Veda which specifically refers to vedic ritual action (*karma*), or 'sacrifice', and the supererogatory ritual actions for gaining wealth and happiness in this world and in the next. The performance of obligatory actions brings in itself no reward; it is expected that one should do this, for their non-performance, that is the performance of that which is not *dharma* (*adharma*), would bring retribution or 'evil' (*pāpa*). The performance of ritual actions for a later reward in heaven, on the other hand, creates an invisible, transcendent force (*apūrva*) which produces the desired result (MS 2. 1. 2). *Dharma*, for the Mīmāṃsā, is identified with vedic obligation or injunction which is eternal, and also with action which is particular. Thus *dharma* has a transcendent, eternal aspect which is expressed at a human level in ritual actions which produce that which is good (*śreyaskāra*).

In order to 'produce that which is good', the Brahman's ritual actions must be pure. The term 'purity' (*śuddha*), Madan (1987: 58) observes, 'refers to the most desired condition of the human body or, more comprehensively, the most desired state of being'. Such a desired state of body or being is achieved through ritual purification, for example by pouring water over the body, and through the avoidance of impurity, for example by avoiding 'polluting' castes and 'polluting' substances such as menstrual blood. 'That which is good' is also related to 'the auspicious' (*śubha*), the importance of which in Hindu culture has again been pointed out by Madan (Madan 1987: 50–58). Thus the optimal conditions for a ritual action, a *dharma*, would be in a condition of purity (*śuddha*) at an auspicious (*śubha*) time such as a particular astrological configuration. However, as with most things in life, these conditions are rarely completely met. For example, Madan discusses the example of childbirth which, if it occurs under the right circumstances, is auspicious, yet it is also hedged about with pollution, and so is impure and, in one sense, inauspicious (Madan 1987: 60, Coward 1991: 11).

The *Dharmaśāstras* are concerned with moral obligation which, in those texts and in Hindu life generally, cannot be separated from ritual obligation and obligations entailed by one's social status and context. These texts are also concerned with *dharma* as justice, and the obligations of the just king to adminster justice and punishment (*daṇḍa*) as befits the circumstance. *Dharma*, while being a cosmic principle, is at the same time particular to each situation. The *Manusmṛti* provides us with many examples of this. The religious duties are different in different ages, and vary according to caste (*jāti*), family (*kula*) and country (*deśa*) (*Manu* 1.85, 119); the obligations of the servant (*śūdra*) are different from those of the higher castes – they cannot, for example, be initiated or learn the Veda (*Manu* 3.156, 4.99, 10.4, 127); and kings must judge according to the customs of and particular duties (*svadharma*) of each region (*Manu* 8. 41).

This idea of *svadharma*, one's own particular duty, is important in understanding the 'context-sensitive' nature of *dharma*. In the *Bhagavadgītā*, Kṛṣṇa, an incarnation of God, responds to the hero Arjuna's reluctance to fight on the battlefield by arguing first that one cannot kill the immortal soul (*ātman*) in any living thing, but secondly, and perhaps more importantly and persuasively for Arjuna, that he must fight because it is his duty, his *svadharma*, as a member of the warrior class. Duty is relative to different contexts; what is correct action for the servant might be incorrect for the warrior, what is correct for a man may be incorrect for a woman, and so on.

Let us illustrate this with reference to *Manu*'s ideas about justice.

People in different castes do not have the same duties or the same rites. A good Hindu's duties are class- and caste-specific, and it is better to fulfil one's own caste obligations, however badly, than to do another's duties well. Justice, similarly, is relative to different contexts. Justice, another translation of the term *dharma*, is administered according to *Manu* by the king through 'the stick' (*daṇḍa*) or 'punishment'. Indeed, ideologically, in the period of classical and medieval Hinduism, the king is the centre of the Hindu universe, and his actions ripple down to the people. The chief function of the king was to protect the people, and to keep the four classes in order and maintain the system of the four stages of life (*Manu* 7.35). Through ensuring the boundaries of caste, the king ensured the prosperity of the communities over which he governed. Furthermore, through the practice of *daṇḍa*, which varied from community to community, he ensured the continued harmony of the state.

The particularity of *dharma* can also be illustrated with regard to marriage. One of the most important moral concerns of normative, brahmanical Hinduism has been the maintenance of caste boundaries through marriage restrictions. Marriage should be endogamous within the caste group, though exogamous within a sub-caste or 'lineage' (*gotra*), and of course marriages were, and continue to be, arranged. In India, as elsewhere throughout the world, people fall in love outside of the permitted social restrictions of who is marriageable. The *Manusmṛti* recognises this to an extent and lists eight kinds of marriage between the four social classes varying in degree of acceptability, the highest kind being the respectable, arranged marriage of a high caste girl to a man of good character, the lowest, 'ghoulish marriage' (*paiśāca vivāhana*), being sexual intercourse with a sleeping, mad or drunken woman (*Manu* 3.21–35).

Indeed, the text is tolerant, though disapproving, of some higher caste men marrying lower caste women. A woman of the servant class (*śūdra*) can marry a commoner (*vaiśya*), who belongs technically to the 'twice born' (i.e., one who has undergone vedic initiation). However, the text says that twice born men who, because of infatuation or delusion (*moha*), marry women of the servant class, reduce their families and their descendants to the status of servants (*Manu* 3.13–16). The text, however, tends to be prohibitive of the purest caste, the Brahmans, marrying lower, more polluting, castes.

Indeed a priest who sleeps with a servant girl goes to hell and loses the status of a priest if he begets a son by her. Again *Manu* recognises the nature of fleeting sexual attraction, and accommodates for this in the idea of the temporary marriage (called the *gandharva* marriage) for the higher classes, when a girl and her lover make love purely out of desire (*kāmasambhava*) (*Manu* 3.17). However, the text also prescribes severe punishments ranging from the loss of two fingers to capital punishment for the transgressing of sexual boundaries or 'sexual misconduct' (*samgrahana*), delineated by caste (*Manu* 3. 32), a category which includes adultery with high caste women and homosexuality (*klība*). Indeed, one passage says that the king should have an adulterous woman eaten by dogs in a place frequented by many people (*Manu* 8.371).

In all of these situations, punishments are more severe for a woman, and the woman is seen to be more passive than a man. In the light of contemporary western sensibilities *Manu*, and indeed many attitudes and practices of contemporary Hinduism, might seem archaic and restrictive of women's rights. *Manu* is quite clear that a high caste woman, whether a girl, young woman or old woman, must do nothing independently (*svatantra*), even in her own house, but must throughout her life be subject to male authority – as a child to her father, as a married woman to her husband and to her sons when her husband (or 'lord') is dead (*Manu* 5.147–8). By leading a life constantly subject to male authority, a woman will attain heaven and so reap the reward of her austerity, though she will be born in a lower form should she neglect these duties (*Manu* 5.161–4).

The ideal woman is reflected mythologically in the famous epic, the *Rāmāyana*. In this text Rāma, an incarnation (*avatāra*) of the supreme God Visnu, has been banished to the forest by his father in fulfilment of a promise to Rāma's stepmother. He is accompanied by his brother Laksmana and his wife Sītā, who is often regarded as the perfect Hindu woman. Rāma and Sītā are role models for the ideal Hindu couple living in accordance with *dharma*. Rāma is robust, honest, and devoted to Sītā who is demure, modest and dedicated to Rāma, her lord. Yet she is also very strong in herself, undergoing hardship and displaying great loyalty to her husband (see chapter on Hinduism in *Women in Religion* in this series). While in the forest Sītā is abducted by the demon Rāvana who takes her to the island of Lanka. Rāma and his brother, with the help of a monkey army, eventually rescue her, the demon is defeated and good triumphs over evil. Now although Sītā has remained faithful to Rāma she has to undergo an ordeal by fire to prove her chastity to the world before Rāma will accept her back – a story which expresses an ambivalent attitude towards woman as a model of virtue, yet at the same time not to be trusted.

In both epic and law book we are presented with ideal images of gender roles and what is regarded as appropriate behaviour. *Manu* presents us with a normative, brahmanical view which may not have reflected social reality, but most certainly reflects the ideology of the Brahman class who composed it and who wielded influence and power in the Hindu world. We see here clearly that *dharma* is not only class-specific but gender-specific as well. The kinds of moral choice open to women are more restricted in both *Manu* and the *Rāmāyaṇa* than for men. Sītā, the exemplar of female virtue, has little choice. Although it is she who chooses to accompany her husband into the forest and who undergoes various vows of religious austerity (*vrata*), she tends nevertheless to be passive, being abducted by a male demon and rescued by her husband! Sītā is the ideal model for the Hindu woman, loyal and deferential to her husband, yet at the same time possessing immense personal strength. Sītā is, however, not the only model or image of women presented in the Hindu tradition. There are the autonomous, ferocious and erotic goddesses such as Kālī, or the 'mothers' (*mātṛkā*), though these tend to be associated with Tantrism and are feared by orthodoxy. There are also historical figures such as Mahādevyakka, a Kanarese *bhakti* poet, who exhibit strength, autonomy and a breaking out of expected gender roles and male dominance, though such figures of female autonomy are rare.

Even allowing for the strength of women portrayed in Hindu mythology, ideologically women would nevertheless seem to be most constrained by the classical Hindu model of social relations. Indeed the low caste woman is probably the most restricted in terms of choice and opportunities open to her, while the high caste male is the least restricted. This traditional limitation of moral choice among Hindu women is again reflected in the institution of *satī* which had developed by the fourteenth century CE, whereby a woman would die on her husband's funeral pyre if he predeceased her. This was certainly practised, though not universally, and, although illegal, is beginning to recur in contemporary India. The very word *satī* means 'good woman' and she who performed it would immediately secure heaven for both herself and her husband. Indeed, the *satī* phenomenon is complex and cannot be seen purely in terms of male oppression of women, but also must be seen in the context of female empowerment; the *satī* becomes like a *yogin*, purifying herself and her family and creating good *karma* for the next life in choosing to assert herself by dying on the pyre.[5] Such a death could feasibly be regarded from within the tradition as a noble and free choice which elevates the status of those participating in it and sanctifies the *satī*.

But to return to the central concept of *dharma* of which *satī* would be an expression. While *dharma* might be regarded as context-sensitive, responding to gender roles and caste, the author of *Manu* is not an ethical relativist. *Dharma* is an eternal principle, a natural law, but its specific laws or codes of conduct vary according to social ranking and, indeed, according to time of year and time of life.

The Hindu hierarchical social structure and the emphasis on duty with regard to class and stage of life (*varṇāśramadharma*), are absolute and sacred for *Manu*. The ideology of caste is legitimated in the first chapter with reference to the myth of the primal sacrifice of the supreme person (*puruṣa*), in the *Ṛg-veda* (10.90), from which the four classes originated: the Brahmans from his mouth, the rulers from his arms, the commoners from his thighs and the servants from his feet (*Manu* 1.31). This structure is absolute, but moral standards are flexible within it, both to allow for the different dispositions of the different classes, and to allow for human fallibility and different responses to existential situations. *Dharma* in principle is absolute, but it functions in particular, practical situations, and *Manu* recognises the fact that people do not universally stick to it; *dharma* has to be context-sensitive in its response to human crises (*āpad*) (Doniger 1991: liii–liv). Sex outside caste-restricted marriage is wrong, but there is nevertheless the institution of the temporary, *gandhārva*, marriage; killing is wrong, but there are circumstances in which it is permitted, for instance in defending oneself. There is then the general principle and universal moral law of *dharma*, but this must meet and adapt to the everyday reality of making moral choices for the Brahman householder. It is this level of the particularity of moral choice and prescription that is addressed by *Manu*.

We have presented a general picture of higher caste males

exercising the widest choice and lower caste females being the most restricted. There are, however, problems here and the picture is a more complex one. The extent to which even high caste males have been autonomous agents is open to debate. In a famous essay, Louis Dumont contrasted the Hindu social agent within the caste system, the man-in-the-world subject to *dharma*, with the world-renouncer beyond the caste system seeking *mokṣa*. The man-in-the-world, the social agent, is subordinated to the collective social order. He is not an 'individual', according to Dumont, being defined purely in terms of his place in a set of social relations. The renouncer, by contrast, is not subject to these social constraints and so is 'invested with an individuality' (Dumont 1980: 274).

Dumont has been criticised, particularly for his idea of the 'individual' in Hindu society. The anthropologist McKim Marriott, by contrast, argues that there are no *in*dividuals in Hindu society, but rather *di*viduals, by which he means that the boundaries of 'persons' are variable and fluid within Hindu social transactions. The Hindu social agent is not individual, but subject to various transferences of his 'coded-substance', the 'form' and 'content', or 'constraint' and 'constrained' aspects of a social actor.[6] Thus the renouncer tries to minimise his transactions with the social world, while the warrior maximises his.

The implication of this is that autonomy, the freedom to have acted otherwise, is contingent upon social standing in a scale which, as we have seen in *Manu*, is regarded as absolute and which is based on the opposition between purity and pollution. According to Dumont, the renouncer has gone beyond this dichotomy and so is outside the social world, while Marriott has argued that, on the contrary, the renouncer is still very much a part of the social matrix. The degree of autonomy of social agents in the Hindu world is important for an understanding of moral decision-making in Hinduism. There is no necessary correlation between high caste – more autonomous, and low caste – less autonomous, precisely because of the purity–pollution spectrum. Indeed, the highest, purest class and caste – the Brahmans – are arguably less autonomous than the commoner (*vaiśya*) class, who are self-supporting and to a large extent independent of the other classes. In contrast to the commoner, because of his purity, the Brahman is hedged around with prohibitions, and fear or anxiety (*śaṅkā*) of pollution and inauspicious (*aśubha*) events or times.

Manu presents a picture of the Brahman as a learned man who performs his correct ritual obligations, and who tries hard to restrain his senses 'as a charioteer his race-horses' (*Manu* 1.88). He is, then, a model of rational self-control and restrained behaviour. His ultimate, distant goal might be liberation (*mokṣa*), but his immediate concern is the fulfilling of his *dharma*, which means particularly the completion of his ritual duties, including the avoidance of pollution. These ritual injunctions (*vidhi*) are the performance of regular, daily rituals (*nityakarma*), occasional rituals (*naimittikakarma*) such as birth, the investiture of the sacred thread (*upanayana*) and funeral rites in the life-cycle, or transformative rituals (*saṃskāra*) of the twice born, and rituals performed for desired results (*kāmyakarma*) such as the obtaining of heaven upon death (Potter 1991: 257).

Alongside these rites are the rites of expiation or restoration (*prayaścitta*) for sins (*pāpa*) committed either with awareness or inadvertently (*Manu* 12.45). By 'sins' the Brahman householder means adharmic behaviour, such as the neglect of the three kinds of ritual or the neglect of caste duties (*Manu* 12.44). Indeed *Manu* lists a variety of sins for which *prayaścitta* would need to be performed, ranging from violating the *guru*'s marriage-bed, which refers to adultery with the *guru*'s wife, to theft and murder. For example, one of the expiations for killing a Brahman would be to build a hut in a forest and live there for twelve years, begging food and using a skull for his emblem (*Manu* 12.72). Indeed this expiation is less injurious than that prescribed for violating the *guru*'s marriage bed. Here the text offers various alternatives, including castration and walking, with the severed organs, to the south west until death (*Manu* 12.105). It is noteworthy that expiation is for 'sin' (*pāpa*) which means 'going against *dharma*', and guilt (*enas*) is specifically related to having violated prescribed dharmic, caste-specific obligations. Indeed there is even a sense of 'conscience' about violated dharmic behaviour in that the body is freed from the wrongdoing (*adharma*), the more the mind (*manas*) despises what has been done (*Manu* 11.230).

Dharma, which embraces caste duties and moral obligations, is the governing force of the Brahman householder's life. This *dharma* is explained in the law books which, although not eternal revelation (*śruti*), are nevertheless regarded as being based on revelation: the laws which texts such as *Manu* expound, while being variable, are based on the eternal law of *dharma* and the Brahman's autonomy is totally constrained by this. The Brahman does, of course, have freedom of action, but this is constrained by *dharma*: if he performs an action which is against *dharma*, he will have to suffer the consequences in this or a future life, or pay for his action by expiation. Alternatively, the Brahman householder, should he be so inclined, could neglect his brahmanical duties and adopt the alien world-view of a tantric practitioner who, as we shall see, espouses a doctrine and practice which would be anathema from the perspective of orthodox *dharma*.

Action and moral retribution

The Brahman's ritual obligations and expiations have continued in Hinduism from the time of the Vedas to the present. The ritual act in vedic times was known as the 'sacrifice' (*yajña*), which became a synonym for many kinds of religious behaviour. Religious rituals were also known by the term *karma* or 'action'. This term initially referred to ritual and its implied invisible effects, but came to be applied, in the *Upaniṣads* and in early Buddhism, to action generally and its consequences, which took effect not only during one life, but over several lifetimes. The theory of *karma* came to be a general explanation of human suffering and a motivation for stepping off the cycle of reincarnation (*saṃsāra*) and seeking liberation through becoming a renouncer (*saṃnyāsin*).

Manu is quite specific about the moral retribution due to action over a period of lives: action, it says, produces 'auspicious and inauspicious fruits' (*śubhāśubhaphalaṃ*) (*Manu* 12.3). An auspicious result would be due to a person having fulfilled their dharmic obligations specific to their caste and stages of life, an inauspicious fruit to their not having fulfilled their *dharma*. Actions, says *Manu*, originate in the mind (*manas*), speech (*vāc*) and body (*deha*), all of which have consequences. Mental actions, such as coveting the possessions of others, thinking about what is undesirable and believing in false ideas; verbal actions, such as lying, abuse, slander and gossip; and bodily actions, such as theft, violence which is against the law, and adultery, all result in a specific kind of retribution in a future life. An inauspicious or sinful mental act will lead to rebirth in a low caste, a sinful verbal act to rebirth as a wild animal or bird, and a sinful bodily act to rebirth as something inanimate or a plant (*sthāvaratām*) (*Manu* 12.5–10).

The text also introduces another scheme of action and its retribution based on the model of the three qualities (*guṇa*) inherent in all manifestations, namely light/goodness (*sattva*), passion (*rajas*) and darkness/inertia (*tamas*) (*Manu* 12.24). The results of actions imbued with these three qualities are reincarnations in, respectively, the realms of the gods, the humans and the animals, each of which is further subdivided into low, middle and high. Thus within the realm of goodness are included ascetics (*tāpasa*) and priests (*vipra*); within the realm of passion we have a range of beings from pugilists to rulers (*kṣatriya*); and in the realm of darkness there are animals, foreigners (*mleccha*), actors and demons (*piśāca*) (*Manu* 12.39–50). The text also deals, with graphic particularity, with the destinies for various moral misdemeanours. A violent man, for example, is reborn as a carnivorous beast; a Brahman killer as an animal such as a dog or an untouchable; various categories of thieves are born as animals (*Manu* 12.59–68), and so on.

Perhaps what is most interesting about this list is that the punishments for misdeeds are caste-specific. That is, the retributions in lower births are due to the failure to perform one's *dharma* correctly. Thus the Brahman who has fallen from his own duty (*svadharma*) becomes a vomit-eating ghost with a flaming mouth (*ulkāmukha-preta*), the warrior who has so fallen becomes a polluted substance and corpse-eating ghost, a commoner who falls from his duty is reborn as a pus-eating ghost who sees through its anus (*maitrākṣijyotika-preta*), while a servant becomes a ghost which feeds on moths or body-lice. Conversely, the high caste Hindu who conforms to behaviour prescribed in the Veda, that is, performs his ritual obligations (*śreyas*), becomes equal to the gods (*Manu* 12.71–90). Indeed, in other law books, Rocher notes, those who fulfil their moral obligations to their *varṇa* are reborn higher up the scale, though the texts do not tell us 'what happens upward after the Brāhmaṇa or downward after the Śūdra' (Rocher 1980: 75–6). Presumably there would be transmigration to higher and lower non-human forms.

There are in classical Hinduism three kinds of *karma*: residues of actions performed in a previous life whose effects have not yet begun to be manifested, a 'store-house' of action (*sañcitakarma*); karmic residues whose effects become manifested in one's present life (*prārabdhakarma*); and the seeds of action sown in this life which will come to fruition in a future life (*āgamin* or *bhaviṣyatkarma*). So in each life a being is working out the results of previous actions and sowing the seeds of future action. The law of action is not therefore fatalistic in the sense that, while *prārabdhakarma* determines one's present existence, this can be changed by an act of will or by some external circumstance such as premature death. Śaṃkara likens this kind of *karma* to an arrow which would continue on its course unless obstructed by some other force (Potter 1991: 256). Only the liberated man (*jīvanmukta*) is free from *karma*, in the sense that his liberation experience has eradicated his *sañcitakarma* and he can no longer produce *āgami-karma* through his actions in the present life. Only his *prārabdhakarma* needs to unfold, which done, there is no more return to the cycle of reincarnation. The liberated man is, therefore, beyond the realm of moral retribution. He can no longer reap the rewards of past actions, nor can he create future actions, having transcended the ethical sphere.

This figure of detachment and transcendence is not, however, the hero of the Hindu law books, which look, rather, to the householder as their exemplar. It is clear from *Manu* that the ideal Brahman householder is one who fulfils his ritual obligations, who keeps free from pollution and whose body and desires are under his rational self-control. The Brahman should make oblations every day, be non-violent (*ahiṃsā*), tell the truth, be without anger and be straight-forward (*Manu* 11.222). The ideal is to become a *tridaṇḍin*, one possessing a 'triple stick', like an ascetic who carried such a trident, to control the actions of body, speech and mind. With this internalised 'triple stick' the Brahman represses emotion, controls lust (*kāma*) and anger (*krodha*), and attains perfection (*siddhi*) (*Manu* 2.10–11). Such a Brahman 'burns down' the fruits of action through knowledge of, and action in accordance with, the Veda. Indeed all other systems or doctrines outside of the Veda bear no fruit for him, being based on darkness.

Dharma and the tantric tradition

In contrast to the controlled Brahman householder presented in *Manu*, other religious traditions within Hinduism, notably the tantric traditions, present very different images, at least at an ideological level. The tantric systems, which the author of *Manu* would no doubt have classified as 'based on darkness' had he known about them, claim a revelation other than the Veda, namely the Āgamas and Tantras. These texts, which generally take the form of a dialogue between the Lord (Bhagvan) as Śiva (though it can be Viṣṇu) and the Goddess as his female energy, śākti, can be dated from between the seventh and eleventh centuries CE, several hundred years after *Manu*, though the ideas they contain and the traditions they express may well be much older.

The locatable origins of the various tantric traditions are the ascetics living in the cremation grounds (*śmaśāna*), the most highly polluting place for the orthodox Brahman householder. These renouncers, living literally on the edges of society, were interested not in the performance of normative Hindu *dharma*, but in the acquisition of supernatural power (*siddhi*) and pleasure in higher worlds (*bhukti*) and, eventually, in liberation. These ascetics would cover themselves in ashes from the cremation ground, have long matted hair, and perhaps go naked in imitation of their terrible gods such as Bhairava, a ferocious form of Śiva (Sanderson 1985: 201). Indeed such people were regarded as highly polluting by the orthodox Brahman, and Sanderson cites the example of such ascetics being classified as 'unseeables': should a Brahman inadvertently see one, he would stare into the sun to purify his eyes so polluting were they considered to be (Sanderson 1985: 211, n. 61).

Confined to the cremation grounds, such traditions, though unpleasant and highly polluting, were not an explicit threat to brahmanical orthopraxy. However, Sanderson has shown how the ideologies and practices of these traditions became absorbed into the orthoprax and orthodox Brahman communities, particularly in Kashmir. This brahmanical tantric tradition, referred to as 'Kashmir Śaivism' or, more accurately, the Trika, drew its inspiration from the cremation ground traditions and was theologically monistic. These tantric ideologies and their concomitant practices were anathema to the orthodox, and threatened to subvert brahmanical ideology, especially once this religion had established a common base among Brahman householders.

Not all tantric traditions, however, were equally threatening, and some indeed were absorbed into quite orthodox and respectable traditions. The Pāñcarātra tradition, which is Vaiṣṇava Tantrism, based on texts called the *Pāñcarātra Āgamas*, became absorbed into the Śrī Vaiṣṇava tradition and exerted influences on the theology of the famous Vedānta theologian, Rāmānuja (d. c. 1137 CE). The Śrī

Vidyā tantric tradition became associated with the non-dualist tradition of Saṃkara (788–820 CE) and was absorbed by the orthodox Smārta Brahman community of South India. Finally the Śaiva Siddhānta, a theistic tradition dominant in South India, initially developed in Kashmir at variance with the monistic Kashmir Śaivism, but accepted caste prescriptions and leaned towards vedic orthodoxy while accepting the dualistic Śaiva *tantras* as its ultimate source of authority.

There have, however, been traditions and texts which have clearly remained outside the vedic fold. Such traditions and texts, which tend to be centred on Śiva and/or the Goddess in one of her forms (and which Sanderson in his publications has called 'hard' tantric traditions), advocate ritual practices involving polluting substances, such as corpses, menstrual blood and semen, and polluting behaviour such as caste-free sexual intercourse. These traditions acted out the prescriptions in the tantric texts 'literally', which became known as the 'left-hand practice' (*vāmācāra*) as opposed to the 'right-hand practice' (*dakṣiṇācāra*) which took such prescriptions only 'symbolically'.[7] These 'left hand' traditions seem so obviously incompatible with *dharma* that they raise challenging questions for the Hindu understanding of morality.

One of the claims of Tantrism is that values are relative, and that transcendent reality, identified with pure, undifferentiated consciousness (*saṃvit, caitanya*) in the systems of Kashmir Śaivism, is beyond the social world and the realm of ethics. The *Kulārṇava-tantra*, a *śākta* text of the Kula tradition, says that values are inverted in the tradition; what is injurious (*bādhaka*) becomes spiritually useful (*sādhaka*) and what is unethical (*adharma*) becomes ethical (*dharma*) (KT 9. 26). The 'subversive' nature of tantric traditions can be seen in the statement that one can be 'internally a Kaula (i.e., a tantric practitioner), externally a Śaiva, while remaining vedic in one's social practice' (Sanderson 1985: 205, n. 130). That is, Abhinavagupta (c. 975–1025 CE), the most famous of the Kashmiri Śaiva theologians, is in one sense agreeing with the *Manusmṛti* that *dharma* is context-sensitive. Values are relative, or rather hierarchical, and here the value system of the vedic brahmanical orthodoxy is ultimately rejected, or, more precisely, relegated to a low position in the tantric hierarchy of traditions. Vedic values, vedic *dharma* of the kind advocated in *Manu*, are entirely relative and of no ultimate value. What is of overarching importance for

Abhinavagupta is the superiority of non-dualism over other doctrines: that Śiva is the one, non-dual reality identified with consciousness.

At first glance there appear to be parallels between the non-dualism of Abhinavagupta and the non-dualism of Śaṃkara's Advaita Vedānta. However, although, as far as I know, Śaṃkara is never mentioned by Abhinavagupta, parallels with Advaita are rejected by the Śaiva tradition on the grounds that the Vedāntic *Brahman* is without *śakti* and so is powerless, a mere 'eunuch' (*ṣaṇḍha*). Furthermore, whereas Advaita Vedānta is a totally orthodox system, accepting the values of *varṇāśramadharma*, Śaiva non-dualism rejects those values and retains the hard tantric traditions at its heart. There is a disjunction here with regard to ethics between the brahmanical emphasis on *dharma*, which means the maintenance of ritual purity, and the tantric rejection of *dharma* as a norm, which means the courting of impurity and the transcending of inhibition (*śaṅkā*).

Of particular opprobrium for the orthodox is the use in tantric rituals of prohibited substances, the five 'm's (*pañcamakara*): meat (*māṃsa*), fish (*matsya*), wine (*madya*), parched grain (*mudrā*) and sexual intercourse (*maithuna*). *Manu* expressly forbids the eating of meat, fish and the consuming of alcohol, as these are substances which pollute the Brahman's purity (*Manu* 10.88). In the cremation ground traditions of 'hard' Tantra, these substances were used as offerings to the terrible deities of the tantrika's pantheon. Liberation or power is attained through the reversal of vedic values; ritual impurity rather than purity becomes the basis for spiritual freedom. In the 'householder's Tantrism' of Kashmiri Brahmans, what became important was the religious experience of the identification of limited, individual consciousness with the unlimited consciousness of Śiva. This identification could be achieved through the esoteric rite of the *kulaprakriyā*, which culminated in sexual intercourse between the male practitioner (*sādhaka*), who was ritually identified with Śiva, for only a god can worship a god (SN: 50), and his female 'messenger' (*dūtī*), identified with Śakti. The emphasis in this particular rite was soteriological and, indeed, aesthetic; the bliss of sexual union transported the practitioners to the bliss of Śiva's pure consciousness. In many left-hand tantric rites the practitioners would not be married, they would not be of the same caste, and the woman would be menstruating – a very polluting condition for the orthodox

Brahman. Some texts even appear to advocate incest, strictly prohibited by orthodox *dharma* (TAV 29. p. 72).

Not only were the sexual practices of Tantrism an offence to orthodoxy, but so also were the consuming of meat and the suggestion of killing. The orthodox Brahman was strictly vegetarian, which means in a Hindu context that no meat, fish, fowl or eggs are to be consumed. *Manu*, however, does allow the consumption of meat which has been offered in vedic sacrifice, though there is some ambivalence about this, given the general emphasis on non-violence (*ahiṃsā*). A Brahman is on the one hand urged to perform vedic sacrifice, yet on the other to befriend all creatures (*Manu* 2.87, 6.75). But, given the ambivalence towards killing in his own tradition, it is little wonder that the tantric rites were quite unacceptable to him. The Brahman's ritual purity would be threatened by the consumption of non-vegetarian food, which has possibly been offered to non-vedic deities, and of alcohol, which would threaten his self-controlled equilibrium.

Tantric ideology is generally an affront to vedic orthodoxy. The Trika Śaivism of Kashmir undermines the social balance and implicitly questions the hierarchical models of the orthodox tradition, offering in their stead initiatory hierarchical models of its own, with its own system at the apex (PH: verse 8). Caste, as having any ontological and soteriological significance, is rejected – both implicitly in tantric ritual's eschewing of sexual controls, and explicitly in saying that tantric initiation eradicates caste (Sanderson 1985: 205). Indeed there are wider questions here, concerning different conceptualisations of the self or person in the two traditions. For orthodox ideology, represented by *Manu*, the person is *prima facie* an actor defined completely by his or her social matrix, in which the highest ideal is the detached, controlled Brahman; for the Kashmir Śaiva the person's true identity is unconstrained consciousness, and the highest ideal is the liberated *yogin*.

Such differences are also reflected in gender. Sanderson points out that there are great differences in models of women presented in the orthodox and tantric traditions (Sanderson 1985: 202). In the former, as we have seen above, they are models of docile dependence, without autonomy, whereas in tantric traditions, women have been regarded as channels of esoteric power and knowledge. The *dūtī* was the 'door' through which the power of the divine was transmitted (TA 29.122–3), and should, according to Jayaratha, Abhinavagupta's commentator, be intelligent, beautiful and displaying signs of possession (TAV 29. p. 68f.). Although the respect and ideological function of women in tantric traditions is higher than that of the orthodox, the extent to which this has been reflected as a social reality is questionable.[8]

Tantric traditions consciously break orthodox taboos in order to offer worship to unorthodox deities and to attain the religious experience of union with Śiva. Indeed, for the tantric ritual to work, Abhinavagupta says that the practitioner must be without desire (TA 29.99–100), which would keep him attached to the world from which he wishes to escape. The end is identification with pure consciousness, and the means is the stripping away or deconstruction of limiting social identities through their trans-cendence. This is significant because here we see how a monistic ideology takes precedence over brahmanical social reality: ethics becomes subordinated to ontology or even aesthetic experience (and the true identity of the person becomes, not the limited subject of first person predicates, but the unlimited subject of universal consciousness).

Ethics and ontology

R.C. Zaehner argued that the monistic philosophies which uphold the idea of the union of opposites, the absolute or ultimate reality conceived as a union of masculine and feminine principles, tend towards unethical behaviour. If the absolute is beyond good and evil, then these are relative concepts which have no bearing on that ultimate state or on the means of achieving it. Thus, conventionally 'wrong' or 'evil' behaviour could lead to or express a transcendent state. Zaehner cited a passage from the *Kulārṇava Tantra* which describes an ecstatic orgy in which usual social codes of behaviour have been abandoned.[9] He then went on to draw parallels between this and the behaviour of the 'Family', a twentieth century quasi-religious group led by Charles Manson, which undertook a number of murders in California in the late sixties, arguing that such behaviour is a consequence of belief in a transcendent state of being beyond good and evil. In *Our Savage God*, Zaehner wrote:

There is much nobility and probably much truth in the theory of the 'union of opposites' proclaimed by Heraclitus and the Upanishads alike . . . But it needs to be rigorously checked by the rational mind which it would destroy. If not then 'all things are lawful'. And is it a coincidence that this particular sect called itself the 'Family' as Charlie Manson called his own devoted band? Or is there a mysterious but real solidarity in what Manson called the 'total experience', which for this Tantric family was 'Bliss' and 'participation in the Divine'?

(pp. 102–103)

The issue of the relation between behaviour and ideology, between action and belief, needs to be addressed here. This is a complex subject and our remarks will be confined to Zaehner's claim in respect of Hinduism. Put simply, Zaehner would seem to be arguing that ethical behaviour is dependent upon belief systems, or more precisely upon ontology. On this account, dualist ontologies, as in Śaiva Siddhānta, in which there is a distinction between the absolute and the particular soul, are more conducive to ethical behaviour, whereas non-dualist ontologies, as in Kashmir Śaivism, are not. Indeed, according to Zaehner, non-dualist ontologies when pushed to their logical extreme, produce murderers.

It should perhaps be remarked that Zaehner was perceptive to an extent, for it is the Śaiva and Śākta monistic *tantra*s which tend to advocate 'left-hand' practices such as caste-free sexual intercourse, whereas the softer Śaiva dualist *tantra*s and the *Pāñcarātra Āgama*s do not. Indeed, monistic texts of Kashmir Śaivism state explicitly the logical development of a pure monism, that if everything is identical with the pure consciousness of Śiva, then, from that absolute perspective, the ideas not only of subject and object, but of purity and impurity are invalid. As has been shown above, ethics in the sense of brahmanical *dharma* are subordinated to a monistic ontology. The *Spanda-kārikā* says that, 'whether in thought (*cit*), word (*śabda*) or object (*artha*), there is no condition which is not Śiva. The enjoyer always and everywhere abides in the condition of the enjoyed' (SK: 2.4). If all is identical with Śiva, then the mind cannot escape from this condition in any state. The *Vijñāna-bhairava* (116) says: 'Wherever the mind goes, whether without or within, there is the condition of Śiva. Because of his all-pervasiveness where [can the mind] go?' This sentiment is again echoed in a verse quoted by Ksemaraja, the student of Abhina-

89

vagupta: 'O dear one, if there are no knowers (*vedaka*) how is there any object of knowledge (*vedya*)? Knower and object of knowledge are one. Thus there is no reality (*tattva*) which is impure (*aśuci*)' (SSV: 8).

This terminology is uncompromisingly non-dualistic. The term *tattva*, which I have rendered as 'reality', can be taken both as 'appearance to consciousness' in a phenomenological sense, and as referring to the hierarchical cosmos comprising the emanation of thirty-six *tattva*s. In saying that there is no *tattva* which is impure, because of the ontological identity of subject and object, the text is saying that there is no appearance to consciousness which is impure and, by implication, no action which is impure or against the 'truth'. Such passages are, therefore, denying the orthodox distinction between *dharma* and *adharma* as a consequence of their non-dualist ontology. The absolute consciousness of Śiva is beyond the distinction of *dharma* and *adharma*.

It has been argued that, far from undermining brahmanical Hinduism, tantric practices serve to reinforce it. Caste restrictions on sex and impurity are suspended during the left-hand rites, but these only serve to underline the differences during everyday worldly transactions. The high caste Brahman in a left-hand rite would not mix with the low caste woman outside of the ritual context. Yet on the other hand it could be argued that left-hand tantrism is surely subversive of brahmanical norms, in so far as it reacts against an ethical and social code perceived to be highly restrictive, particularly of low caste groups and of women. Indeed caste distinctions are said to be eradicated by the Kashmir Śaiva tantric initiation, which is given rational back-up by the un-compromising non-dualism of some tantric scriptural authorities. As Sanderson has observed, the distinction between orthodoxy and heterodoxy is not relative in a tantric context (Sanderson 1985: 211 note 61).

From the perspective of 'orthodox' and 'orthoprax' vedic Hinduism, tantric non-dualistic ideas might lead to 'immorality' in the sense of adharmic behaviour, and Zaehner might be correct here. However, it is not clear that adharmic behaviour would necessarily be the direct consequence of a non-dualist ontology. The most orthodox of Hindu philosophies, Advaita Vedānta, would never advocate adharmic behaviour. Indeed Advaita Vedānta is deeply concerned with the fulfilling of moral and social obligations.

Among the 'great sayings' (*mahāvākya*) from the revealed scripture (*śruti*), namely the *Upaniṣads*, of the Advaita Vedānta tradition, are such statements as: 'I am the absolute' (*aham brahmāsmi*), 'you are that' (*tat tvam asi*) and 'truly this all is the absolute' (*sarvam khalv idaṃ brahma*). Such passages express similar sentiments to those of Kashmir Śaivism cited above, in that both traditions present a non-dualist ontology. However, Advaita Vedānta places itself squarely in the orthodox vedic tradition. While such statements can be existentially realised in the experience (*anubhava*) of liberation, the ultimate identity of subject and object is also known from the vedic scriptures, one of the valid means of knowledge (*pramāna*). For Śaṃkara, the most famous exponent of Advaita Vedānta, knowledge (*jñāna*) is undoubtedly superior to action (*karma*), and sections in the Veda concerning knowledge of the absolute (*jñānakāṇḍa*) are more important than those concerning action (*karmakāṇḍa*). It therefore follows that knowledge of the absolute, which is liberation, is of a higher order than action and, by implication, ethics as *dharma*. Potter's remarks mentioned at the beginning of the chapter are apposite here: *mokṣa* is for Śaṃkara the highest value, higher than ethical duty, though this does not mean that ethical duty is unimportant. For Śaṃkara there are two levels of truth. From the highest perspective (*paramārtha satya*) the liberated person (*jīvanmukta*) has realised the identity of his self (*ātman*) with the absolute (*Brahman*), while from the relative level (*saṃvṛtti satya*) of everyday transaction (*vyāvahāra*), he is a renouncer (*saṃnyāsin*) who behaves in an appropriate, i.e. dharmic, way. Indeed Śaṃkara says that precisely *because* of the identity of subject and object in *Brahman*, the realiser of this cannot perform faults (*doṣa*) such as not doing good (*akaraṇa*) (BSB 2.2.21).

Unethical behaviour as defined within the context of *dharma* does not necessarily follow from a monistic ontology. Advaita Vedānta, which maintains a non-dualistic ontology, has been one of the central ideologies of the Brahman householder. Perhaps one way of looking at this would be to say that Advaita Vedānta, or indeed the Mīmāṃsā, provided the Brahman householder with a belief system while the *Dharmaśāstra*s provided him with a code of ethics and appropriate styles of behaviour. There would be no 'cognitive dissonance' here, for the philosophical systems would not contradict the dharmic system of action. For the Mīmāṃsaka *dharma* is an eternal natural law which is not dependent upon any theistic reality.

Indeed, here we have an atheistic tradition which advocates strict ethical codes of behaviour in accordance with the eternal *dharma*, a fact which militates against Zaehner's claim that theistic systems are more conducive to ethical behaviour.

Zaehner, in his criticism of tantric systems, seems to have been appealing to some universal sense of morality. But the universality of moral statements is in itself a highly contentious issue and its assumption methodologically unjustifiable if understanding rather than judgement is one's aim.[10] To explain and understand tantric traditions and their codes of behaviour it is necessary to locate them in their Indian contexts, rather than discuss them in the light of a presupposed moral discourse.

We can say then that Tantrism might well produce or even advocate adharmic behaviour, but this is not necessarily as a consequence of a non-dualist ontology. Non-dualism, in itself, is neither a necessary nor sufficient condition for an action to be regarded as unethical in Hinduism. As we have seen with the example of Advaita Vedānta, non-dualism does not entail adharmic behaviour, nor even does atheism. It is not simply non-dualism which creates adharmic behaviour in left-hand *tantra*, but rather a different soteriology in which value is located in the ultimate experience of liberation, and in which liberation and pleasure or joy, particularly sexual pleasure, are not seen to be incompatible.

By way of conclusion, I have tried here to locate the semantic equivalent of 'ethics' in the term *dharma* and pointed to some of the term's applications for the brahmanical householder, with particular reference to the *Manusmṛti*. *Dharma* provides the resources for the making of moral decisions in Hinduism. It refers both to a cosmic, eternal principle, and, more importantly, operates within particular situations which require moral choice. *Dharma* is the context in which moral choice operates, determining the kinds of moral choice available. These moral choices are constrained in brahmanical ideology by a person's location in a hierarchical and gender-specific social structure. This brahmanical understanding of *dharma* can be contrasted with some tantric traditions, such as the monistic Śaivism of Kashmir, in which vedic values are undermined and even reversed. Here, while orthodox norms might be superficially adhered to, we have an ideology and practice which directly threaten brahmanical orthodoxy by undermining caste and elevating women to an ideologically higher status. The brahmanical ideology, of ritual duty and eventual liberation through control and purity, is contrasted with the tantric ideology of transcending accepted moral codes in its aspiration for total freedom.

ABBREVIATIONS

(I have not given bibliographical information about Sanskrit texts. For details see the bibliographies of Doniger, Potter and Sanderson.)

BSB	*Brahma-sūtra-bhāṣya*
KT	*Kulārṇava-tantra*
Manu	*Manusmṛti*
MS	*Mīmāṃsasūtra*
PH	*Pratyabhijñāhṛdaya*
SK	*Spanda-kārikā*
SN	*Spanda-nirṇaya*
SSV	*Śiva-sūtra-vimarśinī*
TA	*Tantrāloka*
TAV	*Tantrāloka-vivaraṇa*

NOTES

1. Cantwell Smith, W. (1962) *The Meaning and End of Religion*, New York, Macmillan, pp. 64ff.
2. Weightman, S. (1978) *Hinduism in the Village Setting*, Manchester, Open University, p. 5f.
3. For the application of the idea of context-sensitive rules to ritual acts prescribed by vedic *dharma*, see Staal, F. (1989) *Rules Without Meaning*, New York, Peter Lang.
4. Matilal, B.K. (1991) *Perception*, Oxford, Clarendon Press, p. 17.
5. See Coward et al. (1991) p. 19; Leslie, J. 'Sutee or *Satī*: Victim or Victor', in Leslie, J. (ed.) (1991) *Roles and Rituals for Hindu Women*, London, Pinter.
6. Marriott, M. 'Hindu Transactions, Diversity Without Dualism', in Kapferer, B. (ed.) (1977) *Transaction and Meaning: Directions in the Anthropology of Exchange and Symbolic Behaviour*, Philadelphia, Institute for the Study of Human Issues.
7. There is a problem with the terms 'literal' and 'symbolic', in so far as the 'literal' use of the five 'm's is also 'symbolic'.

93

8. Gupta, S. 'Women in the Śaiva/Śākta Ethos', in Leslie, J. (1991) *Roles and Rituals for Hindu Women*, London, Pinter.
9. Zaehner, R.C. (1974) *Our Savage God*, London, Collins, pp. 102–103.
10. See Donovan, P. 'Do Different Religions Share Common Moral Ground?', in (1986) *Identity Issues and World Religions*, Australia, Australian Association for the Study of Religion.

FURTHER READING

Bharati, A. (1982) *Hindu Views and Ways and the Hindu–Muslim Interface*, Santa Barbara, Ross-Erikson.

Biardeau, M. (1989) *Hinduism, the Anthropology of a Civilization*, Oxford, OUP.

Coward, H.G., Lipner, J.J. and Young, K.K. (1991) *Hindu Ethics*, New York, SUNY Press.

Doniger, W.D. (1991) *The Laws of Manu*, London, Penguin.

Dumont, L. (1980) *Homo Hierarchicus*, Chicago, University of Chicago Press.

Madan, T.N. (1987) *Non-Renunciation*, Oxford, OUP.

Potter, K. (1991) *Presuppositions in India's Philosophies*, Delhi, Motilal Barnarsidass.

Rocher, L. (1980) 'Karma and Rebirth in the Dharmaśāstras', in O'Flaherty, W. (ed.) *Karma and Rebirth in Classical Indian Traditions*, Berkeley, University of California Press.

Sanderson, A. (1985) 'Purity and Power Among the Brahmans of Kashmir', in Carrithers, M. et al. (eds) *The Category of the Person*, Cambridge, CUP.

Zaehner, R.C. (1966) *Hinduism*, Oxford, OUP.

4. Islam

Clinton Bennett

Morals as eternal truths, not human ideas

Muslims sometimes express discontent with the English word
'religion'. They understand 'religion' as a rather private, personal
affair, or perhaps as a set of beliefs, not as a total way of life that
embraces every human activity from, say, the most intimate acts of
sexual relationships, to how to punish people who have committed a
crime, to how the state should organise itself. Islam describes itself as
God's 'straight path' (Qur'ān 1: 5) for the human race, and teaches
that God has revealed, or disclosed, his will – a path for people to
follow, so that they have clear guidance in all areas of life. What is
'right' or 'wrong', 'good' or 'bad', 'permissible' or 'prohibited' –
whether for individuals or for whole societies – are not matters of
mere opinion, subject to fashion or to human convenience, but are
eternal, unchangeable truths. This conviction – that God has
revealed 'right' (or what is permitted, *ḥalāl*) and 'wrong' (or
prohibited, *ḥarām*) – is fundamental to any understanding of the
role played by ethics and morals in Islam. Some writers refer to an
'ethical' or to a 'legal' dimension in all religions; with reference to
Islam, it is quite possible to say that 'Islam' is itself synonymous with
'ethics'. By definition, if you have committed yourself to walking
God's straight path, your conduct and lifestyle must be ethical.

Islam's ethical and legal framework

Before we begin our exploration of moral decision-making in Islam,
it is first necessary to outline the framework within which Muslims
pursue their thinking about moral issues. This framework provides

the context within which public issues – such as law and order, crime and punishment, the economic system, care for the environment, and relations between different states – as well as personal and domestic issues – abortion, sexual relationships, marriage, divorce, and medical ethics – are tackled. In this chapter, we shall examine how Muslims make moral decisions in some of the above 'public life' areas, although we shall also focus on issues of personal morality.

Islam always begins with the Qur'ān, and with the life and example of the prophet Muhammad (570–632 CE), who received this divine revelation. Since God wants men and women to obey him, he has always sent them messengers and prophets to make his will known – otherwise how could he reasonably expect obedience and faithfulness? Islam teaches that every nation, or tribe, has had its own prophet (see the Qur'ān *surah* 10, *āyah* 48). Some of these prophets were also given Books, or scriptures – such as the Torah given to Moses, and the *Injīl*, or Gospel, given to Jesus.

There were, in fact, two types of prophets – *nabī* who operated within existing traditions, and *rasūl*, who brought fresh revelations. This prophetic process is understood as cumulative, a process of education through which God was preparing people for his final, complete, absolute revelation – the Qur'ān. This was revealed to Muhammad between 610 and 632 CE. For Muslims, he is the last of a long line of prophets (perhaps 124,000 of them). Muhammad is called the 'Seal of the Prophets' (*surah* 33: 40). The Qur'ān, as God's final revelation, describes itself as 'a clear guidance for mankind, and clear proofs of guidance, and the criterion of right and wrong' (*surah* 2: 185). It is a book 'in which there is no doubt' (2: 2), completing and confirming all earlier scriptures, such as the Torah and the *Injīl*.

Almost from the very beginning of their existence as an identifiable community (*ummah*, or nation), the Muslims were more than just a group of people who shared certain religious beliefs and practices; they were a nation-state, a social, political and economic as well as a religious entity. Abdur Rahman I. Doi writes, 'Islamic political psychology views *Dār al-Islām* (Abode of Islam) as one vast homogeneous commonwealth of people who have a common goal and a common destiny and who are guided by a common ideology in all matters both spiritual and temporal' (Doi 1984: 5). Although the first twelve years of his preaching at Makkah (Muhammad's home town in Arabia) were ones of persecution and limited success, after he migrated with his companions to Madinah in 622, Muhammad's – and Islam's – fortunes changed dramatically. At Makkah, Muhammad was the persecuted preacher, supported by a small group of companions against the vested interests of the most powerful tribe, whose revenue from the many shrines that dominated the city, and whose concepts of privilege and of racial superiority, were challenged by his monotheistic, egalitarian message.

At Madinah, Muhammad emerged as temporal as well as spiritual leader, exercising authority over non-Muslim (mainly Jewish) as well as Muslim citizens. He gave the city a charter, the Constitution of Madinah, to order its common life, and led the community in all spheres of life. His example, together with his interpretation of the Qur'ān, was carefully observed, and later recorded, by his companions. The Qur'ān itself says that its best interpreter was the Prophet who received it, whose own life, Muslims believe, was also divinely inspired (see *surah*s 4: 59 and 33: 21) and without sin. Muhammad, therefore, while no more than a man in Muslim thinking, is also the perfect man (*insān-i-kāmil*) and, as such, he is unique among men and women.

All this means that Islam, in its classical formulation, makes no distinction between what we might think of as the 'sacred' and the 'secular', between 'religion' and 'State'. Akbar Ahmed usefully points out how, in his life, the Prophet always attempted to achieve 'balance' between worldly and spiritual concerns, between *dīn* (religion) and *dunyā* (world). He also encouraged his companions to live 'in the latter by the principles of the former' (Ahmed 1988: 28). Our concern, then, in this chapter, is to examine how Muslims, in making moral decisions, act out in *dunyā* the principles they derive from *dīn*.

The most fundamental theological principle in Islam is the concept of *tawḥīd* – unity. God is one (see *surah* 112). This principle also involves the idea of interrelatedness between all areas of life, as well as between different life-forms and the created order. Thus, balance (or justice, *al-ʿadl*) is a basic concept – balanced people, balanced societies – a balance between justice and compassion, between wealth and poverty, between the role of women and that of men. *Sūrah* 90: 12–17 says, 'The good is of steep ascent. It consists of freeing slaves. Of feeding the deprived. Of being kind to orphans.

97

And to do so with patience and compassion'. Peace (salām) between people, their creator and their fellow creatures, therefore, lies at the heart of what it means to be Muslim. The origin of the word 'Islam', of which Muslim is the participle, is the same as that of the Arabic word for peace. We shall see how these principles influence and assist moral decision-making when we turn, below, to consider some particular issues in more detail.

After Muhammad's death, Islam continued to spread. Within a hundred years his successors ruled an empire that stretched from the Atlantic to the Indian ocean. John L. Esposito writes;

> As Muhammad was both head of state and messenger of God, so too were the envoys and soldiers of the state the envoys and soldiers of Islam, its first missionaries. They spread a way of life that affected the political and social order as well as the individual life and worship. Islam encompassed both a faith and a sociopolitical system. Ideally, this new order was to be a community of believers, acknowledging the ultimate sovereignty of God, living according to His law, obeying His prophet, and dedicating their lives to spreading God's rule and law.
>
> (Esposito 1991: 35)

Conquered people were not forced to become Muslims (the Qur'ān forbids 'compulsion in religion', 2: 256) but were invited to accept Islam. Those Christians and Jews who chose to remain Christian and Jewish, in return for payment of a poll tax, were guaranteed protection and the right to practise their existing faiths, although some other limits were imposed as part of their minority (or dhimmī) status.

Violence and Islam – the morality of war

This early, rapid and widespread expansion raises the moral question about the use of violence: is war ever ethical, or justified? It is often said by non-Muslim writers that Islam expanded by violent means, by forcibly converting conquered people. However, what actually expanded as a result of the fath, or wars of conquest, was not the Islamic faith, but the Islamic empire. In many areas where Muslims established power and ruled, such as in Spain and India, they always remained a minority. Mohamed Talbi points out that when the youthful Islamic empire emerged as a factor in world history, several superpowers were already competing, through military force, for political domination. Inevitably, the new power joined this struggle and used the accepted means of pursuing it – warfare. Talbi says,

Whether it liked it or not, Islam could not help but fit its own period. The train was already moving; Islam had only to catch it. And so it is a fact that more than one verse of the Qur'ān incites to combat and promises the palm of martyrdom and paradise to whoever falls while striving in God's way. Such combat, however, is always put forward as a second best, a last resort, which must conform to all sorts of material and moral restrictions in order to be acceptable.

(Quoted in Griffiths 1990: 84)

Armed struggle (*jihād*) to extend the borders of the empire could, Muslims believed, be justified if it had a reasonable chance of success. However, as this became increasingly unlikely (perhaps the Ottoman siege of Vienna in 1683 was the last attempt), *jihād* was understood in defensive terms – to defend Islamic territory from external aggression. *Sūrah* 2: 190 says, 'Fight in the way of Allāh against those who fight against you, but begin not hostilities. Lo! Allāh loveth not aggressors'. Under certain circumstances, and as a last resort, aggressive *jihād* to right a wrong, to fight injustice or oppression, can also be justified. Islam, though, views all life (including animal and plant life) as God-given, and its rules governing the conduct of a just war forbid the injury of crops, animals or civilians. They also forbid the destruction of any places of worship.

Many Muslims now question whether, given modern weapons of mass destruction, any war can be considered just. In classical Muslim thinking, there was no place for war between Muslims, unless some Muslims were regarded by the majority as having compromised Islamic principles. Since the early empire was, at least in its early classical period, a united political unit, and nation states only emerged at a later period, even the idea of separate, independent Muslim nations has, arguably, no place in Islamic ideology. Esposito writes: 'The political ideal of Islam was a transnational community that transcended ethnic, racial, and national ties; it was based on an inner cohesion that stemmed from the unity of the community's religiopolitical ideal' (Esposito 1991: 139). We shall refer, below, to some modern reinterpretations of the concept of *jihād*.

The *sharī'ah* (divine law)

In theory at least, the *khalīfah*, deputy or successor to Muhammad's political and judicial authority, although not to his spiritual authority, ruled the entire Islamic empire. A minority (the Shi'ah) believed that spiritual and political authority should have passed from Muhammad to his male descendants, and they emerged as a separate group from the majority party, the Sunni, who follow the tradition (*sunnah*) of Muhammad and not a living, divinely inspired spiritual leader, an *imām*. Some Shi'ah still revere an *imām*. For example, the Nizari Ismailis follow the Aga Khan, a descendant of Muhammad through Ismail (d. 762), eldest son of the sixth Imām, Ja'far (d. 765). The majority of Shi'ah, however, recognised Ja'far's surviving son, Musa al-Kazim (d. 818) as Imām. In 873, their twelfth Imām, while still a child, disappeared from the world. He is believed to be supernaturally 'hidden', and will eventually return as al-Mahdī (Lord of the Age) to rule his people and to establish justice in the world. His followers, the majority of Iranian Muslims, meanwhile, vest authority in their *mujtahids* (religious scholars) who collectively represent the Hidden Imām. They are able to extrapolate new interpretations of *sharī'ah*, and indeed, to add to its content by deducing their own original decisions. They thus become, for their followers, sources of emulation.

The Sunni soon developed an elaborate legal code – their *sharī'ah*, literally, 'a path leading to a watering hole' – which became the official law of the land throughout the Islamic empire. *Sharī'ah* is universal law and covers every area of personal, moral and social life – prayer, fasting, diet, taxation, crime and punishment. The basic source is the Qur'ān, which contains explicit legislation in many of these areas. The Egyptian scholar, Abd al Wahhab ibn Khallaf, has classified Qur'ānic legislation as follows: constitutional provisions, 10 verses; international law, 25 verses; jurisdiction and procedures, 13 verses; penal law, 30 verses; civil law, 70 verses; family and personal law, 70 verses; economic and financial directives, 20 verses (Zakaria 1988: 33). This is supplemented by the *sunnah* (example) of the prophet as recorded in the six 'sound collections' of *hadīth* (sayings and doings of Muhammad – literally 'account', or 'report'). These six collections are those of al-Bukhari (d. 870), Muslim (d. 875), Abu Dawud (d. 875), at-Tirmidhi (d. 892), an-Nasai (d. 915) and Ibn Maja (d. 886).

Strict criteria were employed to judge the authenticity of *ḥadīth*. Much stress was placed on establishing a chain of reliable transmitters that could be traced back to a wife, or companion, of Muhammad. Western scholars tend to underplay the importance attached by the collectors to consistency or plausibility of content. Today, it is more widely accepted that content-criticism, as well as authenticating the chain of transmitters, was an important factor in determining the validity of traditions. Of course, to what degree political or theological considerations may also have shaped the *sunnah* remains the subject of debate. Muslims uphold the integrity of the six collectors, and of the early transmitters' faithfulness to the memory of their prophet.

THE PRINCIPLES OF JURISPRUDENCE

If no ruling or opinion on a particular moral or legal point was found either in the Qur'ān or in the *Ḥadīth*, the early jurists used several methods, or principles (*uṣūl*) of jurisprudence (*fiqh*), to extend the scope of *sharī'ah*. The first principle is known as *ijmā'* (consensus), originally the consensus of the whole Muslim community which, said Muhammad, 'will not agree in error'. *Ijmā'* was also closely associated with the process of *shūrā*, or consultation, and signifies that, for Sunnis, authority is ultimately invested in the whole community, not in certain individuals. Significant examples of *ijmā'* include the office of the *khalīfah*. Sunnis believe that Muhammad did not nominate a successor, or leave any instructions about how the *ummah* should be governed after his death. It was Muhammad's Companions who decided, by mutual consultation and consensus, to elect Abu Bakr as 'Deputy'. Similarly, the authority of the six 'sound' collections of *ḥadīth* was determined by *ijmā'*, as, in the doctrinal area, were such beliefs as the sinlessness of the prophets and the concept of Divine Attributes. Neither doctrine is explicitly found in the Qur'ān, but both can be logically deduced from it. They were confirmed by *ijmā'*. Later, *ijmā'* was restricted to the unanimous consent of the

101

most distinguished or best qualified jurists, the *'ulama'* (plural of *'alīm*).

The next principle used to extend the scope of the law is known as analogy, *qiyās*. An example of *qiyās* is the *sharī'ah*'s prohibition against the consumption of any alcoholic beverage. The Qur'ān itself only refers to *khamr*, an intoxicating drink made from grape-juice, but by analogy the jurists extended the prohibition to include all alcoholic substances. *Qiyās* is also used to extend the prohibition to include drugs and, by some contemporary jurists, tobacco. Not all jurists, though, accepted this total prohibition of alcohol – for example, the Kufa school of law during the Umayyad period (661–750) only forbade grape-wine. The judicial decisions of the first four *khalīfah*s, who are regarded as having been 'rightly guided', and of Muhammad's closest companions, of whom he said 'my companions are even as the stars, whichever of them you follow, you shall be rightly guided', are especially important after the authority of Muhammad's own life.

In fact, the 'ideal' for many Muslims is to imitate Muhammad, and his Companions. This is why the *hadīth* record even the most intimate details of Muhammad's life, since his example – how he ate, washed, dyed his hair, which colours he preferred, how he acted in the company of his wives – provides the ideal model for human conduct. The significance of Muhammad's example in determining the moral life for Muslims cannot be overstated. Based on *hadīth*, it is, for instance, not acceptable for a Muslim to gobble food; eating and drinking should be at a gentle, dignified pace. When a Muslim needs to sneeze, he or she should cover both mouth and nose. Relieving oneself in any public place, or in still water, is forbidden. Unpleasant body-odour is considered *harām*. It is also obligatory to accept a wedding invitation. Muslims should always greet other Muslims with *Assālamu 'alaykum* ('peace be upon you'). It is not considered incorrect to greet non-Muslims, but an alternative formula should be used. These norms are not based on mere opinion, or arrived at by arbitrary choice; they are predicated on *hadīth*. Not observing these norms, for example by gobbling food, swearing or ignoring greetings, is contrary to Muslim ethics.

Finally, very distinguished *'ulama'*, known as *mujtahid*, could also extend the law by special mental effort, exertion or striving (*ijtihād*). In a conversation with one of his own *qāḍi*s (jurists), Muadh ibn Jabal, Muhammad said:

102

Prophet: How will you decide a problem?
Muadh: According to the Qur'ān.
Prophet: If it is not in it?
Muadh: According to the Sunnah.
Prophet: If it is not in that either?
Muadh: Then I will use my own reasoning.

(Ahmed 1988: 24)

Reasoning and rational choice thus play an important part in formulating the content of Islamic law, although any decision made by *ijtihàd* must also be accepted by *ijmā'*. Sometimes, a fourth principle was also applied – *maṣāliḥ*, public welfare.

THE FOUR SCHOOLS OF LAW

By the end of the tenth century, four *imāms* had emerged whose mastery of *fiqh* was thought so complete, that any further extension of the content of *sharī'ah* was thereafter regarded as dangerous. Since the *sharī'ah* is divine not human law, endless human ability to extend its content makes corruption likely. Consequently, the work of the four *Imāms* – Hanafi (d. 767), Malik (d. 795), Shafi (d. 820) and Hanbal (d. 855) – emerged as definitive. Now, instead of extending the *sharī'ah*, a new structure emerged:

> Muslims were simply to follow, or imitate (*taqlīd*) the past, God's law as elaborated by the early jurists. Jurists were no longer to seek new solutions or produce new regulations and law books but instead study the established legal manuals and law books and write their commentaries ... Belief that the work of the law schools had definitively resulted in the transformation of the Sharia into a legal blueprint for society reinforced the sacrosanct nature of tradition; change or innovation came to be viewed as an unwarranted deviation (*bid'ah*) from established sacred norms. To be accused of innovation – deviation from the law and practice of the community – was equivalent to the charge of heresy in Christianity.

(Esposito 1991: 84f.)

Shi'ah *'ulama'*, the *mujtahid*, as noted above, continue to be able to add to the actual content of their *sharī'ah* but Sunni Muslims now

103

follow one of the schools (*madhab*) established by the four *Imāms*. Belief that their work is definitive is itself based on *ijmā'*. Among Sunni, the four schools dominate in certain geographical areas: Hanafi's (which succeeded the Kufa school referred to above) in Turkey and in the Indian sub-continent, Malik's in North Africa, Shafi's in Lower Egypt, and Hanbal's in Saudi Arabia. Different schools give more weight to some of the principles described above. For example, Hanbalis emphasise the *sunnah* and are reluctant to rely on *qiyās*. Imam Hanbal is said to have refrained from eating water melons because no *ḥadīth* recorded that Muhammad ate them. Similarly, Hanbalis regard 'public interest' as a 'controversial principle' which both the Malikis and the Hanafis regard highly but which Shafi rejected. On the other hand, the school founded by Dawud ibn Kahalaf (d. 884) failed to gain official recognition because it refused to accept *qiyās* as an authentic principle of jurisprudence. Shafi preferred *ijmā'*, and laid down strict rules governing the use of *qiyās*.

OBLIGATORY, PERMITTED AND PROHIBITED

The *sharī'ah* legislation classifies behaviour into different categories. *Farḍ* means obligatory duties, including the five pillars of Islam and all their associated rituals – the saying of the *Shahādah* (declaration of faith), the five daily prayers, the fast during *Ramaḍān*, the payment of *zakāt* (the charitable tax) and performing the *ḥajj* (the pilgrimage at Makkah). As we shall see below, marriage, having children, providing for (if you are a man) and caring for (if you are a woman) your family, and caring for elderly parents are also obligatory. *Ḥalāl* refers to that which is permitted, including permitted foods and drinks, but is also subdivided into behaviour which is either neutral (*mubāḥ*), tolerated (*makrūh*) or positively recommended (*mandūb*) – giving to charity, for example, is positively recommended, as are hard work, and pursuit of *'ilm* (knowledge).

Ḥarām behaviour or foods are positively forbidden except under certain (usually life-threatening) conditions. Every action, whether a commercial transaction, eating, or reading a book, has a moral significance in Islam, since 'right action' will be divinely rewarded, 'wrong action' divinely punished. However, reference must also be made to Islam's high regard for 'intent' (*niyyah*). A 'right action' carries no merit unless it is also performed with pious intent, but most jurists agree that even if carried out with 'good intent', a bad act remains bad. Muslim belief in Divine Judgement – in reward and in punishment after death – thus has a direct bearing on their understanding of the interrelatedness of 'theology' and 'morality'. Muslims, though, have discussed at length the degree to which people are morally responsible, and accountable, for their actions.

One early school of thought, the Jabarites, held that if people were capable of acting as independent agents, of their own volition, God's omnipotence was compromised. They taught that all human actions are predetermined by God. Most Muslims were unhappy with this view, since it seemed to remove moral responsibility from people. Another school, the Mutazalites, argued instead that people enjoy absolute freedom of action. They emphasised God's justice over and against his power, which, they believed, was necessarily withheld. The majority, though, thought this too dangerous – reducing God's sovereignty – and developed the alternative theory of 'acquisition' (*kasb*). This theory seeks to uphold God's omnipotence by saying that every human action is caused, or created, by God, but that individuals then acquire moral responsibility for the consequences of these actions. It is perhaps also important to mention the discussion about 'promise and threat', that is, about 'heaven' and 'hell'. What actually happens on the Day of Judgement? Is it simply a matter of arithmetic, a credit-balance of good deeds equals 'heaven', a debit balance equals 'hell'? If so, is God himself not bound to act in a predetermined way, thereby ceasing to be omnipotent? If entry into paradise is 'earned', what role does *īmān* (faith) play? Opinions differ, but the majority of Muslims hold that God is not bound by human action, good or bad (this would almost amount to *shirk* – associating a partner with God), but is ultimately free to exercise his will as he chooses. This ultimate freedom is balanced by divine justice and mercy, but bound by neither.

DIFFERENCES BETWEEN THE SCHOOLS

Based on their preferred *uṣūl* (principles), the four schools do not always agree on every detail of what is *ḥarām* or *ḥalāl*, although it is generally accepted that they fully agree on all major points of law.

105

To give an example, one area of minor difference is how the actual ritual of *ṣalāt* (prayer) is performed. Only Hanifa says that prayer is invalid if a woman is present in a line of praying men. During the fifth prayer position (the kneeling position, or *jalsah*) Malikis say nothing, while Hanafis say 'Lord, cover my transgressions'. Or again, a difference of opinion concerns whether a Muslim who has not yet learnt Arabic can recite the *Fātiḥah* (the opening chapter of the Qur'ān, used frequently during prayer) in any other language. Hanifa declared quite unequivocally that other languages could be used, Shafi that only Arabic was valid. Similarly, both Hanbal and Hanifa saw no difficulty with using a 'translation' of the Qur'ān to teach non-Arabic speakers. Hanbalis and Hanafis today approve of interlinear versions with both English and Arabic, or Persian and Arabic texts. Malik totally rejects this. Shafi, in this instance, sets out arguments for and against but makes no decisive judgement.

Other debates arose from the issue of how literally the Qur'ān should be understood. For example, the verse 'Do not eat anything over which the name of Allāh has not been uttered' (*sūrah* 6: 161): does that mean that flesh slaughtered without a ritual benediction must never be eaten, or that *qiyās* can accept as edible any meat slaughtered by a Muslim, with or without a spoken blessing, since a Muslim is always mindful of God. Also, if it is not known whether the blessing was pronounced, opinions differ as to whether a Muslim should eat, or not. Hanifa rules that only ritually slaughtered meat can be consumed. Most jurists now interpret the blessing as commendable (*mandūb*) but not compulsory. There are also minor differences of opinion about what foods and drinks are *ḥalāl* or *ḥarām*. For example, the Hanafis deem that fish are the only aquatic animals permitted, while Malikis consider all aquatic animals edible. We have already noted that not everyone accepted all alcohol as *ḥarām*. Today, most Muslims regard the consumption of alcohol as unlawful, but some practising Muslims do drink in moderation.

SHARĪ'AH: BRIEF HISTORICAL OVERVIEW

After the classical period of Islamic history (usually said to have ended about 1000 CE with the effective demise of Abbasid authority), *sharī'ah* was often restricted to limited areas, usually to domestic law, and other areas of the law were dealt with under the

106

ordinances or regulations of Muslim rulers (sultans), who often found that the *sharī'ah* did not further, or suit, their economic interests. They carefully avoided using the word 'law', since that is God's province. Consequently, in practice, Muslims' personal conduct and moral behaviour were predicated on the injunctions of the *sharī'ah*, while their political and civil life was largely governed by a quite different set of rules and regulations. In the nineteenth century, many Muslim countries became subject to European domination, and European legal codes, with some accommodation for Islamic domestic law, were imposed. In practice, then, the ideal Muslim society, governed by the *sharī'ah*, has rarely existed, and surveys of Muslim history show how Muslims have struggled to achieve their ideal, as they have also debated what that ideal is and how it can best be achieved. Struggle, or *jihād* (often called Islam's sixth pillar), can refer to this 'obligation incumbent on all Muslims, as individuals and as a community, to exert themselves to realise God's will, to lead virtuous lives, and to extend the Islamic community through preaching, education, and so on' (Esposito 1991: 93). Here, 'struggle', or *jihād*, implies an active, not passive, understanding of human responsibility. People are, according to the Qur'ān, God's 'vice-regents' on earth (6: 165). Their task as 'trustees' is to work with God to steward creation; to achieve balance or harmony between different creatures and ourselves, and between individuals and groups within society.

Many post-independence Muslim countries are today seeking to discover how they can create societies that conform more closely to the Islamic ideal. The *sharī'ah*, they believe, is the blueprint and the guide for creating this ideal. Opinion differs, however, on how the 'ideal' should be achieved. For some, the way to create the ideal Muslim society is to imitate (*taqlīd*) the past. The *sharī'ah*, with all its rules and regulations, laws and prescriptive punishments for specific crimes, must be implemented without change or innovation, addition or deletion. For others, what is truly Islamic are not the particular laws and specific penalties, but the eternal principles that inform and undergird them. In this view, particular legal codes, even those contained within the Qur'ān itself, are of secondary importance – valid for particular contexts; only the principles that informed them remain eternal. Specific legal rulings can, and should, change as circumstances change. Ziauddin Sardar (Anees, Abedin and Sardar 1992), who argues this view, has usefully listed the eternal principles as *tawḥīd* (unity), *khilāfah* (human trusteeship), *'adl* (justice), *'ibādah* (worship), *'ilm* (knowledge) *ijmā'* (consensus) and *istiṣlāh* (public interest). Others would add *al aḥsan* (compassion), *salām* (peace), *īmān* (faith) and *ṣabr* (patience). Doi represents those Muslims who fundamentally reject this approach: 'If a ruler does not apply the Islamic penalty for theft or slander or adultery, preferring judgments of man-made law, such a ruler would be considered definitely an unbeliever' (1984: 39). Other Muslims are happy to separate the political almost entirely from the religious, and claim that you can be authentically Muslim without enjoying any of the traditional Islamic political infrastructure. This is Rafiq Zakaria's thesis: 'History shows that among the Muslims, although there has always been a tendency to oppose the separation of politics and religion in practice, they have inevitably reconciled themselves to the opposite' (Zakaria 1988: 29).

Moral decision-making in public life issues

Given these divergent views, there is more scope than is sometimes imagined for creativity in ethical and public life decision-making within the Islamic world. As Muslims strive to introduce economic systems, for example, that uphold the Islamic principles of equilibrium and compassion – balance between wealth and poverty, between the incentive to work hard (labour and industry are encouraged by Qur'ān and Ḥadīth) and generosity towards those who are unable to work because of ill health or misfortune – there is scope for innovation.

In countries where governments are committed to a process of Islamicisation, such as Pakistan, Malaysia, Iran and the Sudan, there is much debate about how *sharī'ah* should be interpreted. Before we turn in more detail to discuss how individual Muslims actually think about some particular moral issues and dilemmas, and about how they arrive at their decisions or courses of action, we shall examine possible options in one important area of public life. For many non-Muslims, perceptions of Islam are filtered through media images depicting Islam as a world of archaic, obscurantist and barbaric laws and practices. Given these negative images, it is interesting to examine and discuss how Muslims approach the important moral issue of crime and punishment – an area that lies at the heart of any organised, cohesive social unit, especially the nation state.

How should Muslim rulers administer their nations' legal and punitive systems? One option is to be totally bound by the Qur'ānic punishments, or by those prescribed by the classic texts. If we take theft as an example, in this view (argued, as we have seen, by Doi), there would be no alternative but to prescribe amputation of the thief's hand, since this is the *ḥadd* (penalty) prescribed in the Qur'ān: 'And as for the thief, both male and female, cut off their hands. It is the reward of their own deeds, an exemplary punishment from Allāh' (*sūrah* 5: 38). Following the classical judicial system, however, the following factors must also apply (this framework represents the consensus of the four schools).

1. There must be a public trial. Evidence submitted must not be circumstantial but corroborated by two reliable male Muslim witnesses. Strict rules govern the admissibility of eye-witness evidence.
2. The thief must not be a minor, mentally unstable or the subject of coercion.
3. Neither the thief, nor the thief's family, must have been hungry when he, or she, was committing the crime. In this case, the whole Muslim society would be regarded as the real culprit for neglecting its *farḍ* obligations towards the poor and disadvantaged. The thief would not be criminally liable.
4. The thief must be a persistent thief. If there is thought to be the possibility of reform, no amputation would take place. This condition rests on the jurists' interpretation that even punishment by the state is actually an 'evil'. Doi says:

> It is an interesting point that the Holy Qur'an generally adopts the same word for punishment, as for the crime. Thus, in chapter 42:40, both the evil and its punishment are called *sayyi'ah* (evil); in chapter 16:126 and chapter 22:60, the word used is a derivative of *'uqūbah* (punishment) and in chapter 2:194 the word used is *i'tida'* (aggression). The adoption of the same word for the crime and for the punishment indicates that punishment itself, though justified by the circumstances, is truly speaking nothing but a necessary evil.
>
> (Doi 1984: 222)

Punishment is an extreme measure, and is only executed when the limit of society's ability to tolerate the crime has been exceeded. It is regarded primarily as a deterrent to others – as an 'example'. It also depends on the value of the stolen property. Opinions differ about the upper-limit before amputation can be justified. Malik's limit was one quarter of a *dīnār* (a *dīnār* was a gold coin weighing 96 grains of barley), Hanifa's was ten *dirham*s (a silver coin, Joseph was sold for *dirhams* at *sūrah* 12: 20). Such units must obviously be translated into modern currencies, a process which will itself involve an element of relative interpretation in order to adapt them to contemporary value systems.

5. Muslim law gives a high value to the concept of repentance and of forgiveness. This is based on such verses as the one immediately following the verse about theft: 'But whosoever repents after his wrongdoing and amends, lo! Allāh will relent towards him' (*sūrah* 5: 39 and see 3: 134; 42: 40). It is a prerogative of the injured party in Islam to choose to forgive and, if their honour allows, to forego prosecution. This even pertains in cases of murder: 'Do not take life except for just cause. If anyone is wrongfully killed We give his heir the right to demand retribution or to forgive, but let him not exceed bounds in the matter of taking life, for he is bound by the law' (*sūrah* 17: 33).

Muslims who do not accept that amputation must be, for all time, the prescribed punishment for 'theft', would accept the general presuppositions that undergird the above legal framework, but argue that an alternative, though equally severe or extreme punishment, can be substituted. Thus, they retain the eternal principles (justice and patience, for example, and what is *ḥalāl* and *ḥarām*), and adjust the *fiqh* (the particular legislation), which Ziauddin Sardar and others regard as 'outmoded': 'The application of *fiqh* legislations, out of context from their time and out of step with ours, gives Muslim societies a medieval feel' (Anees, Abedin and Sardar 1992: 72). In this view, then, a Muslim jurist faced with deciding whether it is morally right to rule that a thief's hand should be amputated, even after repeated and persistent theft, is not necessarily bound to say that this is irrevocably ordained as part of God's immutable law.

Islam's concept of punishment is usually described as an example of the 'deterrent' theory: that this is the purpose of extreme *ḥadd* punishment is clear from the Qur'ān. However, there is also an element of rehabilitation – the hope is that no thief will persist in criminality because the possibility of amputation should act as a deterrent. Implicit in this framework, too, is the idea that punishment is actually God's prerogative. Punishment is to be seen as only a lesser evil than the type of social instability that crime and lawlessness can engender.

WHO HAS THE MORAL RIGHT TO RULE?

There is also much contemporary discussion within the Muslim world about who actually has the moral right to govern. Since *shari'ah* is God's law, and is believed to be both absolute and comprehensive, any human government can enjoy only limited legislative powers. Who, then, should govern? Can an elected assembly govern, or should the safekeeping and implementation of *shari'ah* be the preserve and responsibility of those who know it best, the *'ulama'*? How Muslims answer this question also depends on how they answer the earlier question about the nature of *shari'ah*. Those who attach primary value to the eternal principles are more likely to advocate some form of democratic, collective government, itself drawing on the principles of *ijma'*, and *shura* (consultation). Those for whom the *shari'ah* is an immutable, universally valid received body of jurisprudence, are more likely to advocate rule by the *'ulama'*. There is not one universally agreed answer to this question, and, as social anthropologists have demonstrated, the world of Islam is actually much more diverse than the classical tradition, which emphases unity and uniformity, suggests. Michael Gilsenan observes:

Anthropologists see the meaning of a particular social role or myth or ritual or event as being the product of its relations and contacts with other roles, myths, rituals and events. The implications of this approach are that Islam will be discussed [in his book] not as a single, rigidly bounded set of structures determining or interacting with other total structures but rather as a word that identifies varying relations of practice, representation, symbol, concept, and worldview within the same society and between different societies. There are patterns in these relations, and they have changed in important ways over time. My aim is not to persuade the reader to substitute a relativised and fragmented

111

vision for one of global unity. Rather it is to situate some of these religious, cultural and ideological forms and practices that people regard as Islamic in the life and development of their societies.

(Gilsenan 1990: 19)

Where Muslims constitute minorities, as they do in India, and in western European countries, questions also arise about the role that *sharīʿah* should play in their lives. If *ḥalāl* meat is not available, can they eat non-*ḥalāl* meat? Traditionally, jurists allowed Muslims to eat *ḥarām* food if otherwise faced with starvation. Malik said, 'The amount of it is what will alleviate his hunger, and he should eat not more than what will keep him alive' (Qaradawi 1985: 50). However, in order to be truly Muslim, must the personal law, or domestic codes of the *sharīʿah* be practised? Some of these are illegal under non-Muslim systems. Since Malik once recommended that the *khalīfah* appoint border guards to prevent Muslims from leaving Muslim territory, it is unlikely that he was thinking about Muslims living outside the Islamic world when he deduced the above point of law. He was probably thinking about Muslims travelling through barren and unpopulated terrain. The idea that you could be a good Muslim without also belonging to a Muslim society, governed by the *sharīʿah*, was alien to his thinking. A classical position would deem it the duty of Muslims living outside *Dār-al-Islām* (the Islamic world) to migrate back to a Muslim country. This raises an interesting point: can you ever be a Muslim in isolation? There is no universally agreed answer, but an assumption behind much moral thinking in Islam is that *ḥalāl* behaviour is easier when the whole society is also striving to function within the same guidelines, predicated on the same assumptions. The fact that marriage is *farḍ*, and that marriage immediately carries with it other family ties and associated obligations, also suggests that the authentic Islamic ethic is best, if not only, lived within an Islamic context.

JIHĀD REVISITED – MORAL RETRIBUTION OR INTERNATIONAL TERRORISM?

Within the contemporary Muslim world, some Muslims have revived the language of *jihād* as violent struggle to establish what they perceive as legitimate Islamic rule, and believe that it is morally justifiable, indeed a religious duty, to combat any ruler whose rule, in their view, is un-Islamic and who has therefore forfeited the right to be regarded as a Muslim. This was the position of the early Kharijites, who opposed the Umayyads as unfit to lead the *ummah*. Such rulers are declared 'unbelievers' or 'infidel'. President Anwar Sadat of Egypt was assassinated in 1981 by the Jihad Organisation. Its leader and ideologue, Muhammad al-Farag, wrote, 'We have to establish the Rule of God's Religion in our own country first, and to make the Word of God supreme . . . There is no doubt that the first battlefield for *jihād* is the extermination of these infidel leaders and to replace them by a complete Islamic Order' (quoted in Esposito 1991: 170). Some also regard aggression, usually terrorism, against western interests, people or property as justifiable since they believe the West, collectively, continues to wage its own crusade against the Muslim world, through neo-colonial exploitation of its oil, through manipulation of its rulers, and through media that portray Islam as a 'force for anarchy and disorder':

> Attacks on Muslim extremists – the fundamentalists of the popular press – easily convert into or carry over onto an attack on the entire body of Muslims. It is difficult to distinguish between the two types of Muslims created in the minds of the media. For non-Muslims, beneath the quiet facade of every ordinary Muslim there is a mad mullah struggling to emerge; the sooner and more effectively he is put down, the better.

> (Ahmed 1992: 39)

Moral decision-making: personal and private issues

Muslims today – in many and in varied contexts, with or without all or some codes of the *sharī'ah* enjoying legal status – are, as Muslims, making moral decisions in several areas of domestic, personal and private lives. In many of these areas they know exactly what, according to traditional Islamic teaching, is morally right and morally wrong. For example, extra-marital or pre-marital sexual relations, homosexual acts, theft, dishonesty and charging interest are, for the vast majority of Muslims, clearly *ḥarām* (prohibited), as are eating pork and drinking alcohol. Differences of opinion between the four schools do not concern individual Muslims, who usually follow the rulings of their chosen school. Today, though, some Muslims, who do not feel bound to accept the tenth century decision that new interpretations are automatically *bid'ah* (innovation), believe that they can deduce new interpretations on moral issues. These will be based on the ethical spirit of the Qur'ān, and on their understanding of Islamic principles. However, Muslims who believe that the *sharī'ah* is a complete, definitive, universally valid code also have some scope for moral decision-making. In order to explore some of the areas where individual choice is possible, issues related to sexual morals, the status of women, abortion and medical ethics will be discussed. Some of the arguments outlined in this section are controversial, although where a viewpoint is radical, or is likely to represent the opinions of only a minority of Muslims, this is clearly indicated.

SEXUAL MORALITY

The Qur'ān permits sexual intercourse between men and women within two types of relationships: marriage, and as master and slave, or concubine. Islam rejects the concept of celibacy (*sūrah* 57: 27). Muhammad once said, 'Whoever gets married has completed half of his faith; therefore let him be conscious of Allāh in the other half of his faith' (quoted in Cole 1991: 126). Most jurists regard marriage as natural and as obligatory, although some view it as *mandūb* (recommended) since certain valid reasons for not marrying, mainly financial, are recognised. Arguably, however, Islam allows men more opportunity for sexual pleasure than women, since while women may marry only one man, *sūrah* 4: 4 allows Muslim men to marry up to four women, and to own as many concubines as they can afford: 'And if you fear that you will not deal fairly by the orphans, marry of the women, who seem good to you, two, or three or four; and if you fear that you cannot do justice to so many, then one only, or the captives that your right hands possess [i.e., concubines]. Thus it is more likely that you will not do injustice'. However, the context of this verse was Madinah in the early years after the *hijrah* (the migration from Makkah in 622) when many men had died in battle leaving behind them dependent widows and children. This implies that the verse permitting men to marry up to four women was specifically intended to safeguard these widows and children, and should not be regarded as a permanent provision. The phrase, 'if you fear that you cannot do justice . . ., [marry] one only', equally implies that monogamy is the ideal. Other important verses also suggest that monogamy, not polygamy, is God's preference, for example, 'Glory to Allāh, who created in pairs all that the earth produces' (36: 36); 'O humanity, be careful of your duty to your Lord who created you from a single soul and from it created its mate' (4: 1), and, 'And among His signs is this, that He created for you mates from among yourselves, that you may dwell in tranquillity with them, and He has put love and mercy between your hearts' (sūrah 30: 21).

From this verse, Muslims derive their understanding that the primary purpose of marriage is companionship and love – as an expression of 'ibādah, worship of God – which includes the act of sexual intercourse. Any lawful activity forms part of a Muslim's worship of the Creator. This view of marriage as primarily a union of love has meant that most Muslims are willing to use contraceptives, not to prevent childbirth altogether, since having children is also regarded as a religious duty, but to help plan financially, or to avoid life-threatening pregnancy. Muhammad was once asked, 'What do you think of coitus interruptus?' He replied, 'Ah well! There's no harm in it, because every single life which God has decided to bring into existence will come into existence' (quoted in Robinson 1991: 43). The consent, though, of both partners is necessary if any form of contraception is to be used; a wife is entitled to decide if she wishes to become pregnant, or not, as she is also entitled to sexual enjoyment.

Creating life?

Since having children is a religious duty, Islam finds it relatively easy to accept modern scientific techniques for enabling childless couples to achieve pregnancy. Muslims are encouraged to use their intellects to pursue scientific knowledge for the common good, although some moral reservations are involved. For example, Muslims have no moral objection to artificial insemination, or even to test-tube babies, as long as the sperm belongs to the husband. However, if a woman were to be impregnated, or implanted with a foetus fertilised by another man's sperm, this would constitute adultery. Rape, incidentally, is considered the equivalent of murder in sharī'ah. Opinions also differ about the morality of surrogacy. No fundamental Islamic principle is obviously breached by surrogacy, but Muslims suspect that social instability could result if the woman

115

carrying the child decided that she would like to keep the baby. What legal, indeed moral, right would she have in this case? The danger of commercialising childbearing also concerns Muslims, as does the possible confusion of identity that could result from surrogacy. Traditionally, it is the bearer of a child who rears and feeds it.

Adultery and extra-marital relations

Where Islamic law is established, both adultery and fornication are criminal offences, punishable – if proven – by sentences ranging from one hundred lashes to death. This, for example, is the law in Saudi Arabia and in Iran. However, as with theft, circumstantial evidence is inadmissible, and both the illicit acts must have been witnessed by four reliable, pious Muslim witnesses. Given this extremely unlikely scenario, it is quite possible to argue that consenting Muslims may, in private, and if their consciences allow, do as they wish. This is not intended to imply that good Muslims habitually engage in extra-marital relationships; the vast majority regard any extra-marital relationship as absolutely prohibited. My intention is merely to point out that those who may – despite this weight of opinion – feel themselves morally able to justify such relationships have, in certain circumstances, the freedom to enjoy them. Muhammad said: 'For every human being, God has fore-ordained an element of adultery which that person will inevitably commit: the glance which is the adultery of the eyes, and the word which is the adultery of the tongue. Men will always be subject to carnal desires, whether or not they gratify them' (quoted in Robinson 1991: 42).

A moral argument in favour of pre-marital sex might rest on the fact that, as we have already noted, the Qur'ānic view of marriage is as a union of love and peace between a man and a woman. The verse cited (30: 21) does not actually mention the words 'husband' and 'wife' – although it is traditionally understood to be speaking about this relationship. Verse 28 of the same chapter says: 'He coins for you a similitude of yourselves: have you from among those whom your right hand possesses [concubines] partners in the wealth we have bestowed upon you, equal with you in respect thereof, so that you fear them as you fear each other'. The meaning of this verse is not immediately obvious, but Muslims could argue that a loving, caring, sexual relationship between consenting adults is morally better than concubinage – which, it must be said, is no longer a common feature of the Muslim world. This is undoubtedly a radical view, but one that is held by some Muslims and it does suggest that while the great majority of Muslims do not regard extra-marital sex as morally acceptable, some may.

Masturbation

While the above view will inevitably attract its critics, it is interesting to note that single Muslims do have more widely agreed scope for moral decision-making about the desirability, or undesirability, of masturbation as an acceptable extra-marital means of sexual relief. The Prophet said: 'Young men, those of you who can support a wife should marry, for it keeps you from looking at women and preserves your chastity; but those who cannot should fast, for it is a means of cooling passion'. Malik regarded masturbation as *ḥarām*, while Hanbal said that, although a weakness, it could be tolerated under two conditions: being in fear of committing sex before marriage or adultery, or not having the means to marry (Qaradawi 1985: 170).

Muslim marriage and non-Muslim partners

Muslim men are permitted to marry Jewish or Christian women (*sūrah* 5: 5), but Muslim women are not permitted to marry non-Muslim men (2: 221). Muslim jurists have never differed on this ruling. The statement in *sūrah* 4: 34 that 'men are in charge of women' would make it difficult to concede that a Muslim woman could maintain her faith while married to a non-Muslim man. In fact, some jurists even advised Muslim men against marrying Christians or Jews, lest un-Islamic habits creep into the household. Given the Qur'ānic prohibition against Muslim women marrying outside the faith, what scope is there for justifying this today? If the argument that Muslim men and women are equal, but different, is maintained, is there any scope for arguing that they are also equal in their ability to remain faithful to Islam while married to a non-Muslim partner? The Qur'ān itself implies such equality of *īmān* (faith) at 33: 35: 'For Muslim men and women, for believing men and women . . . who engage in the praise of Allāh, for them Allāh has prepared forgiveness and a great reward'. It is also possible to argue that the prohibition against marrying 'unbelievers' does not exclude Christians and Jews. Several Qur'ānic verses validate Christian and Jewish 'faith' so unambiguously that the distinction

117

between them, and between Muslims as *mu'minūn* (believers) becomes, at the very least, blurred: 'Lo! Those who believe, and those who are Jews, and Sabaeans, and Christians – whosoever believes in Allāh and the Last Day and does right – there shall no fear come upon them, neither shall they grieve' (*sūrah* 5: 69). Here, and elsewhere, the distinction between Muslims as 'believers' and Christians as 'believers in Allāh' is sufficiently subtle to argue that the traditional interpretation of *sūrah* 2: 221 can be revisited. In Turkey, Muslim women are legally able to marry non-Muslim men. In the United States and in the United Kingdom, some Muslim women who still regard themselves as faithful Muslims, although they are not always, or indeed usually, perceived as such by other Muslims, have married Christian men. Such women have not lightly married outside of their own faith community, but have felt able to do so on both moral and religious grounds.

Divorce

The Qur'ān permits divorce. Men may divorce their wives without necessarily stating why they wish to terminate the marriage, although strict rules, outlined at *sūrah* 2: 226–237 and at *sūrah* 65, must be followed. These rules include not pronouncing the divorce while drunk, or in a rage. Furthermore, the divorce is not official until after the 'waiting period' is over, during which reconciliation may occur and is encouraged. Muhammad said, 'Of all lawful things, divorce is the most hateful to God'. Some Muslims interpret this *ḥadīth* as placing divorce within the 'tolerated', but 'discouraged' category rather than within the 'positively good' *ḥalāl* category.

THE STATUS OF WOMEN

Usually, women may initiate divorce only when ill-treated (*sūrah* 4: 128) unless their marriage contract stipulates additional grounds. Ill-treatment, though, does not mean only physical abuse – desertion, a husband's impotence, insanity, and imprisonment all qualify as ill-treatment. Traditionally, Islam regards men and women as equal but different. Here, though, equality does not mean 'sameness', in the sense of enjoying the 'same rights'. Instead, men and women enjoy those 'rights' appropriate to their God-given duties and responsibilities. The man's role is as provider. Thus, in inheritance, men receive a larger share than women because women are cared for by male relatives. Women do, however, have the right not only to work but also to retain their own earnings (*sūrah* 4: 32). They also have no obligation to contribute to the family upkeep unless they choose to do so.

The position, or status, of women within Islam is one moral issue on which the western media often choose to focus; alongside the amputation of hands, the seclusion of women forms part of the stereotypical image. Leila Ahmed, however, has convincingly argued that both veiling and seclusion, in the Qur'ān, applied only to Muhammad's wives (33: 53 and 33: 59) but were extended to all chaste Muslim women during the classical period of Islamic power and prestige when male attitudes towards women had become misogynist and contemptuous. She blames this negative attitude partly on easy divorce, but especially on concubinage. *Sūrah* 4: 4 allowed Muslim men to own as many captured, non-Muslim female slaves as they could afford. Dr Ahmed says that popular awareness of this common trade in women as 'objects for sexual use' inevitably led to a blurring of any distinction between the words 'women', 'concubine', and 'object for sexual use' in the male mind (L. Ahmed 1992: 85).

Dr Ahmed then argues that if both men and women re-read the Qur'ān, giving primary value to its ethical rather than to its legal voice, interpretations more favourable to women can be heard. In fact, she says, such voices and interpretations did exist, but, representative of oppressed and minority interests, they were drowned by the male-dominated version of the élite, whose views became synonymous with orthodoxy. Other views were dismissed as heretical (L. Ahmed 1992: 239).

Other Muslim feminists, though, such as Rana Kabbani, defend the use of the veil: wearing the *ḥijāb*, she suggests, can liberate women from being looked upon as sexual objects, and from the 'dictates of Western fashion . . . In favour of the *ḥijāb* it can be said that by distancing its wearer from the world, it enriches spiritual life, grants freedom from material preoccupations, and erases class differences by expressing solidarity with others in the same uniform' (Kabbani 1989: 27). The moral 'rightness' or 'wrongness' of the 'total sameness', or 'equal but different and complementary' concepts of the respective status of women and men is an interesting issue to explore. Many Muslims believe that the deterioration, as

119

they perceive it, of moral behaviour in the West stems directly from its abandoning of a more traditional understanding of marriage and of gender roles. Many see the West as immoral, materialistic and largely post-Christian, with no, or few, commonly-shared moral values, in contrast to the Muslim world which is seen as moral, egalitarian and godly, with commonly-accepted, divinely revealed moral principles.

ABORTION

On the morality, or otherwise, of abortion, Muslims have guidance both in the Qur'ān and in the Ḥadīth. The Qur'ān forbids the 'slaying of children' (17: 31); this is understood to include unborn children. Under Islamic law, accidentally induced abortion carries the charge of 'manslaughter', and parents are compensated with 'blood money'. Islamic law also upholds the right of a foetus to inherit property. Muhammad himself said, 'The creation of each of you is brought together in your mother's belly for 40 days in the form of the seed, then you are a clot of blood for a like period, then a morsel of flesh for a like period, then there is sent to you an angel who blows the breath of life in you' (quoted in Cole 1991: 120). Thus, 'quickening', or the beginning of human life, was believed to begin after 120 days. Abortion after this period becomes murder. However, the jurists justify abortion if the mother's life is seriously threatened, if a family's economic welfare is at risk, or, some concede, if deformity is a real possibility. This view was reached by weighing, or balancing, the Islamic principle of the sacredness of life (the foetus's right to a future life) over and against the value of the mother's life and her family's ability to function and to fulfil its duties, within the wider Muslim community. This is the same process of moral decision-making which individual Muslims, as prospective parents, may pursue for themselves.

In the case of a pregnancy caused by rape, when the physical health of the mother is not at risk, but when both her psychological health and her ability to raise the child will inevitably be impaired, abortion may be permitted. Here, the Muslim principle is that of compassion (al-aḥsan). Qaradawi says that Islamic law is permeated by the spirit of such Qur'ānic verses as 2: 185, 'Allāh desires your ease. He does not desire hardship for you'. Islam aims to lift oppressive burdens (Qaradawi 1985: 37). Abortion 'on demand', though, is unacceptable if merely to remove an unwanted foetus without any extenuating circumstances such as those described above.

MEDICAL ETHICS

Another issue that was explored in the classical texts was the question of whether *ḥarām* substances contained in medicine can be consumed. The ruling already cited, permitting *ḥarām* food to be eaten to prevent starvation, is clearly of relevance here. Most jurists allow the medicinal use of *ḥarām* substances when the following conditions apply:

1. If a Muslim's life is at risk unless the substance is consumed.
2. If there is no possible *ḥalāl* alternative.
3. If the physician prescribing the drug is both knowledgeable and pious (see *sūrah* 2: 173).

Conclusion

What I have tried to demonstrate in this chapter is that Islam is an all-embracing way of life, a 'faith' inseparable from 'practice', inseparable from the living of human life, from how one behaves in society. Islam must inform everything one does or it is reduced to something less concerned about the health and harmony, about the 'balance' of creation, and about justice in society, than the Islam of which Muhammad was Prophet and of which the Qur'ān is the revelation. What I have also tried to show, however (with reference, where appropriate, to Muslim history and to contemporary writers and thinkers), is that, in the area of morals and of moral decision-making especially, there is more diversity of opinion among Muslims, and more scope for personal choice, than has sometimes been assumed. For some, whose understanding of *sharī'ah* is more flexible than that of others, there is more scope for independent decision-making, but for all Muslims moral decision-making, and moral behaviour in general, is not only a matter of looking up the rule book: it involves weighing up options against the Islamic principles that inform and undergird their view of the meaning and

121

purpose of human life and destiny, and deciding and acting in the light of these principles.

FURTHER READING

Ahmed, A. S. (1988) *Discovering Islam*, London, Routledge.*

Ahmed, A. S. (1992) *Postmodernism and Islam*, London, Routledge.

Ahmed, L. (1992) *Women and Gender in Islam*, New Haven, Yale University Press.

Anees, A. M., Abedin, S. Z. and Sardar, Z. (1992) *Christian–Muslim Relations*, London, Grey Seal.

Cole, W. O. (ed.) (1991) *Moral Issues in Six Religions*, London, Heinemann.

Doi, A. R. I. (1984) *Shari'ah – The Islamic Law*, London, Ta Ha.**

Esposito, J. L. (1991) *Islam: The Straight Path*, London, OUP.*

Gilsenan, M. (1990) *Recognising Islam*, London, I.B. Tauris.

Griffiths, P. J. (1990) *Christianity Through Non-Christian Eyes*, New York, Orbis.

Kabbani, R. (1989) *Letter to Christendom*, London, Virago.

Pickthall, M. M. (original ed. 1930) *The Meaning of the Glorious Koran*, London, Ta Ha.***

Qaradawi, Y. A. (1985) *The Lawful and the Prohibited in Islam*, London, Sharouk International.**

Robinson, Neal (1991) *The Sayings of Muhammad*, London, Duckworth.***

Waddy, C. (3rd ed. 1990) *The Muslim Mind*, London, Grosvenor.*

Zakaria, R. (1988) *The Struggle Within Islam*, London, Penguin.

Note: Books marked * are useful introductory texts on Islam. Books marked ** focus especially on legal and moral issues and contain some primary texts. Books marked *** contain primary texts only.

5. Judaism

Norman Solomon

Introduction – law and morality

A moral decision is one that the man or woman making it makes in the light of what he or she believes is right or wrong. It is not a decision made simply to gain material advantage or pleasure, or merely to conform with habit, rule or law.

Of course, a moral decision might result in material advantage or pleasure to whoever makes it; being moral does not mean being miserable. Though happiness in this world is not, in Jewish teaching, the *criterion* of right and wrong, it is virtuous to make others happy and, under normal circumstances, sinful to be miserable oneself.

A moral decision might also be made in conformity with a rule or law; after all, the rule or law itself might express moral values. Can moral decisions, then, be distinguished from legal decisions? The relationship between law and morality is complex, and this complex relationship of law and morality is a major factor in decision-making within traditional Judaism. A decision doesn't stop being moral just because it is made in the light of 'divinely revealed law'. On the contrary, since it is a self-evident moral duty to do what God wants, and since he would only want us to do what is good, then if there really is a known 'divine law', obviously we ought to follow it. Traditional Jewish belief is that the Torah (that is, in particular, the first five books of the Bible) is the authentic record of God's self-revelation. The Hebrew word *torah* is by no means co-extensive with 'law', though it is often convenient to translate it as 'law'. When Jews speak of the Torah as 'God's law', what they mean is that it expresses what God wants us to do; it is how God himself formulated the 'moral law' – 'the Torah of the Lord is perfect'

(Psalm 19: 8). It is not law as opposed to morality, but law which *is* morality.

The problem here, for all except the 'true believer', is how to be sure that God commanded this, that or the other. How do we know that the Bible is 'true', or that the rabbis of the Talmud[1] interpreted it correctly? We shall see later that doubts of this kind underlie the sectarian divisions among Jews today. For the time being, however, we will assume the traditional orthodox point of view.

Ought the law to be followed only because God commanded it? Certainly it should not be obeyed with the objective of gain: 'Be not like servants who serve their master in order to receive a reward', counselled Antigonos of Socho[2] (first century BCE). Torah should be observed *lishmah* (for its own sake), ultimately for the love of God. Psalm 119 beautifully expresses the love and joy in the commandments of God as taught by the Pharisees and their successors, the rabbis.

Are moral decisions distinguished from legal decisions by their subject matter? Sometimes people use 'moral' to refer to a decision made on a matter not covered by law, or not enforceable. This, as we shall see, is not a distinction that Judaism can make. Or again, to take another question, does the term 'moral' refer to decisions which exceed the standards demanded by law? The traditional Jewish concept corresponding to this form of morality is *lifnim mishurat ha-din* ('beyond the line of the law'). For instance, although a court cannot demand more than correctness or justice, the individual is called upon to exceed this by restraint from making the full legal demand on the other party, from demanding the 'pound of flesh'.[3] This restraint plays a major role in Jewish ethics. The third century Palestinian Rabbi Yohanan said: 'Jerusalem was destroyed only because people did not act beyond the strict requirement of law'.[4] That the law of Torah did not completely encompass its moral demands was recognised in the traditional *mi shepara'*:

> If (the purchaser) had handed over the money but had not yet taken possession of the goods (the vendor) has the right to withdraw from the sale; but he who punished (*mi shepara'*) the generation of the flood and the generation of the tower (of Babel) will punish him who does not stand by his word.
>
> (Mishnah *Bava Metzia* 4: 2)

Does the concept of *lifnim mishurat ha-din* indicate that the law is not always just, or is *lifnim mishurat ha-din* itself part of one's legal responsibility – that there is, so to speak, a 'law' which tells you to go beyond the law?[5]

Another area of rabbinic Judaism in which the distinction between law and morality becomes fuzzy is that of alms-giving and benevolence. Alms-giving features prominently in Jewish teaching and practice, and the rabbis constantly impressed on their followers the need for compassion and charity. One of the Hebrew words for alms-giving is *tzedakah*, derived from a root meaning to be right, fair or correct. Alms-giving is not so much an act of piety as one of fairness, ensuring correct distribution of the wealth God has entrusted to us. The overall concept within which alms-giving is contained is *hesed*, a biblical Hebrew word which can be translated by 'love' or 'compassion' and has frequently been translated 'loving-kindness'. Yet the rabbis were not content to preach a moral value, but felt the need to formulate the duty of alms-giving in legal fashion, setting down limits as to how much, how often, to whom, and in what manner and form help ought to be given. But even this law-like formulation allows ample space for individual choice.

Isadore Twersky[6] has skilfully used a Talmudic story to illustrate the polarity, in rabbinic Judaism, of law (*halakhah*) and ethics, or morality:

It has been taught: R. Meir used to say: The critic [of Judaism] may bring against you the argument, 'If your God loves the poor, why does he not support them?' If so, answer him, 'So that through them we may be saved from the punishment of Gehinnom.' This question was actually put by Turnus Rufus to R. Akiba: 'If your God loves the poor, why does He not support them?' He replied: 'So that through them we may be saved from the punishment of Gehinnom.' 'On the contrary,' said the other, 'it is this which condemns you to Gehinnom. I will illustrate by a parable. Suppose an earthly king was angry with his servant and put him in prison and ordered that he should be given no food or drink, and a man went and gave him food and drink. If the king heard, would he not be angry with him? And you are called "servants", as it is written, *For unto me the children of Israel are servants.*' R. Akiba answered him: 'I will illustrate by another parable. Suppose an earthly king was angry with his son, and put him in prison and ordered that no food or drink should be given to him, and someone went and gave him food and drink. If the king heard of it, would he not send him a present? And we are called "sons", as it is written, *Sons are ye to the Lord your God*.' He said to him: 'You are called both sons and servants. When you carry out the desires of the Omnipresent, you are called "servants". At the present time you are not carrying out the desires of the Omnipresent.' R. Akiba replied: 'The Scripture says, *Is it not to deal thy bread to the hungry and bring the poor that are cast out to thy house?* When "dost thou bring *the poor who are cast out to thy house?*" Now; and it says [at the same time], is it not to deal thy bread to the hungry?'[7]

The first inference Twersky derives from this passage is that God has, so to speak, abdicated to people part of a function of his own in order to enable them to transcend mere biological existence, to escape damnation. In the practice of *hesed* one does not merely 'imitate' God, one shares directly in his work. The second is that we are all equal, all 'children' of God; even our sin and temporary disgrace do not abrogate this relationship.

Twersky's third point is that the fact that God's judgement has condemned an individual to poverty does not allow us to sit in judgement on that person and to desist from giving help; on the contrary, we are challenged to vigorous ethical response to his or her situation. Fourth, we cannot 'dismiss a destitute person with a counterfeit expression of faith: "Rely on God . . .! He will help you"'. Faith or trust (*bitahon*), to the poor, means trusting in God's mercy; to the rich, on the other hand, 'it suggests the obligation of sustained and gracious liberality'.

Twersky finally draws our attention to the 'dialectic' nature of the halakhic approach to charity. While the essential achievement of *halakhah* is the system of rules by which a principle of faith is anchored into a detailed ethical code, it sought 'to combine the thesis of free, spontaneous giving with the antithesis of soulless, obligatory contribution and produce a composite act which is subjective though quantified, inspired yet regular, intimate yet formal'. This dialectic is indicated in the polarities between the attitude and manner of giving, and the determination of the amount of giving, as well as between individual and community responsibility; both of these polarities are delicately handled within *halakhah*.

The tradition-conscious Jew is thus faced by the need to make a characteristically 'moral' decision whenever he engages in a charitable act; even as *halakhah* sets bounds to the act, he (or, in those commands which affect her, she) is challenged as to its moral dimension.

The Hebrew scriptures

There is some truth in the description of Judaism and Christianity as 'two religions divided by a common scripture'. Both regard the Hebrew scriptures as sacred, yet neither is simply 'the religion of the Old Testament', for both have evolved distinctive traditions of reading scripture.

Rabbinic Judaism reads the first five books of the Bible (Genesis, Exodus, Leviticus, Numbers, Deuteronomy) collectively as 'Torah', often translated 'law', though 'law' must here be understood in a very broad fashion; 'teaching', 'guidance', or 'the way' are possible translations of 'Torah', less misleading than 'law'. The *mitzvot* ('commandments', 'laws') contained in these books cover all aspects of life, from the most personal to the constitution of the state, and ranging from 'you shall love your neighbour as yourself' and 'you shall love the Lord your God' to the minutiae of Temple sacrifice or judicial procedure.

The rest of scripture is secondary to Torah, consisting of history, prophecy and wisdom, which confirm, but neither add to nor detract from, the substance of Torah.

HETERONOMOUS LAW?

The most obvious feature of scripture, when read from this perspective, is that it proclaims a set of laws, or system of behaviour, apparently independent of the observer. The source of law is transcendent; Torah proceeds from the eternal God, who is infinitely greater than the individual human.

Many theologians refer to this as 'heteronomous' law, opposing it to 'autonomous', that which comes from the individual, arising out of his or her own 'nature'. But this is a confused opposition. The distinction between 'outside' and 'inside' just does not apply to the transcendent; in some experiences we may know God as the 'other', but in other experiences we know him through our innermost self. Indeed, it is only when we are divided from our selves that we sense

127

God as imposing, as demanding, from 'outside'. When we are reconciled with our selves, God's demands flow, as it were, from our own being. This is what is meant when humans, both male and female, are said to be made 'in the image of God' (Genesis 1: 27).

Thus even the stringent law code of Deuteronomy is presented, not as a 'scandal' (to use Paul's term) or profound 'mystery', but as totally accessible and in conformity with human understanding:

> The commandment that I lay on you this day is not too difficult for you, it is not too remote. It is not in heaven, that you should say, 'Who will go up to heaven for us to fetch it and to tell it to us, so that we can keep it?' Nor is it beyond the sea, that you should say, 'Who will cross the sea for us to fetch it and to tell it to us, so that we can keep it?' It is a thing very near to you, *upon your lips and in your hearts* ready to be kept.
>
> (Deuteronomy 30: 11–14, New English Bible (NEB), my emphasis)

People, individually or collectively, do not always obey the law, whether it be the 'inner law' of conscience, or some imposed system. Conflicts arise, and that is when authority intervenes, and the individual is deprived of freedom of action and perhaps severely punished. Much as scripture might assume that the individual conscience, freely exercised, would coincide with the 'law of God', it thoroughly disapproves of individuals who 'follow the promptings of [their] stubborn heart' (Deuteronomy 29: 19) to run after false gods. Here we see the essential conflict of religion – rather, of any religious *establishment* – with the individual. The establishment will always characterise as 'stubborn' those who disagree with it. But, assuming integrity on both sides, who is to say the establishment is right and the individual wrong? The establishment may well affirm the freedom of conscience, even primacy of conscience, but so long as it also assumes, 'If you truly followed your conscience you would do as we say', there is no real freedom, no recognition of the autonomy of the individual conscience.

RESOLVING DOUBT

What does one do in circumstances where the Torah offers no clear-cut solution to a problem? In biblical times, one would 'seek guidance of the Lord' (Genesis 25: 22). But what did this mean in practical terms?

In appropriate cases, one would work through the available judicial process, including courts of appeal:

> When the issue in any lawsuit is beyond your competence, whether it be a case of blood against blood, plea against plea, or blow against blow, that is disputed within your courts, then go up without delay to the place which the Lord your God will choose. There you must go to the levitical priests or to the judge then in office; seek their guidance, and they will pronounce the sentence. You shall act on the pronouncement which they make from the place which the Lord will choose.

> (Deuteronomy 17: 8–10, NEB)

An individual, or even the king on behalf of the nation, might turn to some authority figure, for instance a judge, a prophet or a priest, perhaps using an oracle such as the Urim and Thummim (Numbers 27: 21).

There are many instances in the Bible of the 'question and answer'. For instance, Zelophehad had no sons, but five daughters; their problem became the pretext for clarifying the laws of inheritance:

> The heads of the fathers' families of Gilead son of Machir, son of Manasseh, one of the families of the sons of Joseph, approached Moses and the chiefs, heads of families in Israel, and addressed them. 'Sir,' they said, 'the Lord commanded you to distribute the land by lot to the Israelites, and you were also commanded to give the patrimony of our brother Zelophehad to his daughters. Now if any of them shall be married to a husband from another Israelite tribe, her patrimony will be lost to the patrimony of our fathers and be added to that of the tribe into which she is married, and so part of our allotted patrimony will be lost. Then when the jubilee year comes round in Israel, her patrimony would be added to the patrimony of the tribe into which she is married, and it would be permanently lost to the patrimony of our fathers' tribe.'

> So Moses, instructed by the Lord, gave the Israelites this ruling: 'The tribe of the sons of Joseph is right. This is the Lord's command for the daughters of Zelophehad: They may marry whom they please, but only within a family of their fathers' tribe . . .'.

> (Numbers 36: 1–9, NEB)

Centuries later, the same procedure of enquiry from the Lord through a prophet is followed by the Babylonian exiles. Should they continue to observe the fasts by which they had commemorated the destruction of the Temple, now about to be rebuilt? Zechariah, however, hijacks the question as an opportunity to inculcate a moral lesson:

> Bethel-Sharezer sent Regem-Melech with his men to seek the favour of the Lord. They were to say to the priests in the house of the Lord of Hosts and to the prophets, 'Am I to lament and abstain in the fifth month as I have done for so many years?' The word of the Lord of Hosts came to me: Say to all the people of the land and to the priests, When you fasted and lamented in the fifth and seventh months these seventy years, was it indeed in my honour that you fasted? And when you ate and drank, was it not to please yourselves? . . . These are the words of the Lord of Hosts: Administer true justice, show loyalty and compassion to one another, do not oppress the orphan and the widow, the alien and the poor, do not contrive any evil against one another . . . .
>
> (Zechariah 7: 2–10, NEB)

FREE WILL

The rabbinic reading of scripture fairly consistently endorses Ezekiel's statement that it is 'the soul that sins, and no other, that shall die; a son shall not share a father's guilt, nor a father his son's' (Ezekiel 18: 20). The well-known phrase in the Ten Commandments, 'visiting the sins of the fathers upon the third and fourth generations of those who hate me', is glossed by the Targum, 'if they continue in the way of their fathers'.

There are few places where traditional Jewish and Christian exegesis diverges so radically as the story of Adam and Eve. Jewish exegetes understand the sin of Adam as a prototype, not as a burden of guilt to be inherited by his descendants. Though the power of the *yetser ha-ra* (evil inclination) is acknowledged, humans are created with the strength to resist. They should, indeed, turn to God for mercy and help, for true penitence is not easy; but there is no burden of inherited guilt which can only be expiated by vicarious sacrifice. Adam and Eve were themselves penitents.

In this light, it is easy to appreciate Deuteronomy's stress on human ability to choose, and to choose aright:

> I summon heaven and earth to witness against you this day: I offer you the choice of life or death, blessing or curse. Choose life, and then you and your descendants will live.
>
> (Deuteronomy 30: 19, NEB)

> What then, O Israel, does the Lord your God ask of you? Only to fear the Lord your God, to conform to all his ways, to love him and to serve him with all your heart and soul. This you will do by keeping the commandments of the Lord.
>
> (Deuteronomy 10: 12–13, NEB)

There is no suggestion here that humanity labours beneath an inescapable burden of sin, or is destined to suffer.

Equally absent from scripture, on the rabbinic reading, is the notion of fatalism, that certain individuals are fated, or 'predestined', to sin, or that for each individual there is mapped out some inescapable path in life. Some rare individuals – Jeremiah, for instance – might indeed be 'called' to a particular vocation, but this is not the same as being 'fated'; Jeremiah might well have rejected the call, or failed, for there was no compulsion, however much Jeremiah felt it to be so, as a 'fire burning in his bones'.

Against this background it is noteworthy that post-rabbinic Judaism, including Jewish folk custom, sometimes veered away from the rabbinic stress on the freedom of the will. Kabbalah, for instance, developed the concept of the sin of Adam as a cosmic fault. Popular Judaism toys with astrological determinism, reflected in the *mazal tov* (' a good constellation') greeting, and with fatalism, reflected in the common response to events as *beschärt* (cut out, preordained by God).

One of the strongest contrasts between the Hebrew scriptures and the New Testament is the prominence of demonic spirits – 'powers', 'dominions' – and possession (devils being driven out) in the latter. Though demons (*shedim*) figure in many talmudic anecdotes, and are thought to tempt people to sin and to cause damage, their power is very circumscribed. Much the same could be said of Satan who, as in Job, is not a great power challenging God, but rather a 'licensed tempter', whom it is always possible to resist.

Rabbinic decision-making

Towards the end of the second temple period a 'hidden revolution'[8] took place within Judaism. The 'power of decision', previously in the hands of the priests, passed to the scribes, or interpreters of the law, and eventually to their successors, the rabbis. An extraordinary tale referring to events at the beginning of the second century makes plain how the mantle of Torah had passed from men claiming direct inspiration (prophets) and from the priesthood to creative teachers:

> It was taught: On that day Rabbi Eliezer responded to every question (that was raised against his opinion that a certain type of oven was not subject to impurity), but (the other sages) would not accept (his view). He said to them, 'If the law is in accordance with my opinion, let this carob tree prove it!' The carob moved a hundred, some say four hundred, cubits from its place. They said to him, 'One does not prove the law from a carob tree'. Then he said to them, 'If the law is in accordance with my opinion, let this stream of water prove it!' The stream thereupon flowed backwards. They said to him, 'One does not prove the law from a stream of water'. Then he said to them, 'If the law is in accordance with my opinion, let the walls of this House of Study prove it!' The walls of the House of Study began to cave in. Rabbi Joshua rebuked them, saying 'If the learned sages debate with one another, what has it to do with you?' Out of respect to Rabbi Joshua they fell no further; out of respect to Rabbi Eliezer they did not rise . . . (Rabbi Eliezer) then said, 'If the law is in accordance with my opinion, let the heavens prove it'. A heavenly voice then proclaimed, 'What do you want with Rabbi Eliezer! The law is according to him in all matters!' Rabbi Joshua rose to his feet and proclaimed, 'It is not in heaven!'
>
> (Deuteronomy 30: 12) (B. *Bava Metzia* 59b)

Of course, this is not a denial of the need for divine guidance. On the contrary, it is allied with a deep conviction that the correct deliberations of the rabbis are guided by *ruah hakodesh* (the holy spirit). 'Whoever judges one law aright', runs another rabbinic adage, 'is a partner of the Holy One, Blessed be He, in creation'. The correct understanding and application of Torah is a divine task, in which we are humble, if privileged, participants. The part of this process which we can accomplish is the work of study and reflection on that which has already been revealed, a painstaking collaborative work in which decisions are reached by a majority of those competent, not by claims of special divine intervention.

The sources and levels of authority are many. There are laws carrying direct scriptural authority (*d'Oraita*), there are rabbinic enactments (*d'rabbanan*), whether for the protection of the biblical laws or whether directly for the improvement of society, there is customary law (*minhag*) and there are local enactments (*taqqanah*).

God's law has been revealed, and is to be pursued in an orderly and peaceful manner, with faith and love. It is not 'in heaven'; rather, heaven, through the Torah, has come down upon earth.

Freedom of the will

Some indication was given above of how the rabbis read scripture with a hermeneutic of free will. We must now see how the doctrine developed.

'All is foreseen, yet freedom is granted; the world is judged to the good side, and all is according to the effort expended. (Mishnah *Avot* 3: 19) This statement is attributed to Rabbi Akiva (early second century).

The most powerful expression of the doctrine of free will is that of Moses Maimonides (1135–1204), in the seventh chapter of the 'Laws of Penitence' in his great Code, the *Mishneh Torah*. Here is part of it (note that the Hebrew term *reshut* is variously translated as 'power', 'ability', 'freedom' as well as 'free will'):

> Free will is granted to every human being. Should he so wish, he has the power to incline himself to the good way and to be just; should he so wish, he has the power to incline himself to the evil way and to be wicked . . .

> Let that not enter your head, which is claimed by stupid gentiles and by numerous Jewish fools, that the Holy One, blessed be He, decrees on anyone at the time of his birth that he should be just or wicked. It is not so, but everyone possesses the ability to be as just as Moses our teacher or as evil as Jeroboam, or wise or foolish, or compassionate or cruel, or generous or mean, and likewise with other aspects of character. No-one forces him, decrees upon him, or constrains him to either path, but he himself determines of his own free will which path he will follow . . .

> This is a major principle and pillar of Torah and of the commandments, as it is said 'Behold I set life before you this day' (Deuteronomy 30: 15)

133

> . . . that is to say, you have the power, and whatsoever you wish to do of human deeds, whether good or evil, you can do . . .

> If God decreed that any individual should be righteous or evil, or if anything in the formation of a person led him to any (predetermined) path, character or understanding, as senseless astrologers fabricate, how could He command us through prophets 'Do this and don't do that' . . . what would be the point of the whole Torah and what justice would there be either in the punishment of the wicked or the reward of the just . . .?

Notwithstanding Maimonides' example, philosophers such as Cresques greatly narrowed the scope of free will, and where Maimonides had totally ridiculed astrology and reviled those who believed that the stars determined human action, ibn Ezra and most medievals continued to believe that our fate, if not our actions, is determined for us. German Hasidism of the twelfth century, and much liturgical poetry, manifest an overwhelming sense of sin. Yet the fundamental principle of freedom of the will was never abandoned entirely, nor the faith that the sinner, through penitence, could be reconciled with God.

Natural law

The idea of Natural Law (*nomos phuseos*) goes back to Aristotle, to whom ethics was essentially the science of how to fulfil the true nature of humanity. It is reflected in the Roman law concept of *obligationes naturales*. This is 'teleological' ethics, for it presupposes that humans have a 'purpose' – in Aristotle's terminology, a final cause. Jewish theology in the past consistently maintained that God created human beings for a purpose, even if that purpose transcended human reason. Since the Torah was given to help humans achieve the purpose for which they were created, its laws are a teleological ethic; they correspond to the aim of human nature as created by God 'in his own image'.

However, when one actually looks at the detailed provisions of Torah and attempts to explain them, problems arise. Is Torah indeed a rational system which can be related to human nature? Do the dietary laws, for instance, or the precise sexual regulations, correspond to the 'human purpose', or are they, to use the rabbinic term, *huqim* (statutes), which must be observed as 'decrees of the king', but have no intrinsic rationale? One might regard such regulations as 'positive law'. Such questions were discussed at great length by the medieval Jewish philosophers; some argued that these regulations have 'inner meanings', others that, though arbitrary in form, they constituted tests of our obedience, and in this way contributed to the fulfilment of human nature.

Clearly, some concept of ideal human nature underlies the system of Torah. But one may still ask how Torah actually operates as a legal system. Does one, as with 'natural law' systems, make decisions on the basis of broad principles of human nature and purpose? Or do Torah judges adopt a more positivist approach, treating the actual formulation of law as the 'given', and deciding cases by reference to it rather than by reference to human purpose?

TORAH AS NATURAL LAW

Possibly the first Jew consciously to express Torah as a sort of 'natural law' was Philo, who may well have used the term *agraphos nomos* (unwritten law) to refer to that law which did not have to be written down, because it was already in people's hearts.[9] It has been argued by many scholars that the talmudic 'Noahide laws', which constitute the Torah's provisions for gentile behaviour, are a rabbinic attempt at formulating natural law; this question turns on whether the Noahide is expected to follow these laws for their intrinsic merit, or because they are a 'positive law' revealed by God.[10]

Recently, serious consideration has been given to the extent to which Jewish law as a whole is a natural law system. Emanuel Rackman, recognising the artificiality of imposing such a philosophical framework on a legal system which developed in another tradition, observes:

> In halakhic literature one can find support for virtually every theory of legal philosophy known to secular jurisprudence.[11]

Commenting on this, in the following year, the late Julius Stone wrote:

Dr Rackman is concerned to point out that this hospitality of the halakhic tradition to a diversity of legal theories is not inconsistent with the view of Jewish law as commanded by God.[12]

Certainly, many traditional authorities have expounded Jewish law in a manner consistent with a natural law approach. However, they refer not to the law as a whole, but to parts of it, as rational, hence Saadia Gaon's (882–942) distinction between *mitzvot sikhliyot* and *mitzvot shim'iyot* (rational and revealed commandments), or Albo's (fifteenth century) explicit reference to natural law as the basis for the prohibitions of murder, theft and robbery which are essential to the stability of society (Joseph Albo, *Sefer Ha-Iqqarim*, 1: 5).

Among attempts to present Judaism as a whole as a rational, natural law system, is David Novak's extension of the biblical notion of 'covenant' to incorporate even the 'positive law' of revelation into the rationality of covenantal obligation.

ARE THERE 'SECOND ORDER' PRINCIPLES BY WHICH DECISIONS ARE GUIDED?

Another approach to assessing the natural law aspect of Judaism is to examine the way in which 'second order' moral principles are invoked to decide cases.

In his commentary on the verse 'And you shall do what is upright and good in the eyes of the Lord your God' (Deuteronomy 6: 18), Nahmanides (1194–1270) commented:

Our rabbis interpreted this with reference to compromise and to exceeding the bare requirement of law. What they mean by this is that (scripture) first says that you should observe the statutes and testimonies He commanded you, and then it says that even in those matters He did not (explicitly) command you should take care to do that which is good and upright in His eyes, for He loves what is good and upright. This is a very important matter, for it would be impossible for the Torah to mention every detail of man's relationship with his neighbour and fellow, or all his transactions, or every detail of social and political arrangements. But as it gives several examples, for instance 'Do not go spreading tales amongst your people' (Leviticus 19: 16), 'Do not take vengeance or bear a grudge' (Leviticus 19: 18), 'Do not stand on your brother's blood'

(Leviticus 19: 16), 'Do not curse the deaf' (Leviticus 19: 14), 'Rise before the hoary head' (Leviticus 19: 32) and similar things, it repeats in a general manner that you should do what is good and upright in everything, to the extent that you should be ready to accept a compromise and to act beyond the requirement of law . . .

This illustrates that within the Torah itself – for the verse cited is one of the commandments – there is the assumption of a rational ethic, and provision for invoking it in the interpretation and application of other laws. This will be discussed below.

Of principles and cases

GENERAL AND PARTICULAR

One of the most obvious features of the source texts cited by exponents of Jewish ethics is that they tend to consist of anecdotes, rules, examples, rather than generalisations. Even the general exhortations to virtue more often than not take the form of encouragement to observe the commandments, that is, they relate to specific instances of, or rules of low generality about, desirable behaviour. This approach stands in marked contrast to that of the Greek philosophers, or of mainline Christian theologians, who have tended, at least in their theoretical writing, to base ethics on much more general concepts, such as human nature or justice or love. Thomas Aquinas, for instance, utilising the concept of 'natural law', derives the detail of his moral philosophy and the criteria for acceptable legislation from his understanding of human nature.

This dissimilarity is evident in the way in which Jews and Christians today, addressing the identical ethical problem, tend to approach it from opposite directions. In discussions on the environment, for instance, one will find Christians primarily concerned with what they call 'creation theology'; from this they infer the desired attitude towards creation, and they then address themselves, adopting this attitude, to the specific problems of pollution, depletion of resources, threat to species or whatever else they are concerned with.

Traditional Jews tend to reason in the opposite direction, from

137

particular to general. Addressing the problem of depletion of natural resources, they will immediately call to mind the rule of *bal tashchit* (Deuteronomy 20: 19), rooted in the very specific context of the conduct of war; they will then move from the particular to the general, arguing that the rule against destroying fruit trees in time of war implies a general principle of care for the environment, even in time of war; from that, they will make inferences to the specific problems of pollution, depletion of resources, threat to species or whatever else they are concerned with.

I do not wish to imply that Jews and Christians necessarily or always argue along these lines. This would be a form of stereotyping that does justice to neither tradition. Indeed, it is fascinating to observe, among the traditional sources, how the two approaches interrelate. How, for instance, does Aquinas relate his 'moral law' concept to the specifics of Roman law, canon law, the scriptures and the Church's traditions, which effectively tie down the way he argues from general to particular? How does Maimonides accommodate the halakhic system and rabbinic *obiter dicta* on ethics to his adoption of Aristotle's 'doctrine of the mean'?[13]

Moreover, the 'mainline Christian' tendency I have spoken of is Catholic rather than Protestant, and perhaps more strongly characteristic of high medieval and early modern times than of other epochs in church history; at the opposite end of the Christian spectrum, the British-based 'Jubilee Trust' furnishes an intriguing recent instance of 'bottom up' argumentation in basing many of its social policy recommendations on the biblical law of the Jubilee and sabbatical year, and in so doing draws on a strong Protestant tradition of turning direct to the Bible for detailed guidance.

Why are both approaches, the 'top down' and the 'bottom up', needed? For pragmatic reasons: to use either approach on its own would generate great uncertainty. The 'top down' approach used alone means that one has to argue from general to particular without any guidance as to how to proceed. Liberation theologians, for instance, are fond of arguing from the general moral principle, 'identify with the poor' (itself derived from the even more general principle of love), to calling for specific forms of regulation of economic activity. The trouble is that there is no way, at least within the realm of moral discourse, to determine which economic regulations will work to the benefit of the poor, so you cannot argue 'because one should identify with the poor, one should tax the rich heavily' – taxing the rich heavily may well result in the destruction of means of production and the general loss of wealth to the detriment of the poor.

The 'bottom up' approach offers greater certainty at the practical level, but only in the given cases. 'Do not remove your neighbour's landmark' (Deuteronomy 19: 14) is a clear enough rule in its biblical context, but to apply it (as rabbis do) to the copyright of books demands, first, that a fairly general moral principle be supplied as the rationale ('do not act in such a way as to deprive any other person of a proprietary right'), and from that one works 'top down' to the particular case of intellectual property. The 'bottom up' approach, if used alone, leaves one searching for the rationale of the given case, that is, for the general principle underlying it; but without this rationale, it is impossible to proceed to the case under discussion and to know whether it can validly be compared with the original one. Indeed, the rabbinic discussions of the hermeneutic rules of *ribbui umiut* and *klal ufrat* reflect this problem, albeit at a lower level of generalisation than that of abstract moral principles.[14]

THE DATA OF MORAL PERCEPTION

But in fact there is a more profound issue at stake in this question of the direction of moral argument. Presumably, one argues from that which is subjectively more certain to that which is less certain. But at what level is there moral certainty? (I am not committing myself here to 'intuitionist' ethics.) What are the basic known 'data' of ethics? Indeed, at what level do we know or experience *anything*?

The neurologist, Oliver Sacks, reflecting on his experience with people with learning difficulties, is led to assess the relationship between the abstract and the concrete in human psychology. Regarding one patient, he writes, 'He remains a man, quintessentially a man, with all the moral weight and rich imagination of a man, despite the devastation of his abstract and propositional powers . . .'. Sacks adds:

> I believe all this to be true of the simple also – the more so as, having been simple from the start, they have never known, been seduced by, the abstract, but have always experienced reality direct and unmediated, with an elemental and, at times, overwhelming intensity.[15]

139

Sacks should be more careful in claiming 'direct and unmediated' experience, but his remarks serve to remind us of the possibility that all abstract generalisations – and this would include moral principles – are intellectual constructions at a further remove from reality than our already heavily mediated perceptions of particular situations.

Lawrence Kohlberg, from a rather different perspective, has attempted to describe what he refers to as levels of moral development, and he sees these as a progression from the recognition of 'is' to that of 'ought'.[16] The main levels are preconventional, conventional and postconventional, and they are subdivided into six stages. At stage six, decisions are guided by 'logical comprehensiveness, universality and consistency'. Kohlberg sees this as possessing greater 'moral adequacy' than stage five, at which there is 'an emphasis upon the possibility of changing law in terms of rational considerations of social utility'. However, it is unclear just why greater logicality should lead to objective moral superiority (Kohlberg prudently does not claim this), even though it might produce greater consistency. If the 'raw material' of morals – the cases where our moral conviction is strongest that x, y and z ought to be done – is available only at a low level of generality, let alone if it is tied to specific situations, there is a danger that in constructing general rules we will fail to sum the 'data' correctly, and then will make wrong inferences to other cases. Therefore, the maximum of 'known' cases must be recorded and preserved as a check on inference from the general rules.

Stephen R.L. Clarke has aptly written, with reference to philosophical attempts to reduce ethics to a small number of highly general principles:

> The idea that parental obligation, for example, is a minor corollary of some abstract duty, binding on all moral beings, to maximize happiness, or to allow all other moral or potentially moralizing beings an equal liberty, is a quite hopeless fantasy.[17]

It is often said, as Clarke does (citing Macintyre among others), that the detailed interpretations that philosophers put on their general principles are not necessitated by those principles but shaped by their general world outlook. True, but it should also be recognised that the broad outlook itself has meaning only through the very specific commitments that those philosophers, often as members of their class or society, have.

MORAL AND SCIENTIFIC REASONING

An important point arises here in reasoning. In science, one reasons from general to particular by a process of deduction. The well-known laws of Boyle and Charles relate the volume, temperature and pressure of gases, within a certain range of conditions. If the temperature of a gas increases and the volume is held constant, the pressure rises according to a known formula; therefore, if I increase the temperature of this gas, its pressure will increase, according to the formula. This is a deductive inference, and if measurements do not accord with prediction I will call into question either the theory or the measurements.

Moral reasoning is different, especially when mixed up with theology. Consider the recent controversy in Britain about what is popularly referred to as 'virgin birth', but is actually artificial insemination of single women. The Archbishop of York, Dr John Habgood, is alleged to have rejected this practice in the words: 'Single parents who are single by choice play truant from the school of charity, and that is bad for them and bad for their children' (*The Times*, 12 March 1991, p. 2. Undoubtedly this is an inadequate account of Dr Habgood's views). Now this is simply an argument from general to particular. Everyone ought always to practise charity (meaning here, to love their neighbour); *ergo*, if this woman wants a child she ought to be married or in a stable relationship. Put thus baldly, the argument is manifest nonsense; but Habgood's real argument is far more complex, and assumes the desirability of certain forms of social structure and certain forms of child care. Those people who believe that there are ways in which a single mother can provide an adequate environment for her child would not argue from the general principle of love to the particular conclusion that single women ought not to conceive children; indeed, bearing in mind some of the awful things that happen to children in two-parent families, they might be led to argue in favour of single mothers, at least in some cases. Moreover, the argument has no bearing on the method by which the child is conceived. Clearly, there is no deductive inference from the principle of charity to the

141

specific decision about a single woman who cannot find a satisfactory husband and wishes to conceive by artificial insemination. A wide range of decisions is logically compatible with the principle of charity, in sharp contrast with the 'gas laws', where the general law is compatible with only one consequence in the particular instance. Whereas physical laws are generalised summaries of clearly definable classes of observations, moral 'laws' are broad statements of value relating to ill-defined classes of action.

The artificial insemination debate highlights the difference of approach between 'top down' and 'bottom up' moral arguments. Jewish discussions of artificial insemination hinge not on any broad principle of charity (though all Jews subscribe to such principles), but on the permissibility or not of certain acts. One would need to establish whether the introduction of semen into a vagina by means of a syringe constitutes an act of sexual intercourse (it does not), whether the ejaculation of sperm for this purpose is permissible, and whether a child conceived in this way is related to the sperm donor in respect of various consequences, such as inheritance, degree of consanguinity for marriage, and so on.[18] Whatever the overall relationship of *halakhah* to moral principles, it is the *halakhah* and not the principles which would be evoked at this stage of the argument. Only after clarifying these basic *halakhot* would one proceed to consider the more 'social' aspects of the case, and these might well be decided in terms of higher level principles. There is an analogy here with some theories of legal reasoning, according to which hard cases are decided by reference to 'second order rules' which are more general than the actual law, and may well be broad moral assumptions.

Daniel H. Gordis, in a recent essay on Jewish bio-ethics ('Wanted – the Ethical in Jewish Bio-Ethics', in *Judaism* 38/1, Winter 1989, 28–40) has argued that the classic halakhic approach to problems in medical ethics, which he dubs 'precedent-based or formalist', should be replaced by deducing from the halakhic material 'a defensible, positive Jewish conception of human life', and on the basis of this conception the specific problems should be addressed. As an example of the wrong inferences being made by attempting to work directly from the precedent of an existing traditional source, he cites authorities who forbid artificial insemination absolutely on what are obviously spurious grounds. He suspects that their real motive is one of moral repugnance, and rightly observes that if this is the case the correct approach would be to spell out that moral repugnance as a clear moral doctrine and to admit that that is the basis of their judgements. Gordis himself tries to set up a concept of 'humanness', perhaps based on 'God's image', as a basis for judgement of bio-ethical questions. However, apart from the misgivings I have already expressed about teleological ethics, I do not understand how such a vague and ill-defined notion can give any better determination of specific issues than the admittedly strained logic of the halakhists (see Meier, 1986).

IMITATIO DEI

The concept of *imitatio dei* provides an example from within Judaism both of the use of a broad general moral principle and of the difficulty in drawing inferences from it. The Talmud records the following interpretation of the verse 'After the Lord your God shall you walk . . .' (Deuteronomy 13: 5):

> Said Rabbi Hama bar Hanina: How can a person walk after God? Is it not written 'For the Lord your God is a consuming fire' (Deuteronomy 4: 24)? But follow God's attributes. As He clothes the naked . . . as He visits the sick . . . comforts the bereaved . . . buries the dead . . . so should you.[19]

What Rabbi Hama bar Hanina neglects to tell us is how he knows that precisely these attributes of God are to be imitated and no others, for instance God's vengeance (Psalm 94: 1). The answer, of course, lies in scripture, which proclaims 'Do not be vengeful, do not bear a grudge' (Leviticus 19: 18). That is, no deduction can be made direct from the general moral principle that it is good to 'imitate' God; one still needs the check on inference which is provided by the specific laws of Torah.

GENERAL MORAL PRINCIPLES IN LEGISLATION ON NON-JEWS

Further study is needed of the efforts of the rabbis of the Talmud to regulate behaviour towards non-Jews. On the one hand, they tended (not always consistently) to interpret biblical legislation with narrow

143

reference to Israelites. On the other hand, there is a counterbalancing tendency to invoke broad general principles to guide behaviour towards non-Jews, among them *tiqqun olam* (putting the world right), *darkhei shalom* (the ways of peace), *kiddush Hashem* (sanctification of God's name – in the sense of acting in such a way as to bring honour to God's name).

ON MORAL ABSOLUTISM

Are there absolute moral principles or only *prima facie* ones? If it is absolutely wrong to kill people or to tell lies, what happens when some moral duty, for instance to protect the innocent or to avoid deep personal distress, demands that one kill the aggressor or speak an untruth?

Traditional *halakhah*, since it presents itself as a law system rather than as a table of vices and virtues, resists the tendency to moral absolutism. The law of *kiddush Hashem* (martyrdom) does indeed assume three absolutes, for even at the risk of one's life it is forbidden to worship idols, to commit adultery (as defined in the codes) or to shed innocent blood. However, a major part of rabbinic literature is concerned with ranking priorities of obligation, a simple example being that the saving of human life takes precedence over observance of the Sabbath laws.

In terms of moral philosophy we would have to say that Jewish ethics, as expressed in the system of halakhic priorities, is consequentialist; it is never the case, apart from the three exceptions cited, that a virtue is to be pursued or a vice avoided irrespective of the consequences.

Additional contemporary examples

Here are two further examples of the way in which decisions are reached on the basis of traditional Jewish sources.

TERRITORY FOR PEACE

In 1967, defending itself from Arab attack, Israel occupied surrounding territory, including the West Bank and Gaza, both of

144

which lie within the biblical boundaries of the Land of Israel. These territories remained under Israeli control after the 1973 'Yom Kippur' war, and after the accommodation with Egypt under Begin and Sadat in 1978.

Since 1973, a major religious debate has centred on the question of whether the West Bank and Gaza might be voluntarily handed over to Arab control in return for peace. In 1980 a religious peace movement, *Oz Veshalom*, published some papers on this topic, and on the treatment of minorities according to *halakhah*, by Shilo Refael, a *dayan* (judge) of the rabbinical court in Jerusalem. At the front of the booklet stands a summary of the halakhic rulings as agreed by Refael and the then Sefardic Chief Rabbi of Israel, Ovadiah Yosef. The summary reads as follows:

According to the majority of early authorities[20] *they shall not dwell in your land* [Exodus 23: 33] does not refer to Muslims, since they are not idolators.

All authorities agree that nowadays, when Israel does not have power to drive out nations from the land, that the prohibition *they shall not dwell in your land* has no application.

According to many of the greatest authorities, both early and late, the prohibition *lo tehanem*[21] applies only to idolators.

Even if it were prohibited to sell land (in Israel) to non-Israelites, the possibility would remain of exchanging it.

According to all authorities it is permitted to return territories of (biblical) Israel in order to remove the possibility of war, for nothing stands in the way of *pikuah nefesh* (the saving of life).

Even if there were disputes as to (whether this was a case of) *pikuah nefesh*, wherever there is a doubt in a matter of life and death we take the more lenient view (and avoid risk).

In a generation where all are righteous, and immersed in (a life of) Torah, one might trust in God even where there is risk to life, but in our generation we cannot rely on miracles, and therefore we should return the territories to remove enemies from ourselves.

Even according to Nahmanides, who maintains that it is a religious duty to wage war for the conquest of the Land of Israel, there is no religious duty on us today to risk our lives to hold on to the territories we have conquered against the will of the nations of the world.

145

> With the agreement of the leaders of the community not only converts but non-Jews may be appointed to any public office.

What is of interest in the above is the manner in which Ovadiah Yosef and Shilo Refael relate to the classical sources of Judaism.

First, they do not go directly to biblical texts, but to rabbinic interpretation of those texts. Second, they cite a principle formulated by the rabbis, that the safeguarding of life has priority over all of the commandments (except murder, idolatry, and adultery/incest) and use it in a context for which there is no clear talmudic precedent, namely the circumstance where part of the historical territory of Israel is occupied by non-idolators. How is this extrapolation justified? In fact, it would seem that they engaged in a characteristic process by which theologians effect change: they selected one value from a number of available, but conflicting, values in the tradition, and accorded it priority. The selection of the value of *pikuah nefesh* over that of settlement of the land is not dissimilar, for instance, to the selection of the value of human dignity over that of the ownership of slaves. Both represent a creative decision, determining the direction in which the faith and law are to proceed.

Finally, though the *value* priority has been established, nothing very definite follows in practice. Surely they are not suggesting that if Arabs threatened to kill just one person they would relinquish the land rather than run such a risk? Clearly, other priorities come into operation in the actual situation, for we know that Yosef and Refael both support defensive wars and even pre-emptive strikes in certain circumstances. In the end, the decision has to be made in the light of a critical assessment of all circumstances, military and political options, and the like, so although there may be a value input from theology (based on *halakhah*), *halakhah* alone does not determine the decision. We see here another line of demarcation between theology and practical decision-making.

MATERNITY IN FOETAL IMPLANTS

The following example demonstrates the method of rabbinic argument from case law. Note that all areas of law are considered relevant, and are regarded as belonging to a single comprehensive and coherent system.

It is possible to remove an embryo from one woman and implant it in another, who gives birth to the baby. Does conception or birth determine maternity? Dependent on this are questions of inheritance, of personal status, of relationship with other children of the first and second women (see Goldberg in *Crossroads*, 1987, 71–7).

A *prima facie* proof that maternity depends on conception is derived from a responsum of Rabbi Akiva Eger (1761–1837) on the subject of whether the prohibition of cooking milk and meat together applies to the milk of a *treifa* (an animal suffering a defect rendering it forbidden for eating). The relevant part of Eger's responsum runs as follows:

It is questionable whether the milk of a *treifa* is contained in the prohibition, according to the principle that a *treifa* cannot give birth, and hence is unable to be a mother. See *Sanhedrin* 69a (where the Talmud excludes from the laws of the rebellious son one who has reached majority three months earlier, as he is considered to be a (potential) father and not a 'son'. He is capable of impregnating a woman from when he obtains majority and after three months the pregnancy is evident, at which time he is called a 'father'). This implies that the father of an embryo is considered to be a father. Similarly, in our case, the *treifa* is capable of being a mother, since she can conceive, although she cannot deliver. . . . The mother of an embryo is also considered a mother. However, it is possible that the parent of an embryo is considered a parent only if the embryo will be delivered in the future. A *treifa*, however, who cannot deliver, is not considered to be a mother while pregnant. Subsequently, I discovered that the *Issur Veheter* (31, 14) ruled that the milk of a *treifa* is included in the Torah prohibition of milk–meat because if she was impregnated before she became a *treifa*, she is capable of delivering even when a *treifa*. Accordingly, the milk of an animal born *treifa* will not be included in the prohibition.

From this, it would appear that maternity depends on conception; hence the foetal implant would be regarded in law as the child of the first, not the second, woman.

Against Eger, Rabbi Yosef Engel (1859–1920) argued that a distinction should be made between maternity and paternity. Paternity is indeed established at conception. Maternity, however, depends on birth. Engel derives this distinction from a comment of Rashi (1040–1105) on an apparently redundant statement in the book of Esther.

147

Engel proceeds to demonstrate that birth rather than conception determines maternity from the following talmudic passage:

> Twin brothers who are converts or emancipated slaves do not perform *yibum* or *chalitza* (for each other), nor is one prohibited (from marrying) the other's widow. (Rashi – Even if the [first] marriage was contracted after the conversion, as a convert is like a new-born child and therefore he does not have the relationship of brotherhood, even [with a child] from the same mother.) If their conception was before conversion and their birth after conversion, they do not perform *yibum* or *chalitza* . . . but are prohibited from marrying each other's widow.
>
> (Babylonian Talmud *Yevamot* 97b)

Since, in the second case, conception took place before conversion, it cannot serve as a determinant of maternity, for the brothers are like new-born children from the time of conversion. As they are evidently considered brothers from the point of view of incest, it seems that birth, not conception, is the determinant of maternity.

Several similar arguments are considered before reaching the conclusion that the child relates exclusively to the mother who gives birth. It is a matter of speculation as to what extent the argumentation is controlled by unstated assumptions as to moral principles. Certainly, it would not be difficult to show that the arguments are not strictly deductive.

Jewish sectarian differences

In all the preceding we have assumed a position within traditional orthodoxy. Contemporary Jewish orthodoxy is itself diverse,[22] but in its hardest form it treats the words of scripture, from Genesis to Deuteronomy, as verbally inspired, and the words of the talmudic rabbis as guided by *ruah ha-kodesh* (the holy spirit); high authority is accorded to the literature within this tradition, including law codes and responsa still being produced today. Rabbis within this 'hard' tradition are by no means insensitive to the conflicts of conscience faced by Jews today when called upon to follow traditional rulings meticulously. Perhaps their greatest sensitivity is shown in *agunah* cases, where perhaps for some technical reason a woman is prevented from remarriage; undoubtedly they strive hard, within what they perceive as the limits of *halakhah*, to find grounds on which to make permissive rulings. Ultimately, however, in this as in other conflicts between correct Torah rulings (as they see them) and personal compassion, the former has priority. The autonomous individual conscience can never overrule the 'superior wisdom of God' as handed down by the sages.

Conservative[23] Judaism differs from 'hard' orthodoxy in allowing greater rein to historical factors. Historical criticism of the Bible is accepted, and the rabbinic sages and their interpretations placed within historical context. This enables some degree of relativism so that, for instance, Conservatives have permitted mixed seating in the synagogue, and since 1985 they have ordained women rabbis, in the belief that the segregation of women and their diminished role in public life are not of the 'essence' of Judaism, but were related to social circumstances which have changed in modern times. Conservatives nevertheless attach great weight to *halakhah*, and claim that they, rather than the Orthodox, stand in the Hillelite tradition of interpretation in accordance with the needs of the times.

Reform Judaism, originating in Germany in the early nineteenth century and quickly achieving dominance in the United States, takes a more radical approach than Conservativism to the modification of religious observances and to the revision of theological doctrines. Both the 1885 'Pittsburgh Platform' and the 1937 'Columbus Platform' strongly emphasise ethical and moral values at the expense of ritual and tradition. In so doing, Reform has ensured a prominent role for the 'voice of conscience', even where that conflicts with tradition. Recent issues where the autonomy of the individual conscience has claimed recognition include the claim that homosexuals be given equal rights within the community. The range of responses to questions of this type reflects the broad spectrum of opinion within the World Union for Progressive Judaism (founded 1926), of which Reform is the major component.

The greatest freedom of the individual conscience is granted within the Reconstructionist movement, which owes its inspiration to Mordecai M. Kaplan (1881–1982). Though the movement was founded in 1922, it was originally conceived as an 'umbrella' for all Jews, whatever their sectarian attachment. However, in 1967 it set up its own Rabbinical College, in Philadelphia, and since 1970 has

149

had its own congregations. In these, decisions are made collectively by members, who form a democratic *havurah* (society) in which the *rabbi* is no more than a 'resource person'. Autonomy of individual conscience is paramount, however, and it is the individual who is the final arbiter of which rituals or folkways to practise.

Thus the Jewish sects provide between them a full spectrum of approaches to moral decision-making, ranging from the insistence of 'hard Orthodoxy' on a non-historical acceptance of sources, with only limited opportunity for compassionate interpretation, to Reconstructionism, where individual conscience reigns supreme.

NOTES

1. The Palestinian (completed c.450) and Babylonian (completed c. 550) Talmudim are expansions of the Mishnah (completed c. 215), and together form the classical exposition of rabbinic Judaism.
2. Mishnah, *Avot* 1: 3.
3. The early versions of the 'pound of flesh' story, such as that in the tale of the fourth wise master of the 'Seven Wise Masters of Rome' in the Sinbad series, have no Jewish reference.
4. Babylonian Talmud, *Bava Metzia*, 30b. There is an excellent chapter on *lifnim mishurat ha-din* in S. Federbush, *Ha-Musar v'ha-Mishpat b'Israel* (Hebrew) (Mosad Harav Kook, Jerusalem, 5708/1947) Chapter 11.
5. See the discussion in Louis E. Newman's article, 'Law, Virtue and Supererogation in the Halakha', *Journal of Jewish Studies*, XL (1989) pp. 61–88. Newman, following Menachem Elon's Hebrew work *Ha-Mishpat Ha-Ivri* (Magnes Press, Jerusalem, 1978) cites several instances where later authorities have made legally enforceable something which the Talmud referred to as *lifnim mishurat ha-din*.
6. 'Some Aspects of The Jewish Attitude Toward the Welfare State', in I. Twersky, *Studies in Jewish Law and Philosophy* (Ktav, New York, 1982) p. 137 onwards.
7. Babylonian Talmud, *Bava Batra* 10a – Twersky's translation.
8. This is the title of a book by Ellis Rivkin.
9. There are two other interpretations of the term used by Philo in, for instance, *de Specialibus Legibus* IV, 148–9. Many scholars have incorrectly surmised that he was referring to the 'oral Torah', but this is an anachronism. Others, probably correctly, have interpreted it as 'unwritten law as custom'. See John W. Martens, 'Unwritten Law in Philo', in *Journal of Jewish Studies*, 43/1 Spring 1992, 38–45.

10. J. David Bleich, 'Judaism and Natural Law', in *Jewish Law Annual* VII (1988), 5–42. Bleich's article should be consulted for a fuller treatment of the topic of this section. See also David Novak, 'Natural Law, Halakhah and the Covenant', in *Jewish Law Annual* VII (1988), 43–67.

11. E. Rackman, 'Secular Jurisprudence and the Halakha', in *Jewish Law Annual* VI (1987), 45–63.

12. Julius Stone, 'Leeways of Choice, Natural Law and Justice in Jewish Legal Ordering', in *Jewish Law Annual* VII (1988), 210–51, at 211.

13. The *locus classicus* for this difficulty is *Mishneh Torah, De'ot* 2: 3.

14. See Norman Solomon, 'Extensive and Restrictive Interpretation of Terms in Rabbinic Literature', in Rakover (1984), 37–54, and in *Jewish Law Association Studies I*, Scholars Press 1985, 125–39.

15. Oliver Sacks, *The Man Who Mistook His Wife For a Hat*, Gerald Duckworth & Co., London 1983; Picador Edition, Pan Books 1986, p. 165.

16. Lawrence Kohlberg, 'From Is to Ought', in *Cognitive Development and Epistemology*, ed. Theodore Mischel, New York, Academic Press, 1971, 151–235.

17. Stephen R.L. Clarke, 'Abstract Morality, Concrete Cases', in J.D.G. Evans (ed.) *Moral Philosophy and Contemporary Problems*, Cambridge University Press (for the Royal Institute of Philosophy), Cambridge, 1987, p. 42.

18. There is a substantial and growing literature on the subject. See for instance Moshe Drori's article 'Artificial Insemination: Is it adultery?' in Rakover (1984) 203–16. See also the article by Daniel H. Gordis referred to in the text.

19. B. *Sota* 14a. See Maimonides *Mishneh Torah: Hilkhot De'ot*, 1: 6 for a reconstruction of this passage.

20. In this context, 'early authorities' means the post-talmudic rabbis preceding Joeseph Caro (1488–1575); 'late authorities' are any from that time onwards.

21. Deuteronomy 7: 2. Literally, 'do not show them kindness'. By a play on words this was taken to mean 'do not give them dwelling (*haniyyah*) in the land'.

22. On the range of contemporary orthodoxy, see Jonathan Sacks, *Traditional Alternatives: Orthodoxy and the Future of the Jewish People*, Jews' College Publications, London, 1989.

23. Conservative Judaism is strongest in the United States, where it originated early this century in reaction to Reform. The much more recent British offshoot is referred to as 'Masorti' Judaism, the Hebrew name adopted by its Israeli counterpart.

FURTHER READING

Bleich, J. David (several vols from 1981) *Contemporary Halakhic Problems*, New York, Ktav.

Cohn, Haim (1984) *Human Rights in Jewish Law*, London, Institute of Jewish Affairs.

Crossroads: Halakha and the Modern World (1987), Jerusalem, Zomet Institute (no editor given).

Feldman, David M. (1974) *Marital Relations, Birth Control and Abortion in Jewish Law*, New York, Schocken.

Greenberg, Blu (1981) *On Women and Judaism: A View from Tradition*, Philadelphia, Jewish Publication Society of America.

Jacobovits, I. (1976) *Jewish Medical Ethics*, New York, Bloch.

Meier, Levi (1986) *Jewish Values in Bioethics*, New York, Human Sciences Press.

Neusner, Jacob (1988) *The Mishnah: A new Translation*, New Haven and London, Yale University Press.

Rakover, N. (ed.) (1984) *Jewish Law and Current Legal Problems*, Jerusalem, Jewish Legal Heritage Society.

Rose, Aubrey (ed.) (1992) *Judaism and Ecology*, London, Cassell.

Steinsaltz, Adin (1977) *The Essential Talmud*, New York, Bantam Books.

Tamari, Meir (1987) 'With all your Possessions': *Jewish Ethics and Economic Life*, London, Collier Macmillan.

Twersky, Isadore (1982) *Studies in Jewish Law and Philosophy*, New York, Ktav.

6. Sikhism

Indarjit Singh

Truth is high,
but higher still
is truthful living
(Gurū Granth Sāhib, p. 62)

In this single verse is summarised the foundation of Sikh ethics. It is
by no means an abstract principle, but one which, by definition, has
to be expressed in practice. It is, in essence, the answer to the
situation of conflict and frequent cruelty which Guru Nanak found
in the context in which he lived – one in which, in particular, there
was mistrust between Hindus and the Muslim invaders (and rulers):

The age is a knife,
Kings are butchers,
And righteousness has taken wings and flown:
In this dark night of falsehood
No moon of truth is seen to rise.
(Gurū Granth Sāhib, p. 145)

Already, in his first sermon, Guru Nanak had declared that 'there
is neither Hindu nor Muslim, only humanity'. The quest of moral
behaviour is the elimination of *haumai* (self-centredness) and the
realisation in practice of the one human family under God. He
asked, 'How can we see the truth and remove the veil of falsehood?'
To which he answered, 'Abide by his will (*hukam*) and make it your
own' (GGS, p. 1).

Sikhism teaches that if we move in a godly direction, or follow
hukam (the direction of God's will), we will be turned in the

direction of truth and goodness. Equally, if we move away from his *hukam*, we will bring misery and suffering on ourselves, and, importantly, be quite ineffective in making this world a better place for ourselves and our children.

The question that immediately arises is, how can we understand God's *hukam*, how can we find the path of the *gurmukh* (person motivated by godly ideals) as opposed to *manmukh* (person motivated by human passions). The answer is given in the pages of the Gurū Granth Sāhib. Briefly, it requires moving in three dimensions at one and the same time. These are *nām japna, kirat karna* and *vand chakhna*, that is, meditating on God, earning by one's own effort, and sharing one's good fortune with others. What do these mean?

Nām japna

Nām japna, meditation on God, does not mean sitting cross-legged in abstract contemplation. It means reflecting on the eternal truths of religion to give us a sense of perspective, a sense of direction in life that enables us to distinguish right from wrong, good from evil. Meditating on our relationship with God and its implications helps us to distinguish the trivial and petty that so easily obsess us, and focus on the meaningful aspects of life. In this way it helps us to be more effective in helping our fellow beings.

For Sikhs, meditation means reading and reflecting on the teaching of the Gurūs as contained in the Gurū Granth Sāhib. To give an example:

> There is one God.
> Eternal Truth is his Name;
> Maker of all things;
> Fearing nothing and at enmity with nothing;
> Timeless is his image;
> Not begotten, being of his own Being;
> By his grace made known to humanity,
> He was there before time.
> He was present in the earliest age.
> Is present now
> And shall be evermore.
> (Gurū Granth Sāhib, p. 1)

How can we meditate on these lines? What are the implications of these teachings?

First, there is the emphasis on *one* God. Not different gods of different faiths, but one God of all humanity. A God that is common to Indians, the British, French, Russians, whatever, to black, brown or white; to men and women – we are all the children of one father who has equal love for us all.

'Fearing nothing and at enmity with nothing'. This criticises the notion of favoured or less favoured nations.

At a time when people thought that they could make images of God, the Gurū suggested that such people should try to make an image of timelessness. Today, we may not have images to bathe and worship as the people did in Guru Nanak's time, but power, position and material wealth are all too often seen as near objects of worship that blind us to the reality and transience of life.

We respect but disagree with the Hindu and Christian views of God taking birth, and are reminded that God is the only permanent presence in an otherwise finite world.

Important ethical implications flow naturally from this view of God. One God, the father of all humanity, means one human family of equals, and a rejection of all notions of caste or (its modern equivalent) race. Concepts of religious and political tolerance are natural concomitants of these beliefs.

Kirat karna

This, the second of the three dimensions of Sikhism, literally means 'making an effort' and 'earning by one's own effort'. It requires a positive commitment to life and its ethical obligations.

The emphasis on 'earning by one's own effort' is best understood against the background of a holy person in the Gurū's time being considered as someone who had left society and lived by begging for food, or wandering in the wilderness in contemplation of God. Guru Nanak once visited a group of people in the mountains. They asked him, 'How goes the world below?' The Gurū, noting the arrogance implicit in the question, replied that the world was suffering, and how could it be otherwise when those with learning and wisdom deserted it in such a selfish way?

Guru Nanak emphasised that the route to an understanding of God lay not in fleeing from social obligations, but in the service of our fellow humans. He taught: 'Only by the selfless service of others can God be reached' (GGS, p. 26). The Gurū gave Sikhs the example of the lotus flower, which, though having its roots in muddy waters, still flowers beautifully above. He taught that, similarly, Sikhs should live in society, work constantly for its improvement, and yet always be above its meanness and pettiness.

The Gurū's emphasis on positive effort also needs to be set against the enfeebling fatalism of the time. Everything was considered *karma*, or fate, and this was used as an excuse for inaction. The Sikh view on *karma* is best exemplified in the verse by Nathalia Crane:

You cannot choose your battlefields.
That God does for you.
But you can plant a standard
Where a standard never flew.

We are unable to choose our parents, the circumstances of our birth or our early environment, but we are not only able to make the best of our circumstances, we also have a moral duty to do so. It is this life-affirming attitude that has charged Sikhs to enter all the different areas of human activity with characteristic energy and enthusiasm. Sikhs have been pioneers of the green revolution in Panjab, now the breadbasket of India, and they are well represented in medicine, engineering, the arts and all fields of modern technology. It is this zest for life that has taken a small community – no more than fifteen million – to Canada, the United States of America, Malaysia, Australia, Africa, and many other parts of the globe. Wherever Sikhs have gone, one of their first actions has always been to set up gurdwaras, necessary reminders that *kirat karna* is inseparably linked to prayer and dedication (*nām japna*).

Vand chakna

We now come to the third of the three dimensions of the Sikh way of life, *vand chakna*, or 'sharing with others'. In a sense, the other two components, prayer and personal effort, are a necessary preparation for this all-important sharing with others, a sharing not only of material wealth but also of energies, skills and talents in *sevā*, or service to society. The importance of *sevā* to the Sikh way of life cannot be over-emphasised. It manifests itself in *langar* –

'provision of free food', not only in the congregation but also to the needy. It is seen in the setting up of the Pingalwara, a home for cripples in Amritsar, homes for the handicapped in Ranchi, and in many other welfare institutions, both in India and abroad.

Fundamentals

For Sikhs, therefore, morality is placed under the imperative of Sikh teaching. This can be found in two major 'sources':

1. the teachings contained in the Sikh scriptures, which include writings not only from the ten Gurūs, but also from Hindu and Muslim saints – to underline the truth of a single human community under God; and
2. the example of the Gurūs' lives.

The Gurūs lived over a span of more than two centuries, in widely varying social, cultural and political environments. Guru Nanak himself travelled widely in India, the Near East and Tibet. They realised the transient nature of many social customs; they realised that, in the words of the English hymn:

> New occasions teach new duties,
> Time makes ancient good uncouth,
> They must upward still and onward,
> Who would keep abreast of truth.

As a result, while there are some absolutes, ethical guidance in Sikhism is rarely couched in terms of 'thou shalt' or 'thou shalt not'. Instead, we are given guiding principles which do not change with time and place, and these are used to determine action and reaction to the problems and challenges of the day. Of the 'absolutes', the oneness of the human family is paramount, followed by tolerance and democracy.

ONENESS OF THE HUMAN FAMILY

Belief in the oneness of the human family means duty to reject all notions of caste or race.

157

What power has caste? It is righteousness that is tested. Whosoever tastes poison will die, no matter his caste.

(Gurū Granth Sāhib, p. 142)

Know people by the light within them. Ask not their caste. For in the hereafter no one is differentiated by caste.

(Gurū Granth Sāhib, p. 349)

God is not concerned with caste or birth. So let us learn the way of truthful living; for one's deeds determine one's respect.

(Gurū Granth Sāhib, p. 1330)

The pride of caste and the glory of status are futile, for each of us shelters under the one same God.

(Gurū Granth Sāhib, p. 83)

Hereafter caste and power do not count; for every soul appears in its true colours.

(Gurū Granth Sāhib, p. 469)

Sikhism emphasises the oneness of the human race:

The Hindus and the Muslims are all one,
Each has the habits of different environments,
But all men have the same eyes, the same body,
The same form compounded of the same elements,
They are all of one form.
The one Lord made them all.

(Akāl Ustat 86: 16)

The equality of all human beings in Sikhism includes the full equality of women. Guru Nanak taught: 'Why call her low who gives birth to royalty?' (GGS, p. 473).

To emphasise the elevated status of women in Sikhism, Guru Gobind Singh, the tenth Gurū, gave all Sikh women the title *Kaur*, literally 'Princess'. Women occupy a prominent place in all walks of life in the Sikh community, and not only take a full part in Sikh services, but also quite frequently lead them. (See the chapter on Sikhism in *Women in Religion* in this series.)

Let us look at the implications of these teachings for the world of today. If we truly believe in the oneness of our human family, can we countenance deprivation, starvation, and even physical torture being suffered by our brothers and sisters in different parts of the globe? Why should some members of the family be virtually imprisoned in barren and inhospitable regions of the world, while others enjoy both the bounty of nature and the harvest of material progress?

Belief in the oneness of the human family is an imperative, and for Sikhs cannot be conditional in the widespread sense of 'Yes, provided it does not harm my standard of living'. Belief in the oneness of the human race cannot be squared with modern immigration controls which obscenely allow in those with substantial capital assets, while keeping out the less fortunate. Even less should we countenance the niggardly treatment of refugees fleeing cruel and murderous regimes. While any sudden unilateral abandonment of immigration controls is clearly impracticable, and could lead to social unrest, the phased reduction of barriers to freer movement of people must be a natural corollary to any talk of 'one human family'.

TOLERANCE

The English word 'tolerance' is too weak and too negative to describe the Sikh view of tolerance, which is the willingness to give one's life in upholding the rights of others, as exemplified by Guru Tegh Bahadur, the ninth Gurū. He was cruelly martyred for upholding the rights of the Hindu community to worship in the manner of its choice in a climate of fierce persecution by the Islam-professing Moghul rulers.

It was Voltaire who declared, 'I may not believe what you say but will defend to the death your right to say it'. Guru Tegh Bahadur gave this noble sentiment practical utterance. There had been religious martyrdoms before, but his was on behalf of people of another faith.

DEMOCRACY

Belief in the inherent equality of all human beings leads naturally to the democratic ideal. When the tenth Gurū, Guru Gobind Singh, gave *amrit* (initiation) to the first five members of the *Khālsā Panth*, or Sikh brotherhood, he immediately asked them to give him *amrit* also, to emphasise that master and disciples were one.

The Gurūs and the Sikh community have always fought (often literally) against tyranny and oppression. It was Sikhs who initiated the struggle for Indian independence. When the Sikh holy places were freed from political control in the Guru ka Bagh *morca*, Mahatma Gandhi sent a telegram to Sikh leaders: 'Congratulations, the first battle for Indian independence won'. It was the Sikhs again who led the fight against Indira Gandhi's declaration of a state of emergency and suspension of parliamentary rule in 1977. As subsequent events have shown, they were not easily forgiven.

Ethics of personal living

EARLY RISING

Sikhs are enjoined to rise early, wash, and then say prayers or meditate on God. The early morning is considered the calmest time of day, a time when one can properly get one's bearings before the hurly-burly of the day's events – daily pressures which may make it difficult to distinguish between the trivial or transient and the important.

KIRAT AND *SEVĀ*

These have already been discussed. Before we are able to make an effective contribution to the betterment of society, we must become socially and politically aware, and thus there is a requirement for positive involvement.

LIFE OF THE HOUSEHOLDER

Sikhism does not believe in renunciation. Family life is commended, and marriage held sacred. While the equality and individuality of the two partners is recognised, the Gurū also stressed the ideal of a

160

married couple acting as a team, or single soul, in the pursuit of spiritual enlightenment and service to the community:

> They are not husband and wife
> Who only live together.
> Rather they are husband and wife
> Who have one spirit in two bodies.

(Gurū Granth Sāhib, p. 778)

Marriage vows are taken in the presence of the Gurū Granth Sāhib. The couple are reminded of their duty to one another and to society. They pledge to uphold Sikh ideals, and to seek guidance from the Gurū Granth Sāhib. Marriage is considered a sacred partnership. Divorce is not forbidden, but should not be entered into lightly. The responsibility of both partners to their children should take precedence over petty antagonism.

In earlier times, the respective roles of men and women as the providers and the carers of home and children were culturally defined, and marriage was a partnership in which each partner had a clear but separate role. Today, more enlightened attitudes to education and employment mean that both partners may go out to work, and respective roles can become confused or conflicting, leading to strains in a marriage. The concept of equal partnership, of acting as a team, is, therefore, all the more important in today's more complex society. The Gurūs taught that no work is demeaning, and a fair division of household responsibilities should be agreed, rather than assumed, by partners, in a spirit of mutual support.

FAMILY PLANNING AND CONTRACEPTION

Sikhism teaches respect for life, and social responsibility. The concept of family planning is accepted, in that one should not have more children than one can properly care for. Abortion as a means of family planning is contrary to this respect for life but may be permissible in cases of rape or danger to a mother's health or in similar circumstances.

161

CHILDREN

Sikh parents are expected to bring up their children within the teachings and disciplines of Sikhism, and inculcate in them a sense of social responsibility. As parents, they are often accused of being over-protective, and there is some truth in this. However, the balance between this and what may be described as the 'enlightened irresponsibility' of some western parents, is a difficult one, and there is much to be said for erring towards the former. Sikhs, however, are also required to recognise that 'our' children are not *our* children, but individuals in their own right, and a sacred trust.

FOOD AND DRINK

Sikhs are asked to refrain from alcohol, tobacco and drugs or other substances that may injure health or impair mental alertness. No food is specifically proscribed, other than the requirement to abstain from meat killed by ritual slaughter. Dietary habits of Sikhs have over the years been influenced by living in a predominantly Hindu society. A sizeable number of Sikhs are vegetarians; some will not touch beef – sacred to the Hindus – while others, living among Muslims, will feel it is wrong to eat pork.

The debate about meat-eating was particularly strong at the time of Guru Nanak. In the following passage the Gurū makes clear that it is foolish to get over-involved in academic discussion:

> It is men of ignorance that quarrel over eating of meat
> Without understanding what is meat,
> What is vegetation and what constitutes sin.

> (Gurū Granth Sāhib, p. 1289)

There is, he taught, life even in vegetation, and such matters should be left to the individual. More generally, no food is considered 'sinful', and the advice is simply, 'eat only that which agrees with you'.

CLOTHES

Many will be familiar with the Sikhs' Five 'K's, so called because the Panjābi word for each of the five begins with the sound 'k'. These are *keś* (long hair), chosen as a reminder of the need for saintliness (long hair in the Gurūs' times was worn by saints), *kangha* (comb), to remind one of the need for cleanliness, *kirpān* (short sword), as a reminder of the duty to defend the weak or oppressed, *karā* (steel bracelet), worn on the wrist as a link or symbol of dedication to godly ideals, and *kaccha* (shorts or trousers), to replace the cumbersome Indian *dhoti*, a garment considered unsuitable for an active life. Together, these symbols constitute a uniform that enables Sikh men to be recognised as individuals dedicated to a particular way of life. Wearing these symbols does not in any way suggest a moral or spiritual superiority.

Modern social issues

EUTHANASIA

In the excellent play, *Whose life is it anyway?*, by Brian Clark, a young man paralysed in an accident argues the right to take his life on the grounds that it is *his* life. Sikh teachings, however, suggest that 'our life' is not *ours*, but a gift from God to be used responsibly. Responsibility is, then, the key factor that determines Sikh attitudes to euthanasia. Individuals who are suffering and contemplating taking their own life should consider their responsibility to others, particularly their loved ones. While the burden of care should never be used to rationalise the termination of a life, the artificial prolonging of the life of an individual who is brain-dead would be difficult to justify.

THE ENVIRONMENT

Having obliterated rainforests, polluted the air, soil and water, squandered natural resources and driven many life-forms to extinction, the industrialised West has suddenly discovered 'the environment'. Much of the poetry of the Sikh Gurūs is couched in

163

terms of wonder and respect for God's creation. Responsibility is again the keyword – particularly responsibility to future generations. Sikhism teaches that human life is a rare gift, and the blessings of nature are God's gift, to be used with responsibility to both ourselves and others, particularly to generations yet unborn.

THE 'SEVEN' DEADLY SINS

In Sikhism there are only five! These are referred to as the five thieves, namely: lust, anger, greed, undue attachment and pride. The way to guard against these bars to spiritual development is to live a life rooted in prayer, free from obsession with self, and dedicated to the service of others.

Attitudes to violence and injustice

Some dictionaries and encyclopedias still refer to Sikhs as a 'martial race'. This is an inaccurate and misleading definition. As discussed earlier, Sikhism strongly disagrees with the whole concept of the human family being composed of different races with inherently different characteristics. We are, as Guru Gobind Singh taught, all members of one human race. The appellation 'martial' also does a disservice to the essentially peaceful teachings of Sikhism. Sikhs have, however, suffered almost continuous persecution since the time of the Gurūs. At one time there was a price on the head of every Sikh caught – dead or alive. Sikhs had to put up a robust resistance to survive. This robustness, culminating in the fiercely fought Anglo-Sikh wars, is probably responsible for the reputation of Sikhs as a martial people.

Having cleared away this misconception, let us look more closely at Sikh attitudes to violence and injustice. First, the correct Sikh response to personal injury or affront is very similar to that of the Christian. Instead of turning the other cheek, they are asked to 'kiss the feet' of those causing affront. Sikhs are, however, duty bound to intervene when violence or injustice is directed at the weak or disadvantaged. The Sikh teaching, where human rights are being infringed or innocent people oppressed, is remarkably similar to that contained in the preamble to the 1948 UN Universal Declaration of Human Rights: 'it is essential, if man is not to have recourse, as a last resort, to rebellion against tyranny and oppression, that human rights should be protected by the rule of law'.

Centuries earlier, Guru Gobind Singh had taught: 'When all other means of righting injustice have been tried and failed, it is legitimate as a last resort to turn to the sword'. It must be emphasised that violence must be used only as a last resort to combat injustice. The Gurūs taught the importance of peaceful protest and non-violent response. As already stated, two of the Gurūs were martyred in non-violent protest, and this historically has been a strong aspect of the Sikh fight against injustice.

SOCIAL ETHICS

Sikhism stresses the importance of positive involvement. We have all come across people who boast of never having done any harm to anyone. The response from Sikh teachings is that countless sticks, stones, rivers and mountains could make a similar claim. Can the real aim of human existence be to do no one any harm? Guru Gobind Singh, in a famous prayer, reflects: 'May I never be deterred from doing positive good'. The following verse by the poet Charles McKay accurately reflects Sikh teachings:

You have no enemies you say:
Alas, my friend, the boast is poor:
If you have none, small is the work you have done,
You've struck no traitor on the hip,
You've dashed no cup from perjured lip,
You've been a coward in the fight,
You've never turned the wrong to right.

We have seen how Sikhs, starting with personal cleanliness and a recharging of spiritual batteries through meditation, are duty bound to make every effort to 'turn the wrong to right', to make the world a happier and safer place for ourselves and our children. The 'no harm' philosophy is the catch-phrase of our times. It is used to justify pornography, and gratuitous sex and violence in the media. Apart from the moral bankruptcy and glibness inherent in such an attitude to life, the harm is often not apparent or easy to prove; but we are all influenced by our environment, and an environment of

165

violence or immorality is bound to influence an individual or whole society in a *manmukh* (unethical) direction. At best, such living is a squandering of the precious gift of human life.

FOUNDATIONS FOR A JUST WORLD ORDER

The present world order is built not on sound ethical imperatives but on the unsure foundations of conquest, exploitation and greed. While some progress has been made in moving towards the democratic ideal, it is all too often forgotten that 'majority rule' does not always equate with 'just rule'. The agenda for world rulers must no longer be: how we can fudge things to preserve the status quo, but, what we need to do to ensure peace, prosperity and justice for our children. Sikh teaching is that violence and injustice will continue until we understand that there is a higher vision of justice than that resulting from political alignments and short-term expediency. Guru Nanak taught:

> The final vision of justice
> Lies not with man
> Nor any creature of the universe.
> It lies with God alone.

Putting this another way, human justice will always be influenced by human failings, and thus be crude and imperfect unless it is refined by spirituality and the ethical input of religion. The challenge to religion, so clearly seen by Guru Nanak, is to provide this input, this sense of direction.

FURTHER READING

Cole, W.O. and Sambhi, P.S. (1978) *The Sikhs: Their Religious Beliefs and Practices*, London, Routledge and Kegan Paul.
Kohli, S.S. (1975) *Sikh Ethics*, New Delhi, Munshiram Manoharlal.
McLeod, W.H. (ed. and trans.) (1984) *Textual Sources for the Study of Sikhism*, Manchester, Manchester University Press.
Rahit Maryādā (1978), Amritsar, Shiromani Gurdwara Prabandhak Committee.

Singh, Avtar (1970) *The Ethics of the Sikhs*, Patiala, Punjabi University.

Singh, Sohan (1975) 'Ethical Aspects of Guru Nanak's Thought', in Harbans Singh (ed.), *Perspectives on Guru Nanak*, Patiala, Punjabi University.

Singh, Taran (1977) *Teachings of Guru Nanak Dev*, Patiala, Punjabi University.

Singh, Teja (1964) *Sikhism, Its Ideals and Institutions*, Calcutta, Orient Longmans.

Talib, Gurbachan Singh (1969) 'The Basis and Development of Ethical Thought in Sikhism', in Joshi, L.M. (ed.) *Sikhism*, Patiala, Punjabi University.

7. Chinese and Japanese Religions

Stewart McFarlane

The moral influence of Confucius and Confucianism

Confucianism is the dominant ethical influence on traditional religious and social life in China and Japan. The term 'Confucianism' is based on the latinised form of the name of the sage K'ung Fu Tzu 551–479 BCE. This usage correctly reflects the importance of K'ung Fu Tzu and his teaching for later Chinese thought and society.[1]

K'ung Fu Tzu (551–479 BCE) was not the founder of a religion but a would-be social and ethical reformer who turned to teaching in the hope of implementing his ideas through students who, it was hoped, would gain office in the feudal states of Chou China. While he was sceptical of, or indifferent to, many of the traditional religious ideas of his day, he was a firm advocate of filial piety and ancestor rites.

He felt a sense of mission which he derived from *T'ien* (Heaven), a power which he regarded as a positive moral force (*te*), and on which he relied at times of personal threat or political failure (*Lun Yu* [Analects], Lau (trans.) 1979: 69 v13, 89 v23, 113 v5, 129 v35). From these and many other passages in the *Lun Yu*, or '*Analects*', of Confucius, it is clear that he was not a total sceptic, but had a developed sense of a sacred power which he understood in specifically moral terms. Not all later Confucian scholars have subscribed to such an interpretation of *T'ien*, but it is unquestionably present in both the *Analects* and the teachings of Mencius (Meng Tzu 371–289 BCE).

Even later Confucians and scholars sympathetic to Confucian traditions have not sufficiently acknowledged the challenge and originality of his moral insights, in the context of the society in which they were developed. A significant example of this can be seen in a list of approved attitudes and behaviour patterns derived from the *Lun Yu (Analects)* by a respected scholar of Chinese history and thought.[2] The list is as follows:

1. Submissiveness to authority-parents, elders and superiors
2. Submissiveness to the mores and norms (*li*)
3. Reverence for the past and respect for history
4. Love of traditional learning
5. Esteem for the force of example
6. Primacy of broad moral cultivation over specialised competence
7. Preference for non-violent moral reform in state and society
8. Prudence, caution, preference for a middle course
9. Non-competitiveness
10. Courage and a sense of responsibility for a great tradition
11. Self respect with some permissible self pity
12. Exclusiveness and fastidiousness on moral and cultural grounds
13. Punctiliousness in treatment of others.

Wright's account is not incorrect in terms of the attitudes identified, but it fails to acknowledge how innovative Confucius' teaching was in relation to the society and dominant values which he lived among. It appears that Confucius virtually invented the idea of literary and moral education in ancient Chou China. Prior to him, an education for scholars seems to have been haphazard and unsystematic, more attention being devoted to a thorough training in archery and warrior skills. It appears that early Confucian moral teaching was appropriated by later Confucian orthodoxy; the Confucian formulation of the 'Golden Rule' is a perfect example.

> Tzu Kung asked, 'Is there a single word which can be a guide to conduct throughout one's life?' The master said, 'It is perhaps the word "*shu*" [reciprocity]. Do not impose on others what you do not desire.'
>
> (*Analects*, Lau (trans.) 1979: 135 v24, cf. 112 v2)

Such a teaching is as much a commonplace of later Confucian

169

moralising as it is of Christian moral teaching. But set in the context of Warring States China, when many rulers exercised power with ruthless brutality, and when the notion of a moral action guide, extending across social and feudal state boundaries, was unknown, then its radical impact is considerable.

Similarly, many of the key terms in Confucius and later Confucian moral teaching seem to have been creatively redefined by the master himself. The term *jen* (goodness, benevolence, authoritative person), which is rare in pre-*Analects* texts and seems to have applied to relationships within specific social groups (usually the nobility), becomes a key term in the *Analects*. Here it is employed as a disposition or attitude reflecting human solidarity across any social or class boundaries. Similarly the term *te* in pre-*Analects* usage seems to refer to the exercise of power, often in a political context, with no connotation of a moral dimension to such a function. In the *Analects, te* refers specifically to morally authenticating power or moral character. The term for ritual action, *li*, which was used to refer to formal rites and sacrifices correctly performed, was extended by Confucius to refer to the appropriate disposition which all formal interactions should embody.[3] Finally, the term *chun tzu* ('son of a noble' or 'gentleman') is redefined by Confucius to refer to the person of moral worth regardless of birth (*Analects*, Bk 4 Lau (trans.) 1979: 73–5).

Confucius and his early followers did not develop their teachings and methods in the context of abstract theory or academic debate. Rather than asking abstract questions about how moral principles are formulated and arrived at, they dealt with concrete or potentially real situations which were likely to occur in ministerial office. The question then was, 'How would a sage (*sheng jen*) or exemplary person (*chun tzu*) respond with *te*, and accord with *jen* and *li*, in such situations?'

Early Confucian thought did not value consequentialist calculations or the weighing up of opposing principles. It was much more an intuitive process of responding with one's *te* (moral power, derived from heaven) and harmonising one's actions with it. These would then inevitably be in conformity with the *li* and with the actions of the sages of the past. This conformity was not necessarily a conscious state. Conscious decision-making and consequentialist thinking would have been regarded as at a lower or preliminary stage of ethical development. The morally accomplished sage or exemplary person would not be in 'two minds'. Moral decision-making and the imposition of externally constraining moral rules are actually seen as features of a preliminary and immature stage of moral development. At a more advanced stage of moral development the Confucian sage would be at ease and unconstrained in his behaviour, yet he acts appropriately and in accord with *li*.

> The master said 'At fifteen my heart and mind were set on learning; at thirty I took my stance; at forty I was no longer of two minds; at fifty I realised the will of heaven; at sixty my ear was attuned; at seventy I could give my heart and mind free rein without overstepping the mark'.
>
> (*Analects*, Bk 2 v4 Lau (trans.) 1979: 63)

The way this kind of moral thinking is applied in practice can be seen in cases where moral decisions have to be made when there are conflicting principles or loyalties at stake. For example, where filial or family loyalty conflicts with loyalty to the ruler or the state, Confucius is in no doubt that family loyalty always takes precedence. In one striking passage he praises as 'upright' those who cover up for the crimes of their fathers or sons (*Analects*, Bk 13 v18 Lau (trans.) 1979: 121). Such a position has puzzled many commentators. But it becomes intelligible if we acknowledge that for Confucius filial piety and brotherly love are actually the model for good government, and constitute in themselves a form of public service (*Analects*, Bk 2 v21 Lau (trans.) 1979: 66). This can, of course, lead to the criticism that Confucius' model of government is deeply paternalistic and patriarchal. Both charges certainly carry some force in a contemporary perspective, but in the context of late Chou and early Warring States China the *de facto* method of government was frequently one of brutal dictatorship.

Developmental intuitionism and moral argument in Mencius

Many of the key concepts and moral themes present in the *Analects* are taken up, developed and refined in the thought and teaching methods of Mencius (374–289 BCE). Mencius provides the basic arguments and models for an intuitionist or innatist moral theory, in which the positive moral qualities are already present in a person's mind/heart (*hsin*), and simply need to be identified and correctly refined and developed. It is a theory which characterises the more optimistic or idealistic tradition of Confucian moral thinking throughout later Chinese history. While Confucius seems to have been the only teacher of his day to offer a moral teaching and systematic instruction to students, Mencius was one philosophical and moral teacher among many. This meant that he had to consciously define and defend his position against rival teachers and would-be advisers to the rulers of his day. By the time of Mencius, the so-called feudal states of China were functioning as independent kingdoms.

Mencius spent many years wandering from kingdom to kingdom, attempting to persuade rulers and advisers to pursue humane and just methods in their administering of the kingdom. He was not permanently successful in any kingdom, but in the course of his wandering he attracted a large following of students, some of whom succeeded in gaining office.

Mencius' basic argument for the innate moral capacity of all humans is set out very clearly in the following passage, which was known to every educated Chinese from the Han dynasty (206 BCE – 220 CE) onwards. The passage is worth quoting in full.

Mencius said, 'No man is devoid of a heart sensitive to the suffering of others. Such a sensitive heart was possessed by the Former Kings and this manifested itself in compassionate government. With such a sensitive heart behind compassionate government, it was as easy to rule the Empire as rolling it on your palm.

My reason for saying that no man is devoid of a heart sensitive to the suffering of others is this. Suppose a man were, all of a sudden, to see a child on the verge of falling into a well: he would certainly be moved to compassion, not because he wanted to get in the good graces of the parents, nor because he wished to win the praises of his fellow villagers and friends, nor yet because he disliked the cry of the child. From this it can be seen that whoever is devoid of the heart of compassion is not human, whoever is devoid of the heart of shame is not human, whoever is devoid of the heart of courtesy and modesty is not human, whoever is devoid of the heart of right and wrong is not human. The heart of compassion is the germ of benevolence; the heart of shame, of dutifulness; the heart of courtesy and modesty, of observance of the rites; the heart of right and wrong, of wisdom. Man has these four germs just as he has four limbs. For a man possessing these four germs to deny his potentialities is to cripple himself; for him to deny the potentialities of his prince, is to cripple his prince. If a man is able to develop all these four germs that he possesses, it will be like a fire starting up or a spring coming through. When these are fully developed, he can take under his protection the whole realm within the Four Seas, but if he fails to develop them, he will not even be able to serve his parents.

(Mencius Bk 2 pt A, (Lau trans.) 1970: 82–3)

Notice how Mencius concentrates on the initial response of alarm on the part of the observer. He does not even describe the man rescuing the child in this hypothetical case, but appeals to the force of the initial reaction as indicating the positive fundamental orientation of human nature. He does not conclude with a naive assertion about the goodness of human nature in practice. It is clear from this, and many other passages in the text, that Mencius was insistent on the need for the moral cultivation and refining of this basic human moral potential. As a practical teacher and adviser Mencius used these types of argument to show the kings who granted him audience how they too had the moral capacity to institute just and compassionate government. On one occasion he used an incident, where a king felt sympathy for the fate of a sacrificial ox, to demonstrate to the king that he had the capacity to extend his sympathy for the ox to sympathy for the suffering of his subjects. In doing so, Mencius cleverly manoeuvres the king into wanting to extend sympathy and compassion to his subjects and so qualify as a 'true King' (Mencius Bk 1 A 7, Lau (trans.) 1970: 54–6).

In some rather more obscure passages in the text, Mencius also provides clues as to how the heart of compassion, once it has been discovered, can be nurtured and developed into true benevolence (*jen*). Here Mencius' notion of moral reflection (sometimes described as meditation) and his development of the notion of *ch'i* (life force) as a factor in moral cultivation, are fundamental. For Mencius, the purpose of learning is to recover the lost mind/heart (*hsin*) (Mencius Bk 6 pt1 v11, Lau (trans.) 1970: 167). Once the heart/mind is discovered, it becomes the means of moral reflection or meditation, which is understood as a process of quietening and steadying the mind and focusing the will, which in turn controls the functioning of *ch'i*. According to Mencius *ch'i* can actually be nurtured and accumulated by the sustained performance of moral acts in accordance with propriety (Mencius Bk 2 pt A v2, Lau (trans.) 1970: 77–8; Lau translates *li* as 'rightness').

What Mencius appears to be saying is that stilling the mind and acumulating *ch'i* both facilitate and result in the performance of correct behaviour and moral acts. This fusing of cosmological, psychological, ethical and political themes represents a tendency which became typical of much later Neo-Confucian thought.

The tendency to literalism and rigidity does emerge in later Confucian thought and action. Later morality tales, where loyal ministers, sons and particularly women kill themselves over minor breaches of propriety, become models and ideals for upright Confucians to emulate or revere. The principle of dying rather than compromising on duty is established in Mencius (Bk 6 pt A v10, Lau (trans.) 1970: 166), but he applies it with discrimination and discretion (Bk 4 pt A v17, Lau (trans.) 1970: 124).

Mohism and Taoism as ethical alternatives

It is important to recognise that Confucian values and concerns were not the only influences on traditional life, thought and ethical behaviour. Two teachings, which emerged partly as protests against Confucian propriety and moral rigidity, went on to influence the nature of Chinese moral and political thinking, and provided an intellectual alternative, or at least temporary respite, from Confucian formalism. The earliest of these was the teaching of Mo Ti (Mo Tzu 470–391 BCE). His teaching was pragmatic or utilitarian in nature. He argued that a determining factor in any policy or moral decision should be the value it has in promoting the welfare of the family, group or nation. He called into question any ethical position, policy or institution which did not materially benefit the people. This led him to criticise directly the ancient rites and rituals and elaborate funerals (Chan 1963: Ch. 9). He also rejected the Confucian elevation of filial piety, and argued that universal love (*chien ai*) was a higher virtue. He maintained that it was decreed by Heaven, and that even Confucians who rejected universal love in theory actually endorsed it in practice. He pointed out that if a Confucian had to leave his family in the care of a stranger, he would ensure their protection by leaving them with someone who practised universal love, rather than with one who practised partial love and would therefore favour his own family in times of hardship.[4]

Mo Tzu was forthright in his condemnation of expansionist military campaigns, and condemned warfare on utilitarian grounds, because it impoverished the state and kept people from productive work. He not only condemned military aggression theoretically, but also organised his followers into a disciplined military force, whose duty it was to go to the aid of weak states who were being attacked by stronger aggressors. Mo Tzu's ideal model of government seems to have been an authoritarian theocratic state, which required a military style discipline and organisation to maintain itself. Although the Mohist movement seems to have died out by the early Han (206 BCE – 9 CE), later alternative states did occasionally emerge, apparently inspired by a fusion of Taoist and Mohist ideals.[5]

Much of the early Taoist attack on Confucian ethics involved a rejection of the conservatism, literalism and moral rigidity referred to above. This should not obscure the fact that the early Taoists and Confucians appear to have shared an optimistic view of human nature, and an innatist and positive view of human ethical potential. In Lao Tzu's *Tao Te Ching*, authentic moral power (*te*) is regarded as so integral and natural to humans that to seek to nurture, instruct, or require it is to injure it (Lao Tzu, Chs 38 and 57). Lao Tzu states that it is the imposition of external rules and constraints on people that obscures their innate sense of what is right. People come to rely on the rules rather than on their own *te* (moral power). When the inevitable situations arise in which the rules or laws are inapplicable, or conflict, or can be broken without detection, then inevitably chaos and disorder result (Lao Tzu, Ch. 57). Lao Tzu blames not the people themselves for such disorder but those who imposed the rules and rites of propriety in the first place. The Confucian establishment and its methods and values are rejected, and are seen as the causes and indicators of moral weakness and decay (Lao Tzu, Chs 19 and 20). As an antidote to this chaos and disorder, Lao Tzu recommends that the sage ruler should reduce his desires, avoid manipulative interference in government, and practise *wu-wei* (non-doing) or taking no action which is not natural and spontaneous (Chs 1, 3, 7, 19, 25, 59, 60, 63).

In self-effacement and self-emptying, and acting without schemes and intentions, the sage is actually modelling himself on the functioning of Heaven and earth, and of that which gives rise to them. In the text it is called the 'nameless' or 'Mother' or *Tao* (Ch. 1). The early Taoist fusion of a self-emptying mysticism with a political programme of radical non-intervention and de-centralising

175

of power (Ch. 80), along with an innatist moral perspective, has justifiably been compared to some forms of radical western anarchism.[6] Ironically some of the rebel movements leading to alternative states which were inspired in part by Taoist ideas became highly autocratic, ritualised and hierarchical in structure.

Ethics in the *Chuang Tzu*

Many regard the *Chuang Tzu* as the greatest Chinese philosophical work ever written. Some of its insights, humour and poetry are unequalled in the Chinese tradition. Modern scholarship tends to question both the 'authenticity' of many of the later chapters of this work, and their early dating to the fourth century BCE. Even accepting that the work is a compilation of different editors over a fairly extended period, the conscious interlacing of themes throughout the work still means that there is considerable value in reading it as a whole (Allinson 1989: 10–13).

Some modern scholars have sought to interpret the *Chuang Tzu* in contemporary intellectual categories. By concentrating on the specifically philosophical content of the 'inner chapters' of the work (Chs 1–7), they label its fundamental message as a form of linguistic relativism and as an early Chinese version of contemporary analytic and linguistic philosophy. Unfortunately, such interpretations neglect the passages in the inner chapters which clearly refer to experiential questions and insights derived from what can only be described as mystical or meditational experience (*Chuang Tzu*, Chs 2, 4, 6, 7. Watson (trans.) 1968: 36, 57–8, 90–91, 97). What is also lacking in the linguistic and relativistic reading of the *Chuang Tzu* is an appreciation of the moral insights offered.

Chuang Tzu is deeply sceptical of philosophical or 'common sense' claims to valid knowledge and moral certainty (Watson (trans.) 37, 47–8). This is why it rejects absolute claims, including Confucian appeals to universal principles, and prescriptive moral statements and judgements on the basis of such principles (e.g., the *li* – Confucian rites and rules of propriety). The work insists that such judgements and prescriptions fail to take account of the individual differences and needs of the recipients of such judgements and prescriptions, and also fail to take account of how much the perspective and judgement of the prescriber or law-giver may change over time and circumstances. In a typical humorous and evocative style, Chuang Tzu uses a mythic story to highlight the weaknesses of the Confucian method of moralising and governing. It is the story of Hun Tun (Chaos), the ruler of the central region, who showed great kindness to his neighbours, Shu and Hu, the rulers of the South and North. In discussing how to repay Hun Tun for his kindness, they noticed that he lacked the seven openings which all men possess, so they decided to bore him some openings so he could be like other men. They bored a new hole in him each day and on the seventh day he died (*Chuang Tzu*, Ch. 7 Watson (trans.) 1968: 97). In Chuang Tzu's view they acted inappropriately and failed to allow for Hun Tun's distinctive nature and characteristics. This was the Confucian failing of trying, from the best motives, to enforce rules and standards which cannot apply in all cases.

In Chapter two *Chuang Tzu* indicates the importance of allowing for individual variations and even opposites. It recommends resorting to 'clarity' (*ming*) and the 'light of Heaven' (*T'ien*) as the guiding perspective in determining the appropriate way to act (Watson (trans.) 1968: 39–41). Chuang Tzu rejects any notion that appropriate or moral action (*te*) is about the formulation of, and obedience to, moral rules and obligations. The work seems to follow a more natural and innatist sense of morality, which combines situational flexibility with a reference to a higher perspective which issues from what is 'heavenly' (*T'ien*) or with power/virtue (*te*). The distinction between the contextually limited human moral judgement and behaviour, and the perspective of Heaven, is clearly articulated in Chapter seventeen.

Hence it is said: the Heavenly is on the inside, the human is on the outside. Virtue resides in the Heavenly. Understand the actions of Heaven and the human, base yourself upon Heaven, take your stand on virtue, and then although you hasten or hold back, bend or stretch, you may return to the essential and speak of the ultimate. 'What do you mean by the Heavenly and the human?' Jo of the North Sea said, 'Horses and oxen have four feet – this is what I mean by the Heavenly. Putting a halter on the horse's head, piercing the ox's nose – this is what I mean by the human'. So I say: do not let what is human wipe out what is Heavenly; do not let what is purposeful wipe out what is fated; do not let [the desire for] gain lead you after fame. Be cautious, guard it and do not lose it – this is what I mean by returning to the True.

(Watson (trans.) 1968: 182–3)

The exemplar of such appropriate behaviour is variously described in the text as the 'great man', the 'true man' or the 'man of virtue' (*te*). Extensive accounts of his way of demonstrating the above methods and qualities occur in Chapters six and seventeen. One brief passage indicates the kind of exemplar Chuang Tzu is commending.

> Therefore the Great Man in his actions will not harm others, but he makes no show of benevolence or charity. He will not move for the sake of profit, but does not despise the porter at the gate. He will not wrangle for goods or wealth, but makes no show of refusing or relinquishing them. He will not enlist the help of others in his work, but makes no show of being self-supporting, and he does not despise the greedy and base. His actions differ from those of the mob, but he makes no show of uniqueness or eccentricity. He is content to stay behind with the crowd, but does not despise those who run forward to flatter and fawn. All the titles and stipends of the age are not enough to stir him to exertion; all its penalties and censures are not enough to make him feel shame. He knows no line can be drawn between right and wrong, no border can be fixed between great and small. I have heard it said, 'The Man of the Way wins no fame, the highest virtue wins no gain, the Great Man has no self.' To the most perfect degree he goes along with what has been allotted to him.
>
> (Chuang Tzu, Ch 17. Watson (trans.) 1968: 178–9)

Buddhist ethics in traditional China and Japan

Buddhism was first known in China at about the beginning of the Christian era, but its growth and initial period of popularity really occurred at a time when China was politically divided after the collapse of the Han dynasty in the third century CE, and remained so until reunification under the Sui dynasty in the late sixth century. The introduction of Buddhism into Japan in the middle of the sixth century was also a period of political division and interstate rivalry and conflict. Buddhism with its strong universalist and fundamentally moral teachings offered the basis for what could be seen as a unifying ideology. The moral dimension of *buddhadharma* had strong appeal to rulers who wanted to encourage the population to peaceful compliance with their rule. In Japan particularly, Buddhism offered a new and specifically moral dimension to religious life. In pre-Buddhist Japan, religious life focused on the multitude of spirits and powers called *kami*. The *kami* and the rituals of purification associated with them were not concerned with any formally defined moral code or even with informal moral behaviour. Avoiding ritual pollution, maintaining purity and ensuring the continuation of the natural cycle of growth, harvest and decay, and ensuring the blessing of one's ancestral *kami*, were the concern of pre-Buddhist Japanese religion. No word for this religion existed: the term, 'Shinto' (Way of the Gods), is derived from Chinese concepts, and was used only to refer to the indigenous Japanese religion in later times. Interestingly, two of the great unifying rulers, Yang Ti of the Sui dynasty in China and Prince Shotoku (573–621 CE), were both dedicated Buddhists who used Buddhism as a unifying moral teaching and ideology. Significantly, the Buddhism of their official statements and constitutions was heavily influenced by Confucian moral and political concepts (Ch'en 1964: 194–209; De Bary 1958: 36–53). This identifies a typical feature of the relationship between Buddhism, Confucianism and other teachings of traditional China and Japan; it is that they are generally treated as existing in a harmonious and functionally complementary relationship. The implications of this will be explored further below.

For ordinary people in China and Japan, exposure to Buddhist moral and cosmological ideas brought new and promising dimensions to their lives. The Buddhist notions of *karma*, merit and rebirth were positively attractive features in the early period of the establishing of Buddhism in China and Japan. Heavens or improved rebirths were more attractive to ordinary people than the rather bureaucratic 'Confucian' afterlife. While the fate of people inadequately provided for after death was even more unpleasant, because they were thought to be destined to wander as sorrowful and lonely ghosts, or even be punished in hell, Buddhism provided ritual expertise in the form of monks who could preside over funerals and 'universal salvation' rites (*pu t'u*), and could thus help lonely ghosts or save the newly dead from hell.

The annual performance of 'universal salvation' rites at the Yu Lan P'en (China) or Bon (Japan) festival became a central role of the Buddhist *sangha* in these countries. The fact that one could facilitate a pleasant future for one's parents in the afterlife, thus conforming to ancient Confucian as well as Buddhist values, is another factor in explaining the popularity of these rites and the respect for Buddhism in traditional China and Japan (Ch'en 1973: 24–64, 271).

The operations of *karma* could be seen as offering compensation for suffering and hardship in the present life. The possibility of acquiring merit, and so ensuring a pleasant future existence, was another powerful factor which explains the moral appeal of Buddhism in these countries. Such ideas soon led to formal and systematic methods of accumulating merit as well as to some highly organised charitable activities (Ch'en 1973: 294–303).

Elaborate systems of 'merit accountancy' were developed, similar to those observed by Spiro in use in Burma (now Myanmar), (1971: 111–13). The proliferation of 'ledgers of merit and demerit' seems to have occurred during the Ming dynasty (1368–1644 CE), partly as a result of increasing literacy among the general population, and as an extension of the popular Confucian morality books. The ethical asumptions underlying the ledgers of merit and demerit were Buddhist in that they were concerned with the operation of *karma* and the prospect of a pleasant rebirth, and also Taoist in that they were concerned with the perceived link between a person's interior hygiene and ritual purity, and between their moral behaviour and longevity (Welch 1966: 130–51). The ethical content of the morality books and ledgers of merit and demerit was a blend of Confucian and Buddhist values, with large measures of agricultural or business common sense (Tadao Sakai, in De Bary (ed.) 1970: 341–62). Clearly a significant part of the appeal of Buddhism in practice and on a popular level was for its 'kammatic' and 'apotropaic' dimensions (Spiro 1971). Improving one's future state through moral practice and merit acquisition, and using the magical and ritual power of *dhamma* to improve one's present life, are actually strong motivational factors. They were far stronger considerations than the rather abstract soteriological appeal of Buddhist *nirvana* or supreme enlightenment. Such 'kammatic' and 'apotropaic' considerations are far more typical popular Buddhist practice in Buddhist countries than the 'nibbanic' considerations.

The emperors and ministers who supported monks and Buddhist activities also expected some tangible benefits from such arrangements. It was argued by Buddhist apologists that the presence of Buddhist teachings and the *sangha* helped to maintain an orderly population and, therefore, political stability (Hui Yuan, in De Bary (ed.) 1960: 281). This in itself was not enough for many rulers. The chanting of texts and performing of protection rituals by monks on behalf of the state were frequently required by Chinese and Japanese emperors from the sixth century on (Ch'en 1973: 105–124; De Bary 1958: 94–110). Such services could be seen as fulfilling both magical and ideological functions. Whether the emperors believed that the protection gained from such rituals was effective can be questioned. But the majority of the population certainly did, and the obvious role of the monks in state procedures added to the legitimacy and authority of the emperors.

The ethical interrelatedness of traditions

It was unusual for most of the population of pre-Communist China or traditional Japan to identify themselves in terms of exclusive religious affiliations such as 'Buddhist', 'Taoist', 'Confucian' or 'Shinto'. Even the allegiance of religious professionals was not necessarily exclusive. It is possible to identify a general demarcation of spheres of influence and responsibility, in terms of how the different traditions functioned in society and served the needs of the people:

Confucian teachings regulated the traditional rites of passage and moral behaviour, particularly in relation to family and public life.

Taoism, in traditional China, regulated many communal festivals, and Taoist priests performed healing/exorcism rites as well as their own versions of the 'universal salvation' (*pu tu*) rites, initially developed by the Buddhists.

Shinto, the indigenous Japanese religion, served a similar role to that of Taoism in China: ritual purity and protection, exorcism.

Buddhism emphasised the more universal moral values of compassion and generosity. The practice of these provided the opportunity to acquire merit, and a happy afterlife. It also provided the ritual means of serving one's parents and ancestors in the afterlife.

Because, for ordinary people, all these functions were important in maintaining a stable and harmonious social and private life, the different traditions were generally seen as complementary rather than antagonistic.

Ethical reflection and decision-making in Japan

This complementarity of traditions was even more evident in Japan than in China. Some of the reasons for this are historical ones, concerned with the nature of the transmission of religious, philosophical and moral teachings from China to Japan. A fundamental difference between the countries is that in China, the teachings of the Confucian, Taoist and later Buddhist texts and authorities were recognised as distinct in terms of their origins and initial distinctive identities; in Japan these distinctions were not so apparent because the teachings were transmitted to Japan in their mature forms, which were already integrated. A further important difference is that Buddhism arrived in China after distinctive Chinese moral and religious teachings had developed and matured, and Buddhism had to accommodate to them. In Japan it was Buddhism which was the first major foreign religious and moral influence, and it was in association with Buddhism that other Chinese teachings and institutions became known in Japan. The outcome of these processes was a tendency to regard the complementarity of traditions as even more natural and self-evident in Japan than in China.

The Constitution of Prince Shotoku, who served as regent under his aunt, Empress Suiko, from 573 to 621 CE, provides a perfect example of this. Although he was a Buddhist, much of the content of his constitution and the legal and political reforms he tried to introduce, were based on Chinese Confucian models and ideals (De Bary 1958: 36–53). This attempt to introduce Chinese ideals and institutions was repeated in the great Taika reforms of 645 and 647 CE. It included the deliberate process of elevating and empowering the role of the emperor, along the lines of the T'ang Chinese emperors. In the Japanese context, this meant endorsing the Chinese concept of the Heavenly Mandate and the title 'Son of Heaven', and applying them to their own emperors. The particular Japanese refinements of these concepts in the seventh century involved seeing the emperor as bearing the particular approval of the *kami*, and the identification of the emperor himself as having the status of a living or manifest *kami*.

From the late fifteenth century in Japan, Neo-Confucianism began to be identified as a powerful intellectual tradition, and it appealed to some Japanese scholars as an alternative to Buddhism, which some regarded as too otherworldly, and too mystical for practical affairs or moral life. But even they were unable to divest themselves of the Buddhist influence. Much of Neo-Confucian thought itself is powerfully influenced by Buddhist concepts. Ironically, it was largely scholarly Buddhist monks who were responsible for bringing Neo-Confucian learning from China to Japan. Much of the language of Japanese Neo-Confucian critiques of Buddhism was infused with Buddhist terminology and concepts (De Bary 1958: Ch 18).

Conclusion

To conclude this chapter, we shall look in more detail at three examples of teachers, one Buddhist and two Confucian, who reflect in different ways the irenic and synthesising perspective which emerged as so characteristic of later Chinese and Japanese moral and social thought. The first is Takuan Soho (1573–1645 CE), a famous Zen Master who was teacher and adviser to some of the most important political and military leaders of his day. He combined traditional Buddhist and Zen teachings with those of Confucian, particularly Mencian, moral theory, as well as incorporating Taoist notions of non-volitional action and spontaneity. He even incorporated an ecumenical reference to Shinto (Takuan (trans.) Wilson 1987: 28, 38, 47–75). He argued that the 'lost mind' discussed by Mencius is none other than *jen* (benevolence/human-heartedness) and *li* (propriety), and that these are none other than functional names for the 'no-mind' (*mushin*) state of Zen, the fundamental nature of which is 'emptiness' or 'no-self'. Takuan's ecumenism extended to other Buddhist schools, particularly Shingon (True Word, i.e. Vajrayāna Buddhism) as well as Pure Land Buddhism, both of which he cited with approval in his writings (Dumoulin 1990: 279–88). Some of Takuan's writings were originally addressed to particular individuals, in particular the general and sword master, Yagyu Munenori, who was Takuan's Zen disciple. In these works, Takuan tried to demonstrate how Zen meditation and the unfolding of *prajñā* (Buddhist insight) can be

183

achieved through the rigours of sword training and the demands of the daily life of a *samurai.*

This move to develop a Zen practice which is applicable to daily life and secular pursuits is characteristic of Japanese Zen. It was partly a response to the common Neo-Confucian criticism of Buddhism – that it is too otherworldly and introspective to be of value to ordinary people. This criticism was sometimes specifically levelled at Zen in seventeenth- and eighteenth-century Japan, and some Confucians felt that Zen's supposed lack of an explicit ethical teaching made it a harmful influence, or at least rendered it impractical for ordinary life (Dumoulin 1989: 284). Such a criticism was earlier developed in the works of the great Chinese Confucian teacher magistrate and military leader, Wang Yang-ming (1472–1529 CE) (Chan 1963: 667). Ironically, even when rejecting particular characteristics of Buddhism as it was perceived and practised in medieval China, Wang's Confucianism reflects Buddhist influences. The practice of quiet sitting, practised by many Neo-Confucians, is undoubtedly influenced by Ch'an (Zen) meditation techniques, albeit given a particular moral psychological interpretation derived from Mencius. Furthermore, Wang's holistic moral vision, which strongly influenced Japanese Neo-Confucian thinking, contained distinctly universalist Mahāyāna Buddhist themes as well as traditional humanistic Confucian teachings (Chan 1963: 659–67).

Like Buddhism, Confucianism persists as a living tradition. In a fine recent study by Rodney Taylor, the thought and practice of the contemporary Confucian teacher, Okada Takehiko, is described in considerable depth. The account is particularly important because it discusses Okada's view of the nature of meditation or 'quiet sitting' (*seiza*) in that tradition, and includes transcripts of interviews with Okada himself on a range of contemporary moral and social problems, as well as on the issues that have exercised Confucian thought since the sixth century BCE (Taylor 1988: 123–62, 189–212). Of particular interest is Okada's advocacy of 'quiet sitting' and Confucian style self-cultivation (though not necessarily employing Confucian terminology to teach them) as basic elements of educational programmes, and as means of overcoming the dehumanising effects of technology (Taylor 1988: 204–206). What emerges very clearly from these discussions is the ancient Confucian principle of human dignity, and the need to maintain it in the face of technological and industrial change.

184

NOTES

1. The terms 'Confucian' and 'Confucianism' in western writings on China and Japan are used in a variety of ways. I list some of the more common uses here:

    (i)   The ethical, social and ritual teachings of K'ung Fu Tzu or his successors (Hall and Ames 1987).

    (ii)   Anyone conforming to traditional values such as loyalty to the Emperor, filial piety, righteous and upright behaviour (Thompson 1979, 37–43).

    (iii)   Scholars preparing for the official examinations based on the Confucian classics, officials in office or retired (Yang 1961, 134–64).

    (iv)   Anyone participating in the officially sanctioned state cult of Confucius (Shryock 1966).

    (v)   Anyone participating in rites and rituals that were officially sanctioned by the state, either at central or local level (Thompson 1979, Ch 5).

    (vi)   Neo-Confucian thinkers such as Chou Tun-yi (1017–1073 CE), Chang Tsai (1021–1077 CE), Chu Hsi (1130–1200 CE) and Wang Yang-Ming (1472–1529 CE), who produced new syntheses, combining traditional Confucian ethics with traditional Chinese cosmological concepts, along with elements of Taoist and Buddhist theory. Their syntheses became the dominant intellectual and ethical influences in China and Japan from late medieval times until the late nineteenth century (De Bary 1960: Chs. 17, 18, 19; De Bary 1958: 25–49; Thompson 1979: Ch. 7).

    None of the above uses of 'Confucian' is necessarily incorrect or misleading, but it is important to understand something of the context and associations authors have in mind when they use the term.

    The most common term in Chinese for a Confucian in the sense of an educated scholar committed to traditional ways and values is *Ju* (pronounced 'roo'), which is often rendered in English as 'scholar/s' or 'literati'. The general term for the tradition is *Ju Chia*, 'Confucian school' or 'Confucian philosophy'. Laurence Thompson provides a clear introduction to the main terminology and concepts used in referring to Confucian ethical ideals and goals (Thompson 1979: Chs 3 and 7).

2. Wright, A.F. and D. Twitchett (eds) (1962) *Confucian Personalities*, Berkeley, Stanford University Press.

3. See Hall, D.L. and R.T. Ames (1987) *Thinking Through Confucius*, State University of New York Press.

4. See Watson, B. (1963) (trans.) *Mo Tzu. Basic Writings*, New York, Columbia University Press, p. 42.
5. See Bauer, W. (1976) *China and the Search for Happiness*, New York, The Seabury Press, pp. 110–30.
6. See Ames, R.T. (1983) 'Is Political Taoism Anarchism?', in *Journal of Chinese Philosophy* Vol 10, No 1 (March), pp. 27–47, and Bender, F.L. (1983) 'Taoism and Western Anarchism', in *Journal of Chinese Philosophy* Vol 10, No 1 (March), pp. 5–26.

FURTHER READING

Allinson, R.E. (1989) *Chuang-Tzu. For Spiritual Transformation*, Albany, State University of New York Press.

Chan, W.T. (1963) *A Source Book in Chinese Philosophy*, Princeton University Press.

Ch'en, K. (1964) *Buddhism in China*, Princeton University Press.

Ch'en, K. (1973) *The Chinese Transformation of Buddhism*, Princeton University Press.

De Bary, W.T. (1960) (ed.) *Sources of Chinese Tradition*, New York, Columbia University Press.

De Bary, W.T. (1958) (ed.) *Sources of Japanese Tradition*, New York, Columbia University Press.

De Bary, W.T. (1970) (ed.) *Self and Society in Ming Thought*, New York, Columbia University Press.

Dumoulin, H. (1989–90) *Zen Buddhism: A History*, 2 vols, Japan, London, Macmillan.

Lau, D.C. (1979) (trans.) *Confucius. The Analects*, Harmondsworth, Penguin.

Lau, D.C. (1963) (trans.) *Lao Tzu. Tao Te Ching*, Harmondsworth, Penguin.

Lau, D.C. (1970) (trans.) *Mencius*, Harmondsworth, Penguin.

Shryock, J.K. (1966) *The Origin and Development of the State Cult of Confucius*, New York, Paragon.

Spiro, M.E. (1971) *Buddhism and Society*, London, Allen & Unwin.

Tadao, S. (1970) 'Confucianism and Popular Educational Works', in W.T. De Bary, (ed.) *Self and Society in Ming Thought* New York, Columbia University Press, pp. 331–66.

Takuan Soho (1987) *The Unfettered Mind. Writings of the Zen Master to the Sword Master*, (trans.) W.S. Wilson, Tokyo, Kodansha.

Taylor, R.L. (1988) *The Confucian Way of Contemplation*, Columbia, University of South Carolina Press.

Thompson, L.G. (1979) *Chinese Religion*, 3rd Edition, California, Wadsworth.

Watson, B. (1968) (trans.) *Chuang Tzu. The Complete Works*, New York, Columbia University Press.

Welch, H. (1966) *Taoism. The Parting of the Way*, Boston, Beacon Press.

Yang, C.K. (1961) *Religion in Chinese Society*, University of California Press.

Index